Massive Retaliation

A Declassified Documentary History of American Military Plans for Nuclear War 1950-1985

by Lenny Flank

Red and Black Publishers, St Petersburg, Florida

Introduction © Copyright 2015 by Red and Black Publishers

These documents were declassified after the end of the Cold War. Areas which are [*contained within brackets in bold italic type*] represent sections which were originally censored by the Defense Department, but were released later when the documents were declassified. Areas which are blank spaces within brackets:

[censored]

are still classified and were removed by the Defense Department prior to release.

Contents

April 25, 1950   5
January 30, 1957   21
May 22, 1957   27
November 20, 1958   37
December 31, 1958   43
August 17, 1959   49
February 19, 1960   61
April 26, 1960   65
July 14, 1960   69
January 18, 1961   93
May 1961   99
September 5, 1961   115
August 29, 1964   153
September 23, 1964   159
January 27, 1969   161
February 1, 1969   171
May 29, 1969   175
November 8, 1969   197
January 29, 1971   205
January 3, 1972   213
April 3, 1974   255
July 25, 1980   271
November 3, 1986   277

April 25, 1950

At the end of the Second World War, the United States possessed one complete atomic bomb ready for use and was making enough plutonium to potentially produce two more bombs per month. But, President Truman thought, there was no need for that number – no country, he thought, could withstand an attack by more than five or six atomic bombs without being forced to surrender. One year after Hiroshima, the entire US nuclear stockpile stood at 9 weapons, and by July 1947 this had grown to only 13 bombs and 34 specially-modified B-29 bombers to deliver them.

In 1949, however, the Soviet Union test-detonated its own atomic weapon (a virtual copy of the Nagasaki bomb). The US, in a panic, ordered increased production of its own nuclear weapons, and a crash program to develop bigger and better bombs and delivery systems, eventually culminating in the Intercontinental Ballistic Missile (ICBM) capable of delivering hydrogen thermonuclear weapons halfway around the world with over one-million tons of explosive power. The next forty years would see a nuclear arms race on a massive scale, which drained treasuries, hobbled economies, and threatened the entire planet with instant nuclear annihilation.

At the beginning of the Cold War, US plans for a potential nuclear war against Russia were a simple continuation of the strategy that had won the Second World War against Japan: the US would launch continuous bomber attacks using nuclear weapons until the enemy's cities were destroyed and surrender was offered.

This declassified memo is a description of US nuclear strategy as it stood in 1950. It was prepared by the Strategic Air Command, a section of the US Air Force dedicated to the long-range delivery of nuclear weapons. The plan called for nuclear bombers stationed in the US to move within five days to bases in Britain and staging areas in Alaska or, if weather in Alaska was too severe, in SAC bases at Rapid City and Goose Bay, accompanied by six assembly teams to ready the bombs for delivery. There were 123 target cities in Russia, of which 60 would be hit in the opening stages of the war and the remainder would be struck after being examined by reconnaissance flights. A total of 32 targets would be bombed in the first attack wave. It would then take about 30 days to destroy all 123 targets.

Presentation By The Strategic Air Command

General Vandenberg and gentlemen,

In brief order I will cover the current operational plan for the atomic offensive and the present status of forces within the Command. Following this, General LeMay has asked that I point up the major deficiencies which impair, or threaten to impair, the execution of the plan.

Items to be discussed include:
Organization and location of units
Personnel
Aircraft
Plan of overseas movement
Planned disposition of deployed forces
Latest target system
First atomic strike
Notes on bombing accuracy
Current "soft spots"

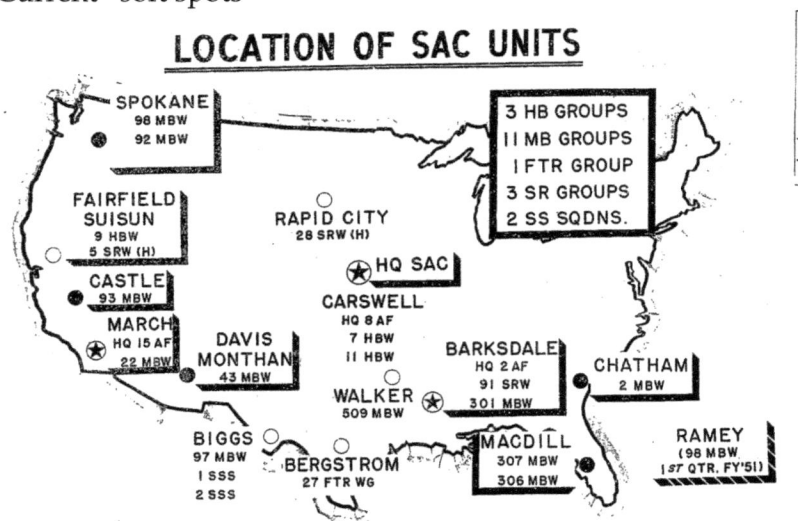

As shown by this chart, Strategic Air Command is composed of the following:

Three (3) Heavy Bombardment Groups
Eleven (11) Medium Bombardment Groups

One (1) Fighter Group (with one additional group to be assigned in the near future)

Three (3) Strategic Reconnaissance Wings

Two (2) Strategic Transport Squadrons

These units are organized as follows:

Shown in green are units of the Fifteenth Air Force, commanded by General O'Donnell with headquarters at Match Air Force Base.

Units of the Eighth Air Force shown by yellow are located in the central part of the country. The Eighth Air Force is commanded by General Ramey, with headquarters at Carswell AFB, Fort Worth, Texas.

In the eastern part of the country are located units of the Second Air Force. These units are shown in blue. General Atkinson commands the Second Air Force with headquarters at Barksdale, Louisiana.

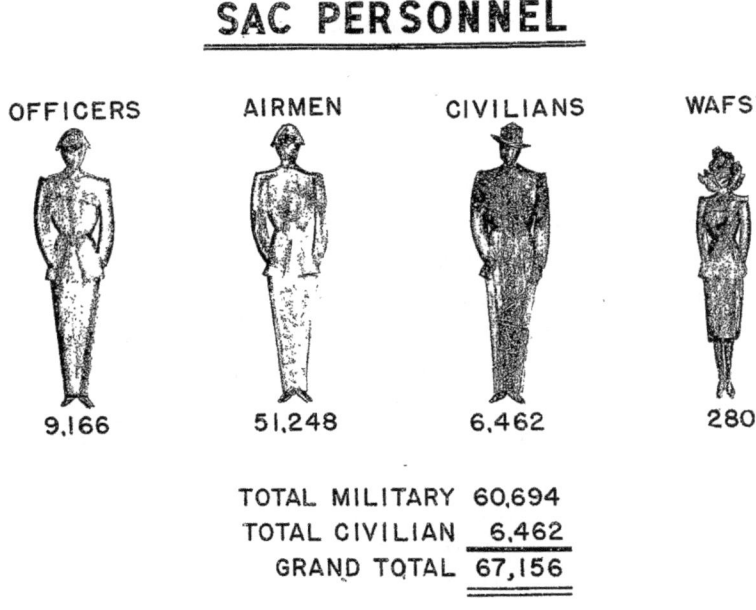

As shown by next chart, the command has a total personnel strength of 67,156, composed of:

9,166 Officers

51, 248 Airmen

6,462 Civilians, and

280 WAFs

Massive Retaliation

This amounts to approximately 16% of the total strength of the Air Force.

Although fully manned, body-wise, SAC is only 85% effectively manned.

SECRET

SAC AIRCRAFT

B-36	27	HEAVY BOMBERS	27	TOTAL BOMBERS	512	"A" CARRIERS	256
B-50	148	MEDIUM BOMBERS	485			STANDARDS	256
B-29	337						
KB-29	77			TOTAL TANKERS	77		
RB-29	62			TOTAL RECON	62		
F-82	77			TOTAL FIGHTERS	104		
F-84	27						
C-54	19			TOTAL CARGO	29		
C-97	10						
				TOTAL SAC	784		

SECRET

As for aircraft, exclusive of administration types, we have a total of 784, broken down as follows:

512 <u>Bombers</u>, including 27 Heavies and 485 Mediums (note that the 485 Mediums consist of 148 B-50s and 337 B-29s)

Also note that of the 512 total, 50% are equipped to carry the A-bombs.

Our total <u>Tanker</u> strength is 77. All of these are equipped with the British type refueling system.

Our total <u>Reconnaissance</u> strength is 62. All of those are the B-29 type. We have not yet received our first RB-36 or our first RB-50.

At present we have 104 <u>Fighters</u>. With the assignment of the 31st Fighter Group, this figure will be approximately doubled.

In our <u>Transport</u> units we have a total of 29 aircraft.

So much for assigned aircraft.

At exercise "DUALISM", conducted at Maxwell Field in December 1948, we outlined in detail the plan for moving our forces overseas. Although the size of our deployment has changed, the general scheme of movement remains the same.

The present plan calls for rapid movement overseas of seven (7) Bomb Groups, one (1) Fighter Group, one (1) Reconnaissance Group, and five (5) A-Bomb Assembly Teams.

One additional Assembly Team goes to Alaska.

On E-Day only a limited number of movements occur, all of which are in the Zone of the Interior. The large scale movement starts on E+1 with the departure of the initial squadrons.

By E+3 the intensity of movements will reach its peak. To refresh your memory, I have a chart showing movements scheduled for E+3.

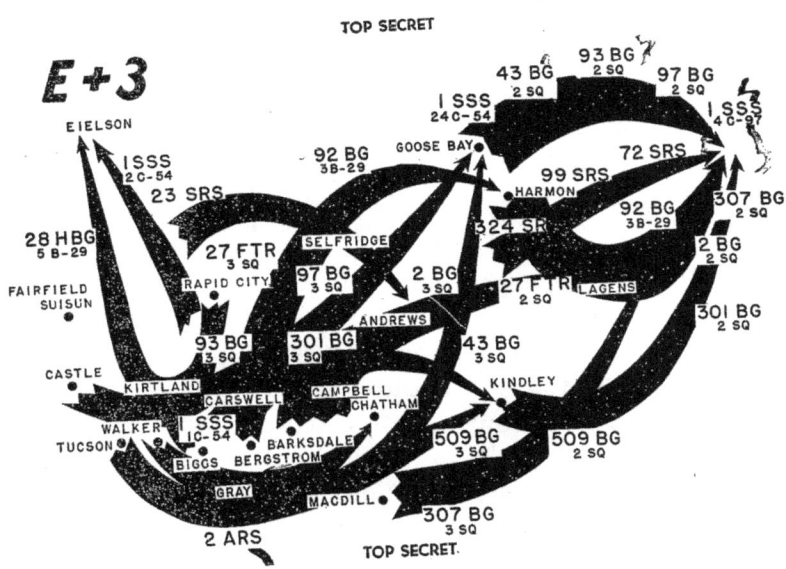

As shown by this chart the second squadrons of each deployed group are moving into position in the United Kingdom; the third squadrons are shown departing home stations for staging bases. Staging bases include: Goose Bay, Harmon, Selfridge, Andrews, Kindley, and Lagens. Tactical aircraft will be routed through storage sites to pick up A-bombs and components.

En route to Alaska, five (5) B-29s from Rapid City carrying A-Bomb components, and two (2) C-54s carrying assembly team personnel and equipment.

By E+5, all movements are scheduled to be completed.

Our plan calls for the utilization of eight (8) air bases in the United Kingdom. The disposition on those air bases is shown by the next chart.

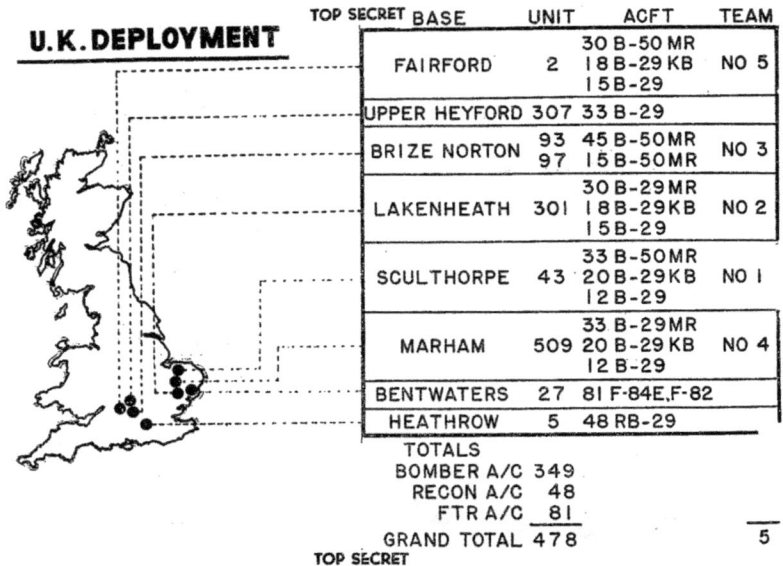

Fairford – the 2d Group with 30 B-50s, 18 tankers and 15 B-29s, and Assembly Team 5.

(Note: A-Bomb carriers are shown in red.)

Upper Heyford – the 307th Group with 33 B-29s.

Brize Norton – two groups, the 93d with 45 B-50s, the 97th with 15 B-50s, and Assembly Team 3.

Lakenheath – the 301st with 30 modified B-29s, 18 tankers, 15 B-29s, and Assembly Team 2.

Sculthorpe – the 43dGroup with 33 B-50s, 20 tankers, 12 B-29s, and Assembly Team 1.

Marham – 509th Group with 33 modified B-29s, 20 tankers, 12 B-29s, and Assembly Team 4.

Bentwaters – the 27th Fighter Group with 81 F-84Es and F-82s.

Heathrow – the 5th Reconnaissance Wing with 48 RB-29s.

The total force will consist of 349 bombers, 48 reconnaissance, and 81 fighter aircraft for a grand total of 478.

As mentioned previously, Assembly Team No. 6 will be deployed to Alaska, to handle bombs for the B-36 staging operations.

As for targets, plan "TROJAN" listed a total of 70 industrial centers. Plan "OFF TACKLE" lists a total of 123.

With the target material we now have, we are prepared to strike 60 of the 123 targets. Pre-strike reconnaissance is required on the remaining 63. The location of targeted and un-targeted areas is shown by the following chart.

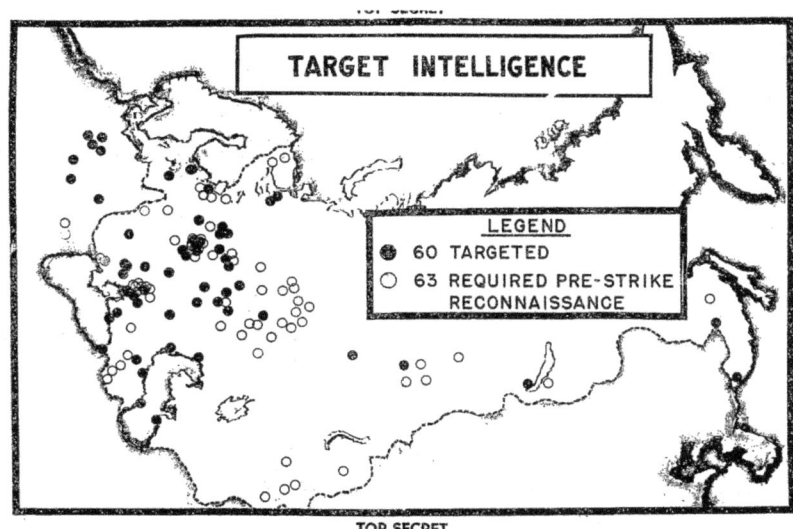

Red discs indicate areas on which we now have target material, and blank discs indicate areas which will require pre-strike reconnaissance.

The magnitude of the reconnaissance effort can be appreciated by noting the numbers of untargeted areas and their geographical spread. Several of the target areas assigned by "OFF TACKLE" lie outside the boundaries of Russia proper.

The first atomic strike is scheduled to be launched on E+6.

Medium bombers will attack from the United Kingdom and B-36s will attack from either Alaska, Goose Bay, or Rapid City. In the event that B-36s are launched from Rapid City, it will, of course, be necessary to stage them through the Middle East. Experience to date indicates that, with present facilities at Eielson, we will not be able to operate B-36s through Alaska during mid-winter when temperatures are below about –30.

The next chart shows the scheme of attack for medium bombers based in the United Kingdom. Let me emphasize that this is only the first strike, involving a total of 26 target areas. Also let me point out that it is only one way of conducting the strike. There are, of course, many variations involving the size of the force as well as tactics to be employed.

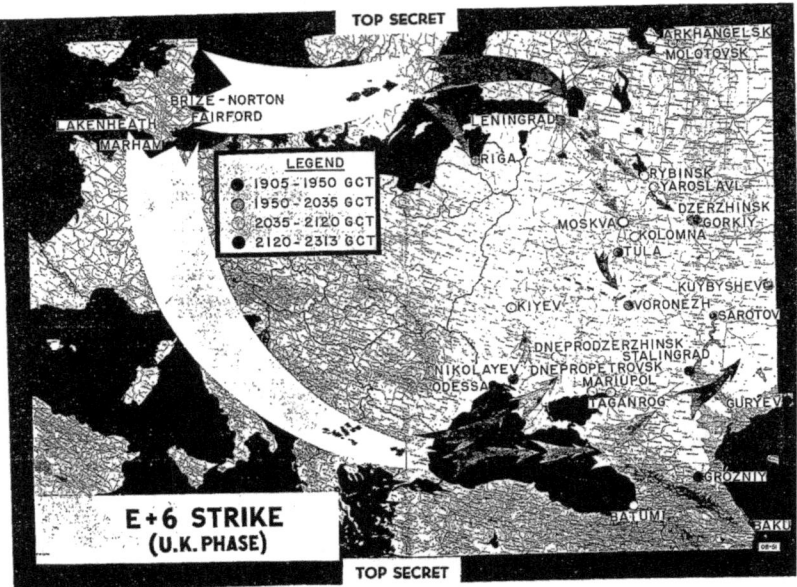

The attack plan calls for Soviet borders to be penetrated simultaneously by two major forces attacking from the northwest and southwest.

The total force will includes 201 UK-based medium bombers and 10 North American-based B-36s. Only the UK phase is shown on the chart. 112 will attack along the northern route and 89 along the southern route. The northern force will approach along southern Scandinavia and southern Finland, the penetration occurring in the area northeast of Leningrad. The southern forces will cross central France, central Italy and the southern Balkans, and will penetrate along the Black Sea area.

We have resorted to color to show the scheme of maneuver by indicating successive positions of the two forces as the attack develops.

For instance, at the time that the northern force is crossing southern Scandinavia, the southern force will be crossing Greece.

During the period 1905-1950 GCT, forces will be positioned as shown by brown. At this time, borders will be crossed and periphery targets bombed.

During the period 1950-2035, the forces will be positioned as shown by the blue areas. Seven targets will be bombed during this period.

During the period 2035-2120, positions are shown by green. Five targets will be bombed.

The most remote targets, totaling ten, will be struck during the period 2120-2313, as shown by the red.

Within approximately four hours after borders are crossed all targets will have been bombed.

We have not attempted to indicate the withdrawal routes. However, forces attacking targets north of the dotted red line will withdraw to the United Kingdom; while those attacking targets south of the line will withdraw to staging bases in the Middle East.

We believe that this general scheme of attack will give us the maximum degree of saturation in so far as fighter defenses are concerned.

To dilute AA defenses as much as possible, we plan to compress each attacking cell to approximately one minute between successive aircraft. A cell would normally comprise from two to four supporting bombers and one A-carrier.

Simultaneous with the United Kingdom strike, B-36s are scheduled to strike six targets from North American bases, making a total of 32 targets included in the first strike.

The timing of later strikes will be determined by the tactical situation. However, we plan to launch the second strike not later than E+9. If United Kingdom bases remain tenable, it is planned to complete strikes against 123 targets within a period of 30 days.

Since exercise "DUALISM", much interest and effort has been devoted to the problem of bombing accuracy. Many questions have been asked concerning the capability of our crews to hit assigned targets. The Weapons System Evolution Group has completed an intensive study of our capability, and has rendered a favorable report.

As a matter of information, General LeMay asks that I review quickly the progress we have made during the past year on radar bombing accuracy.

Before presenting actual figures, a few words on the background of this problem.

During the past year, we have conducted a number of evaluation exercises designed to measure bombing accuracy capability. These exercises consisted of radar bombing runs against a variety of industrial areas within the United States. Ground radar units were used to track the bombers and measure bombing accuracy.

All attacks were conducted at 25,000 feet and above.

In addition, a system of "first runs" was instituted, a "first-run" being the initial approach on any one day against a particular target. This was done to isolate and eliminate the advantage gained through successive runs.

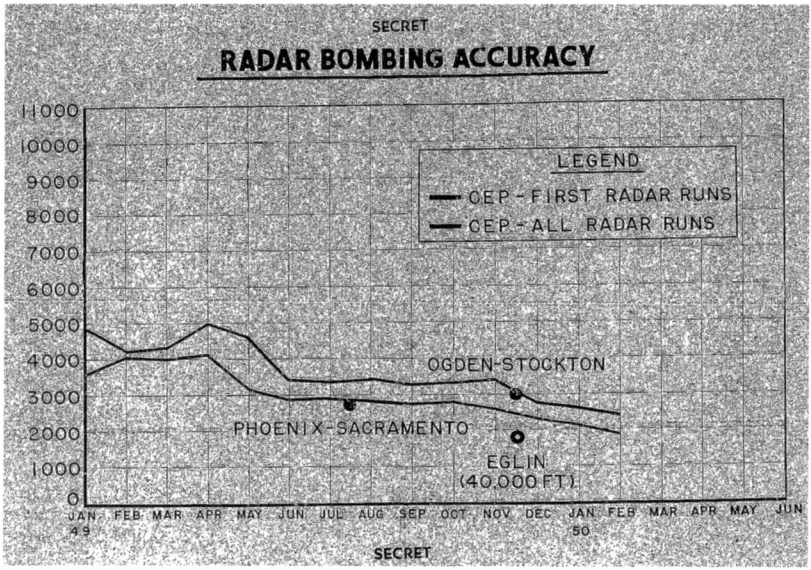

As shown by this chart, the trend of all SAC first runs has dropped from around 5000 feet last year to a present level of around 2500.

In all radar runs, including practice runs, the error has fallen from approximately 5000 feet to 1800.

During the early part of 1949, we experienced some rather high bombing errors in the neighborhood of from eight to ten thousand feet. Close scrutiny indicated that these high errors were due to faulty techniques, poor mission preparation, and lack of experience at high altitudes on industrial type targets.

Accordingly, an intensive training program, both air and ground, was instituted on the subject of radar bombing.

It also became apparent that especially selected crews would have to be ear-marked as A-carriers and subjected to intensive training. This was done and a Lead Crew School was established for this purpose.

In the summer of 1949 an exercise was conducted utilizing lead crews. A number of missions were run against Phoenix and Sacramento, producing an average CEP of about 2500 feet.

In the winter of 1949, the final two exercises were conducted against Ogden and Stockton. One hundred and fifty nine first runs produced an average error of around d 3000 feet. For this exercise all SAC crews were scheduled. Note that the results confirm the accuracy trend line.

Also a controlled experiment was conducted by SAC and APG, utilizing B-36s at 40,000 feet altitude. With the improved Q-24 equipment, B-36 crews were able to average 1925 feet for a total of 114 radar runs. Targets included Eglin, Tampa and Birmingham.

Our Lead Crew School is still in operation and is being used to train evaluated crews selected as A-carriers. This will be a continuing program. By careful screening of A crews, by continued training, and with improved bombing equipment, such as the Q-24 and K series, we believe that bombing accuracy can be improved below the 2000 foot level.

With a weapon radius of 5000 feet, we are confident the targets can be accurately bombed.

Approximately 18,000 radar runs, all conducted above 25,000 feet, provide the basis on which those figures were based.

So much for bombing accuracy.

The foregoing gives a brief picture of SAC resources and the planned utilization of those resources, in the event of an emergency. You can appreciate the need for a high degree of readiness and preparation, if the Plan is to be carried out on schedule. There are a number of deficiencies which threaten to impair, to varying degrees, its execution.

Current deficiencies include:
Advanced bases
Reconnaissance
Fighters
Airlift available for deployment
ECM
Electronic Maintenance Personnel and Material

On the subject of <u>Advanced Bases</u>:

You will recall that the recent plan contemplates the use of eight (8) Air Bases in the United Kingdom and two (2) staging bases in the Middle East. For discussion I will use a chart previously shown.

The three bases in the Oxford area – Fairford, Upper Heyford and Brize Norton, have runways of only 6000 feet in length. These are inadequate for B-29 operations and extremely marginal for B-50's. The use of these bases in the immediate future would necessitate staging a number of sorties through the eastern bases. Although arrangements are under way for lengthening the runways, considerable time will be required before the work is completed.

So far as runways are concerned, Lakenheath, Sculthorpe, Marham and Heathrow are satisfactory.

Bentwaters has 6000-foot strips which are inadequate for F-84Es, operating with four external tanks.

Base personnel complements are now considered adequate for Lakenheath, Sculthorpe, and Marham. However, none are available for the additional bases at present.

Essential base equipment is in place only at Lakenheath, Sculthorpe and Marham.

Plans for <u>base defenses</u> and ground security are not satisfactorily developed. AA-defense is limited to only a few 50-caliber guns and no concrete plans have been developed for fighter cover and ground troops for protection against sabotage.

<u>Avgas</u> distribution is a problem. Fuel lines connecting tank farms with operating bases are not currently in use. Until pipe lines are activated, it would be necessary to resort to rail and motor transportation, with obvious disadvantages.

The RAF now plans to station approximately 70 B-29s at Marham which complicates present deployment plans.

The next soft spot is <u>reconnaissance</u>. The picture can be summed up briefly.

Although three reconnaissance wings are presently programmed, we now have the equivalent of one wing, and, considering the basic equipment of this wing, the RB-29, we are stretching a point to assess our present strength as the equivalent of one wing. Looking at the job required by "OFF TACKLE", we estimate that at least four reconnaissance wings would be required on a minimum basis.

The accomplishment of such essential photography as pre-strike and post-strike missions would be require approximately 750 sorties. In the event of an early emergency, it would be necessary to draw heavily on the bomber forces to supplement the effort of our present reconnaissance forces.

As for post-strike reconnaissance, the tactical difficulties involved in operating RB-29 aircraft during daylight hours are obvious. The RB-47 will greatly alleviate the bomb damage assessment problem, but the airplanes will not be with us in numbers until early 1953.

So much for reconnaissance.

Next is the matter of <u>fighters</u>.

Since this discussion involves fighter escort over routes to target areas, I will call your attention to the strike plan chart.

We require fighter escort protection along both principle routes; the northern route along southern Scandinavia and the southern route across France. These routes are critical inasmuch as daylight passage is unavoidable during a large part of the year. Also, because of the long range involved, our bombers must operate at medium altitudes over these approach routes.

In addition to close escort, we need fighter cover over UK bases during critical periods of loadings and take-offs.

The entire job, if accomplished efficiently, would call for four fighter groups. At present, we have one group assigned, and one additional group to be assigned in the near future. These groups are to be equipped with F-84E type aircraft. A test program, utilizing four external tanks, is soon to be conducted. Based on the results of this test, we will submit requirements for long range fuel tanks. However, at present there are no stocks of long range fuel tanks in the United Kingdom.

In summary, we have no long range fighter escort capability at present. Inasmuch as escort groups will be required for a period of only 30 to 45 days, it is felt that some arrangement could be worked out to provide them. After this time they could be reassigned for other duty.

<u>Airlift available for deployment.</u>

The present emergency plan calls for approximately 360 C-54 equivalent sorties to be accomplished by E+8. Staff discussions with MATS indicate that they can provide approximately 260 during this period. We are therefore examining the situation to determine how much of this deficit can be made up by using B-29s. Use of the relatively small bomber force for airlift during this period is undesirable for many obvious reasons.

An exercise designed to test SAC-MATS mobility is scheduled for June. MATS will provide 126 C-54 equivalents scheduled for the first four days.

<u>Electronics Counter Measures.</u>

The present war plan calls for the use of chaff and electronic jammers. We plan to use B-29s to support the atomic carriers by strengthening our ECM effort and by diluting enemy defenses.

Our present ECM capability is about 35% effective. This condition is due to a shortage of electronic jammers, a type of chaff that is not altogether suitable, and the fact that automatic chaff dispensers are not yet installed so that they can be operated from pressurized compartments. Steps have been taken to improve the overall ECM picture but months will be required to achieve any material improvement.

The next item is <u>Electronics Maintenance Personnel</u>.

Although the command is fully manned – body-wise – we are not 100% effectively manned.

Certain critical shortages continue to hamper operations, the most critical being electronic maintenance personnel.

In this category, the command is a little over one half manned. Steps have been taken to train out all present personnel shortages, however, some categories will not be completely filled until late 1951.

The last "soft spot" is <u>Materiel</u>.

In January we presented to the Air Staff the major engineering and supply problems which then confronted us in the conversion of our units to new types of aircraft. Some of the problems presented at that time have since been solved or partially solved; however, there are still many confronting us.

A few of our major engineering problems have been:

In connection with the B-50, major engineering and maintenance difficulties have been encountered with the turbo superchargers and the electrical system.

With the B-36, the major deficiencies fall in four categories; power plant, fuel leaks, radar, and armament.

In addition we have various items limiting operations with B-29, RB-29, F-86 and F-84 aircraft.

Our supply support problems have not been greatly alleviated since the January presentation. We are still plagued with an excessive number of B-50 and B-36 critical spares, a serious lack of current supply and maintenance publications, and critical shortages of personnel and survival equipment. These supply deficiencies, of course, add up to an unsatisfactory situation insofar as supply support is concerned.

In closing let me emphasize that I have by no means covered all the problems facing the command. There are many others of somewhat less importance than those covered. They have all been assembled and made known to appropriate agencies.

Also, may I emphasize that I have discussed only those deficiencies which face us today. As the enemy builds up his atomic capability, the mission of the command, and its ability to execute its mission, will be basically effected.

General LeMay will cover this part of the presentation.

January 30, 1957

In 1956, neither the USSR nor the US had a ballistic missile capable of reaching the other's territory. It was assumed that bombers would be the primary delivery vehicle for nuclear weapons

By the end of 1956, however, a large amount of research had been done on mounting a nuclear-armed ballistic missile aboard a submarine, which could then approach Soviet shores undetected and reach targets deep inside the country.

On January 30, 1957, the Naval Warfare Analysis Group released a memo concerning the role that Fleet Ballistic Missiles (FBMs), later known as submarine-launched ballistic missiles (SLBMs), would play in American planning for nuclear warfare.

The "Q-Ships" mentioned in the document were a British anti-submarine tactic used in both World Wars, in which merchant ships were secretly fitted with guns which were hidden on deck, to be used to surprise and sink enemy U-boats.

There is also a brief mention here of "salted" weapons – these referred to early efforts to develop "dirty bombs" which would contain an amount of cobalt. Upon detonation, the cobalt would be irradiated and scattered over a wide area, producing a band of high radiation which, it was thought, might be utilized to act as a barrier to enemy troop movements.

Naval Warfare Analysis Group
Study No. 1
Introduction Of The Fleet Ballistic Missile Into Service
Extracts From CNO Memorandum
(Secret serial OO11P03 of 15 January 1957)
Subj: Introduction of the Fleet Ballistic Missile into Service

1. Reference (a) (NAVWAG Study No. 1) is a study of the introduction of the FBM into the naval family of strike weapon systems. It contains the following salient points:
   a. The SSG(N) (FBM) is the optimum launching vehicle in terms of survival and economy of force.
   b. The mission of the FBM system should be expressed as a deterrent capability.
   c. The initial force requirements for SSG(N) (FBM) should be modest, with a 1965 objective of six such submarines in inventory. Acceptance of this program will require modification of the current five-year shipbuilding program.
2. The concept of FBM utilization as expressed in paragraph 1 above is approved and accepted as the basis of navy planning for the introduction of the FBM into service. This is specifically applicable to the drafting of the operational requirement, development characteristics and ship characteristics, and shall be used as a guideline by the Standing Committee on Shipbuilding and Conversion.
3. Studies are currently under way to determine what type surface combatant ship is best suited for task force employment of the FBM, how many such ships should be planned, and in which Shipbuilding and Conversion Program years such ship or ships should be included. Decisions in these matters will be forthcoming subsequent to the completion of the studies.
/s/ Arleigh Burke

I. INTRODUCTION

This study examines those matters which require prompt decisions, for the Navy to achieve a rapid and orderly development of a deterrent capability using the fleet ballistic missile. Among the subjects included are a study of the optimum launch vehicle for the first operational introduction, a concept for employment, and an estimate of force requirements. In preparing this analysis the following assumptions have been used:

a. The problems of operating early increments of an FBM force contribute as much to determining first generation requirements, as do considerations of the ultimate composition of the force.

b. Adequate test and evaluation facilities will be provided by Mariners I and II, so that only the early operational vehicles need be considered.

c. Only the most elementary force requirements can be intelligently considered at present, since the eventual requirement will probably involve decisions by higher authority as to composition of the national deterrent capability, and considerations of different weapons systems which can diversify our effort and make more difficult the enemy problem of countermeasures.

II. CONCLUSIONS AND RECOMMENDATIONS

LAUNCHING VEHICLE

1. The nuclear powered missile submarine (SSG(N)-FBM) is the only missile-launching vehicle capable of providing assurance of survival when deployed in small numbers.

2. Since considerable "growth potential" is anticipated for both the vehicle and the missile, quantitative specifications are not deemed sufficiently important (within rather broad limits) to warrant delay in introducing the earliest types.

3. Characteristics other than submerged endurance, quiet operation and rapidity of launch require only routine emphasis, since submarines can operate near friendly or neutral shores. Submarine size should be that which is most economical per missile; it should carry at least 3 but not over 10 missiles. Surface launch is acceptable, but submerged launch is preferable and should be developed.

4. Later SSG(N's) should emphasize reduced cost, through the use of smaller submarines, possibly with external missile stowage. Development of a subsurface-to-air weapon system would make a larger submarine acceptable in the more distant future.

5. Initial force requirements for submarines should be fairly modest: a capability to maintain two or three on station will contribute significantly to 1963-65 requirements, will furnish valuable operational experience and will demonstrate unique Naval capabilities.

6. Increased SSG(N) forces should be contingent upon the availability of increased funds, so as not to interfere with other vital Naval missions.

7. If pressures to attain an earlier capability than the SSG-Polaris combination should enforce adoption of an interim surface vessel configuration, it is recommended that conversions of combatant hulls be made, unless new construction can be available sooner or would be cheaper in absolute cost.

8. Other launching vehicles, such as Q-ships, and combatant surface vessels, should be considered for development only for later phases of the program when longer range missiles become available; they would be of value in forcing the enemy to divert his initial attack to many targets.

THE MISSILE

1. A range of 1150 miles is adequate for the initial missiles. Later versions should be capable of 1500 miles, with 2500 miles as the ultimate goal. Initial specifications of minimum range are not critical (800 miles would be acceptable); ultimately, a range band of about 1000 miles is desired.

2. Accuracy and yield should be the best available in a small warhead. For the first generation a yield of 0.4 MT and an over-all system accuracy of 4-mile CEP would be acceptable. Subsequent generations should increase yield and accuracy. Ultimately yield requirements might even be decreased as accuracy increases, to a minimum of about one-third MT, depending on target damage criteria.

3. High launch rates, submerged launch, and longer range should be programmed for development to enhance submarine safety and permit penetration to more distant targets. One ultimate goal, which may not be technologically feasible, is a delayed-launch to be planted by a submerged SSG(N) about an hour in advance. Longer ranges are necessary to permit the missile to be used on surface vessels without restrictions on location of operating areas.

4. Conventional two-stage warheads are adequate. A separate study, soon to be completed, demonstrates no dramatic increase in radiological warfare effectiveness by using "salted" weapons, although there is a minor decrease in strontium-90 world-wide contamination.

PROGRAMMING AND OPERATIONAL REQUIREMENTS

1. A small FBM capability will permit penetration of the limited number of targets, such as Moscow, whose defenses will be difficult to penetrate with other weapons. Missile characteristics desirable for other targets should be deferred beyond this initial stage. CNO should emphasize only the desired early operational capability and desired trends in missile design, and should only specify minimum acceptable missile performance.

2. Very highly defended population or industrial targets should be specified by CNO as the target for the initial FBM capability. A large fraction of targets of naval interest are more suitably attacked by aircraft, or air-breathing missiles of the Triton type.

May 22, 1957

In 1957 President Eisenhower gave "pre-authorization" to several military commanders, granting them the authority to use nuclear weapons on their own initiative, without any previous communication with the President, in the event of a major surprise attack on the United States.

Modern nuclear weapons have complicated coded locking systems called PALs (Permissive Action Links) that prevent them from being activated by any unauthorized person without the proper codes (the President always has with him the suitcase, known as "the football", containing the computer codes for releasing nuclear weapons and authorizing an attack).

In 1957, however, no such system existed, and any local commander who had actual possession of nuclear weapons could, in theory, load a nuclear bomb onto an aircraft and deliver it to a target. The PAL system was designed to prevent any such unauthorized use.

Eisenhower's "pre-authorization" policy was designed to allow military commanders to launch a counter-strike on the Soviet Union if a surprise first-strike was able to knock out the President and other national commanders. Significantly, however, it made no distinction between a Soviet nuclear attack and a major conventional attack – if the Soviet Union were to move into Germany with a large conventional military invasion, commanders in Europe were pre-authorized to use nuclear weapons against the invading troops. For the rest of the Cold War, it remained US policy to initiate the first-use of tactical nuclear weapons to oppose any conventional Soviet invasion of Europe.

INSTRUCTIONS FOR THE EXPENDITURE OF NUCLEAR WEAPONS IN ACCORDANCE WITH THE PRESIDENTIAL AUTHORIZATION DATED MAY 22, 1957

BASIC INSTRUCTIONS

1. <u>AUTHORITY</u>. These instructions are issued pursuant to paragraph 4 of the President's "Authorization for the Expenditure of Nuclear Weapons" dated May 22, 1957.

2. <u>PURPOSE</u>. These instructions establish policies in the implementation of the Presidential Authorization.

3. <u>DEFINITIONS</u>. The following definitions are established for the purpose of these instructions:

a. The term "nuclear weapons" includes all types of weapons and devices which release atomic energy.

b. The term "United States, its Territories and Possessions" includes the Canal Zone.

[*c. The term "Authorizing Commander" is a commander empowered to expend nuclear weapons pursuant to subparagraph 5c of the Presidential "Authorization for the Expenditure of Nuclear Weapons."*]

d. The term "major US forces" refers to those organized units of US military forces comprising the essential operational military strength of the United States, including the numbered field armies, fleets, and air forces and (see subparagraph 6a below) [*the forces of Authorizing Commanders.*]

e. The term "attack" refers to a major hostile assault of such magnitude and against such areas or forces as to constitute an immediate and vital military threat to the security of the United States or to major US forces, as defined above.

f. The terms "expend", "expending", and "expenditure" refer to the firing or launching and detonation of a nuclear weapon.

g. The terms "foreign territory" and "territory of foreign friendly countries" include the territorial waters and air space thereof.

h. The term "international waters" includes the air space above.

[*4. AUTHORIZED EXPENDITURES. When the urgency of time and circumstances clearly does not permit a specific decision by the President, or other person empowered to act in his stead, the Armed Forces of the United States are authorized by the President to expend nuclear weapons in the following circumstances in conformity with these instructions:*]

a. For the defense of the United States, its Territories and possessions:

1. In the United States, its Territories and possessions, and its coastal air defense identification zones, against attack by air – (Special Additional Instructions in Section "A" below).

2. In the United States, its Territories and possessions, and in international waters adjacent thereto as defined in Section "B", against attack by sea – (Special Additional Instructions in Section "B" below).

3. In the territory of friendly foreign countries near the United States, its Territories and possessions, subject to applicable agreements or understandings, if any, with the government exercising sovereignty over the country or countries concerned, against attack by air – (Special Additional Instructions in Section "A" below).

b. For the defense of United States forces in foreign territory and in international waters against Sino-Soviet Bloc attacking forces, subject to applicable agreements or understandings, if any, with the government exercising sovereignty over the country or countries concerned - (Special Additional Instructions in Section "B" below).

c. In the event of nuclear attack upon the United States, in retaliation against the enemy identified as responsible for the attack, subject in the case of retaliation from friendly foreign territory to applicable agreements of understandings, if any, with the government exercising sovereignty over the country or countries concerned – (Special Additional Instructions in Section "C" below).

5. <u>OPERATIONAL LIMITATIONS</u>. Because of the serious international implications of the use of nuclear weapons by US military forces, it is essential that particularly strict command control and supervision be exercised, and that the use of nuclear weapons be limited to the circumstances of grave necessity. *[The authority to expend nuclear weapons in the event urgency of time and circumstances clearly does not permit a specific decision by the President, or other person empowered to act in his stead, is an emergency measure necessitated by recognition of the fact that communications may be disrupted by the attack. It is mandatory to insure that such authority is not assumed through accident or misinformation. The authorization to expend nuclear weapons should be regarded as an authorization effective only until it is possible, in light of time and circumstances, to communicate with the President, or other person empowered to act in his stead.]* In the expenditure of

nuclear weapons pursuant to these instructions, the following limitations will be observed:

[a. *An Authorizing Commander may expend nuclear weapons only when the urgency of time and circumstances clearly does not permit a specific decision by the President, or other person empowered to act in his stead.*

b. *Under this authorization, Authorizing Commanders may not expend nuclear weapons for defense against minor assaults nor against assault upon minor US forces wherein damage inflicted would not constitute an immediate and vital threat to the security of the United States or to major US forces.*

c. *Any expenditure of nuclear weapons pursuant to these instructions will be limited to such size and numbers of weapons and to such targets as are necessary. Further, nuclear weapons will be used in the manner best calculated to avoid expanding hostilities and with due regard for the safety of friendly forces and people.*

d. *Nothing in these instructions shall be construed as preventing any responsible commander from taking such actions as may be necessary to defend his command, with the exception that the expenditure of nuclear weapons may be authorized only by Authorizing Commanders, utilizing the criteria and procedures set forth in these instructions.]*

6. RESPONSIBILITIES AND PROCEDURES. [*Responsibilities and procedures applicable to the expenditure of nuclear weapons, when the urgency of time and circumstances clearly does not permit a specific decision by the President, or other person empowered to act in his stead, are:*

The Authorizing Commanders are designated in the appropriate Sections below for the purposes set forth therein. In addition, commanders of joint task forces and of other commands, equivalent in stature to the numbered forces, as specifically approved by the President and the Secretary of Defense, may from time to time be designated as Authorizing Commanders by the Joint Chiefs of Staff. Further, in regard to the air defense of the United States, its Territories and possessions, these instructions do not limit the authority granted to operational commanders pursuant to the "Authorization for the Expenditure of Atomic Weapons in Air Defense" approved by the President on 18 April 1956 and the "Policy Statement on Interception and Engagement of Hostile Aircraft", approved 24 September 1952, which were implemented in accordance with the revised "Interception and Engagement Instructions and

Procedures", dated 7 December 1956. Previous authorizations to expend atomic weapons in accordance with the revised Interception and Engagement Instructions and Procedures dated December 7, 1956 (attached hereto as Appendix A) are continued in full force and effect.]

[censored]

[f. An Authorizing Commander expending nuclear weapons pursuant to these instructions shall immediately report his action to the President through the Joint Chiefs of Staff and the Secretary of Defense and advise directly all commanders of commands established by the Joint Chiefs of Staff utilizing the most expeditious means available.

g. Upon approval by the Secretary of Defense, the Secretary of State and the President, separate authorizing instructions will be transmitted by the Joint Chiefs of Staff to the Authorizing Commanders designated herein and may be disseminated to subordinate commanders have been designated as Authorizing Commanders pursuant to the procedures of paragraph 6a above.]

[censored]

The existence of these instructions and the provisions thereof are TOP SECRET classified information and must be safeguarded accordingly. No authority exists short of the President to modify this classification or make disclosures inconsistent therewith. In addition to the classification of TOP SECRET, the fact of the existence of these instructions will be limited to a highly restricted group of people.

[censored]

[h. The Joint Chiefs of Staff will keep the Authorizing Commanders informed of the current status of agreements or understandings with friendly foreign countries regarding the expenditure of nuclear weapons in their respective territories.

i. The expenditure of nuclear weapons over Canada will be in accordance with the terms of the interim agreement between the governments of Canada and the United States which was forwarded to the Joint Chiefs of Staff by the Secretary of Defense on 16 March 1957. The current agreement is effective until 1 July 1959. Any expenditure after 1 July 1959 will be in accordance with then existing agreements.]

7. <u>EFFECTIVE DATE</u>. These instructions are effective upon receipt.

Section "A"

<u>Special Additional Instructions for the Defense of the United States, its Territories and Possessions Against Attack by Air</u>

PURPOSE. These special instructions provide additional guidance applicable to the expenditure of nuclear weapons for the defense of the United States, its Territories and possessions, against attack by air:

a. In the United States, its Territories and possessions and in the coastal air defense identification zones (ADIZ's).

b. In the territory of friendly foreign countries near the United States, its territories and possessions, subject to applicable agreements or understandings, if any, with the government exercising sovereignty over the country or countries concerned.

2. PROCEDURE.

a. The expenditure of nuclear weapons in the United States, its Territories and possessions and in the coastal air defense identification zones (ADIZ's) will be in accordance with the revised "Interception and Engagement Instructions and Procedures", dated 7 December 1956, which are attached hereto as Appendix "A" and are continued in full force and effect.

b. The expenditure of nuclear weapons in the territory of friendly foreign countries near the United States, its Territories and possessions will be subject to applicable agreements or understandings, if any, with the government exercising sovereignty over the country or countries concerned and will be in accordance, as closely as the situation permits, with the procedures set forth in the revised "Interception and Engagement Instructions and Procedures", dated 7 December 1956, or such other rules as are applicable in the areas concerned.

c. As regards the expenditure of nuclear weapons in the air space above international waters outside of the coastal air defense identification zones for the defense of the United States, its Territories and possessions against attack by air, the provisions in Section "B" below will apply.

3. *[AUTHORIZING COMMANDERS. Authorizing commanders for the purposes set forth in paragraph 1a of this Section are those military commanders authorized to declare aircraft as "hostile" pursuant to the revised "Interception and Engagement Instructions and Procedures", dated 7 December 1956. Authorizing Commanders for the purposes set forth in paragraph 1b above will be designated in subsequent instructions.]*

Section "B"

Special Additional Instructions for the Defense of the United States, its territories and Possessions Against Attack by Sea and for the Defense of the United States Forces in Foreign Territory and in International Waters Against Sino-Soviet Bloc Attacking forces

1. PURPOSE. These special instructions provide additional guidance applicable to the expenditure of nuclear weapons:

a. In the United States, its Territories and possessions and in international waters adjacent thereto, as defined herein, for the defense of the United States, its Territories and possessions, against attack by sea.

b. For the defense of the United States forces in foreign territory and in international waters, against Sino-Soviet Bloc attacking forces, subject to applicable agreements or understandings, if any, with the government exercising sovereignty over the country or countries concerned.

2. DEFINITION. The following definition is established for the purpose of these instructions:

The term "international waters adjacent to", as used in subparagraph 1a above, is defined to include all international waters and the air space above within effective enemy striking range of the United States, its Territories and possessions.

3. *ENGAGEMENT. [When the urgency of time and circumstances clearly does not permit a specific decision by the President, or other person empowered to act in his stead, any decision to expend nuclear weapons against attacking forces is the responsibility of the Authorizing Commander in consonance with the criteria set forth in these instructions.]*

a. In amplification of these criteria, the situations below may be considered examples of an attack, as defined in these instructions:

1. A submarine or surface craft engages in launching or controlling missiles against the United States, its Territories and possessions.

2. A Sino-Soviet Bloc force engages in launching or controlling missiles, bombing, air-to-air attack, or strafing attack against a major US force in international waters or in foreign territory.

3. Sino-Soviet Bloc ground, paratroop or other forces make a major assault and thereby effect a significant penetration of an area occupied by major US forces in foreign territory with the evident intention of rendering them militarily ineffective or of continuing the advance.

b. The above list of situations is not all inclusive and does not preclude expenditure of nuclear weapons against assaulting Sino-

Soviet Bloc forces under other situations consonant with the criteria set forth in these instructions.

c. Unidentified submarines or aircraft which are engaged in an attack as defined in these instructions may be assumed to be Sino-Soviet Bloc attacking forces.

d. In defending against attack by air, commanders shall conform as closely as the situation permits to the procedures set forth in the revised "Interception and Engagement Instructions and Procedures", dated 7 December 1956, or such other rules which are applicable to the areas concerned.

4. OPERTIONAL LIMITATIONS.

a. *[When the urgency of time and circumstances clearly does not permit a specific decision by the President:]*

1. [An Authorizing Commander, as designated in subparagraph 5a below and as contemplated in subparagraph 5b below, may order the expenditure of nuclear weapons in international waters and in foreign territory [censored   ] subject to applicable agreements of understandings, if any, with the government (except for a government involved in attack on US forces) exercising sovereignty over the country or countries concerned, to eliminate the local threat of Sino-Soviet Bloc forces engaging in an attack against United States forces, when in his judgment this is vital to the security of his forces.

[censored]

b. [Authorizing Commanders will bear in mind that the above authority to expend nuclear weapons is an emergency measure necessitated by recognition of the fact that communications may be disrupted by the attack. It is mandatory to insure that such authority is not assumed through accident or misinformation. The authorization to expend nuclear weapons should be regarded as an authorization effective only until it is possible, in light of time and circumstances, to communicate with the President, or other person empowered to act in his stead.

5. AUTHORIZING COMMANDERS.

a. Authorizing commanders for the purposes set forth in this section are: The Commander in Chief, US-Europe; The Commander in Chief, Alaska; The Commander in Chief, Caribbean; The Commander in Chief, Atlantic; The Commander in Chief, Continental Air Defense; The Commander in Chief, Pacific; The Commander in Chief, Strategic Air Command. The Commander in Chief, US Naval Forces, Eastern Atlantic and Mediterranean (CINCNELM) will be an Authorizing Commander for the purposes set forth in this section only when he has been directed to conduct operations as a Specified Commander by the President through the Secretary of Defense. This limitation does not preclude his designation as an Authorizing Commander by CINCEUR in accordance with paragraph 5b below.

b. In addition, commanders of numbered field armies, fleets, and air forces, and commanders of Joint Task Forces and of other commands equivalent in stature to the numbered forces may from time to time be designated as Authorizing Commanders by recommendation of a Specified or Unified Commander to the Joint Chiefs of Staff or by the Joint chiefs of Staff, with the approval of the Secretary of Defense and the President in each instance.

Section "C"

Special Additional Instructions Regarding Retaliation in the Event of a Nuclear Attack Upon the United States

1. <u>PURPOSE</u>. These special instructions provide additional guidance applicable to the expenditure of nuclear weapons in the event of a nuclear attack upon the United States in retaliation against the enemy identified as responsible for the attack, subject, in the case of retaliation from friendly foreign territory, to applicable agreements or understandings, if any, with the government exercising sovereignty over the country or countries concerned.

2. <u>POLICY</u>. In the event of a nuclear attack upon the United States, it is assumed that the President would have approximately the same information as the Department of Defense regarding the strength and character of the attack and the identity of the nation launching it. *[Retaliation for such an attack, therefore, will be on order of the President, except in circumstances where immediate communications have become impossible between the President and responsible officials of the Department of Defense. In such circumstances, the Secretary of Defense or the next official in the chain of responsibility, acting in the name of the Secretary of Defense, is authorized to expend nuclear weapons in retaliation against the enemy identified as responsible for the attack, subject, in the case of retaliation from friendly foreign territory, to applicable agreements or understandings, if any, with the government exercising sovereignty over the country or countries concerned.]*

3. DEPARTMENT OF DEFENSE PROCEDURE AND RESPONSIBILITIES

a. [When retaliation is ordered by the Department of Defense such orders will be issued through command channels by the Secretary of

Defense or by the next official in the chain of responsibility, acting in the name of the Secretary.

b. In the event that a nuclear attack has in fact occurred, as authenticated through prescribed procedures as approved by the President, on the United States, and it is impossible to communicate with the Secretary of Defense and the Joint Chiefs of Staff, expenditure of nuclear weapons for retaliatory purposes may be ordered by an Authorizing Commander. Before ordering such an expenditure under this authorization, an Authorizing Commander will adhere to the following conditions:

(1). Comply with applicable international agreements or understandings, if any, in expending nuclear weapons for retaliatory purposes from friendly foreign territory.

(2). Alert his retaliatory forces to the fact that they may be recalled prior to their arrival in the target area.

4. <u>OPERATIONAL LIMITATIONS</u>. The authority to expend nuclear weapons for retaliatory purposes is an emergency measure necessitated by recognition of the fact that communications may be disrupted by the attack. It is mandatory to insure that such authority is not assumed through accident or mis-information. The authorization for expenditure of nuclear weapons for retaliatory purposes should be regarded as an authorization effective only until it is possible, in light of time and circumstances, to communicate with the President or other person empowered to act in his stead.

5. <u>AUTHORIZING COMMANDERS</u>. The Authorizing Commanders for the purpose set forth in this Section and approved by the President are listed below:

a. The Commander in Chief, Atlantic.

b. The US Commander in Chief, Europe.

c. The Commander in Chief, Pacific.

d. The Commander in Chief, Strategic Air Command.

e. The Commander in Chief, US Naval Forces, Eastern Atlantic and Mediterranean, will be an Authorizing Commander for the purpose set forth in this section only when he has been directed to conduct operations as a Specified Commander by the President through the Secretary of Defense.

November 20, 1958

By 1958, Intercontinental Ballistic Missiles (ICBMs) based in the Soviet Union and the United States allowed each to reach the other with nuclear warheads. The number of ICBMs on both sides grew quickly throughout the 60's.

This classified memorandum reports on the results of a study carried out by analysts to determine what the effects would be of a hypothetical Soviet first-strike in 1961, and a full retaliation by the US. According to the scenario, every Soviet city with a population greater than 25,000 people would be the target of a nuclear weapon; larger cities would receive more than one warhead.

During the meeting, Eisenhower remarked that he remembered when the nuclear-warfare plan contained only 70 targets within the USSR, thought that the capacity to inflict that level of damage was enough for deterrence, and wondered whether we really needed the capacity for "100% pulverization".

MEMORANDUM
SUBJECT: Discussion at the 387th Meeting of the National Security Council, Thursday, November 20, 1958
1. REPORT BY THE NET EVALUATION SUBCOMMITTEE.
Mr Gordon Gray introduced General Thomas, the Director of the Net Evaluation Subcommittee Staff, and explained the general

purpose of the meeting. (A copy of Mr Gray's remarks are included in the Minutes of the Meeting and another is attached to this Memorandum.)

General Thomas summarized the methodology of the report that was about to be given. He pointed out the change which had been made last year by the President in the directive to the subcommittee and also referred to the use made by the Subcommittee of the current National Intelligence Estimate of Soviet intentions and capabilities. General Thomas also pointed out the assumptions under which this year's evaluation had been developed and noted the participation in the evaluation of representatives from all four of the military services as well as representatives of each of the other responsible Government agencies.

General Thomas then introduced Brig General Willard W Smith, Deputy Director of the Net Evaluation Subcommittee Staff, who discussed the basic assumptions concerning the assumed Soviet attack on the US which was mounted by the Soviets in mid-1961 with strategic surprise. This was followed by General Smith's discussion of the detailed assumptions made by the USSR with respect to the nature of the attack which it made on the continental US. General Smith followed with a discussion of the detailed assumptions underlying the US retaliatory attack on the Soviet Union.

Upon the conclusion of General Smith's portion of the report, Colonel William R Calhoun, USA, described the Soviet attack on the continental US. Captain Edward L Dashiell, USN, subsequently described the US retaliatory attack on the Soviet Union as well as the US military posture after the attack on the US by the Soviet Union.

Colonel Calhoun next expounded the estimate of the damage inflicted on the US by the Soviet attack and Captain Dashiell described the damage inflicted on the Soviet Union by the US retaliatory attack. Dr RJ Smith of the Central Intelligence Agency, also a member of the Subcommittee Staff, discussed the potentialities of the Soviet clandestine attack on the US which concluded the formal presentation.

In his concluding statement General Thomas emphasized the difficulties involved in attempting to achieve realistic assumptions with regard to the evaluation as a whole. There were obviously many uncertainties with respect to the military capabilities of the US at a period as distant as mid-1961 and of course even more uncertainty as to the military capabilities of the Soviet Union at the same time.

Despite these uncertainties, General Thomas believed the assumptions were sufficiently realistic to bear out the essential validity of the evaluation.

General Thomas also invited the council to take a backward look at the previous reports of the Net Evaluation Subcommittee in relation to the findings of the report just rendered. There was, he pointed out, an essential similarity to the findings of all the reports since the first one was delivered in 1954. These findings were listed in a chart described as "Recurrent Conclusions".

Mr Gray reminded the President and the Council that this was General Thomas' last appearance as Director of the Subcommittee Staff, and that his successor, Lt General Thomas F Hickey, was present this morning. Thereafter, Mr Gray presented a recommendation in substantially the following language:

"You will recall that the 1957 report involved a retaliatory attack confining itself to a primarily military target system. For 1958, the President directed that the exercise concern itself with the retaliatory objective of [*immediately paralyzing the Russian nation, rather than concentrating on targets of a military character although not entirely ruling out particular military targets which the Subcommittee believed would significantly contribute to paralysis of the Russian nation.*

"*The presentation you have just heard has concluded that a substantial reduction of the capability of the USSR to recover would be accomplished by the concentration of a US retaliatory effort against a combined military-urban industrial target system as opposed to a strictly military target system. The conclusion also was that such an effort would destroy the Soviet nuclear offensive capability.*]

"A central aim of our policy is to deter the Communists from use of their military power, remaining prepared to fight general war should one be forced upon the US. There has been no suggestion from any quarter as to a change in this basic policy. However, as you know, NSC 5410/1, the so-called 'war objectives' paper, is in the process of review. These matters are inextricably interwoven.

"In the light of these facts, it seems to me that it is important for you, Mr President, to have before you, for your consideration, an appraisal of the relative merits, from the point of view of an effective deterrence, [*of retaliatory efforts directed toward:*

"*1. Primarily a military target system; or*

"2. *What might be felt to be the optimum mix of a combined military-urban industrial target system.*]

"Such appraisal should also take into account the requirements of a counter-force capacity which might conceivably be called upon in the case of unequivocal strategic warning of impending Soviet attack on the US. The question here might be whether the character and composition of such a force would be adequate to the purposes of 1 or 2 above, and vice versa.

These matters have been under intensive study in the Department of Defense. If it agreeable to you I shall be glad to work with Mr McElroy and General Twining to determine the best way to accomplish such an appraisal, relating it as necessary to the review of the so-called War Objectives Paper, bearing in mind that the knowledge and views of the State Department and other Federal agencies would be importantly involved."

When Mr Gray had concluded his suggested Council action, the President said he was convinced that what Mr Gray proposed to have done was essential for the obvious reason that in today's presentation of the US retaliatory attack on the Soviet Union, [*the US had as targets every city in the USSR with a population of over 25,000 people. In view of this very large number of urban targets, the President believed that we must get back to the formulation of the series of targets in the Soviet Union destruction of which would most economically paralyze the Russian nation.*] Turning to General Twining and addressing him and other members of the Joint Chiefs of Staff, the President said that he could remember well when the military used to have no more than [*70 targets in the Soviet Union and believed that destruction of these 70 targets would be sufficient. Now, however, a great many more targets had been added.*] He accordingly expressed his approval of the suggested action by Mr Gray.

[*Secretary McElroy expressed his view that the dispersal of the hardened Soviet ICBM bases introduced a new element in the picture because even if we succeeded in destroying the cities and urban centers of the Soviet Union, these missile sites would still enable the Soviet Union to retain an add-on capability with their long-range missiles.*

In response to Secretary McElroy's point, the President commented that in this morning's presentation the Soviets delivered all of their ICBMs in the first two hours of their attack on the US. Secretary McElroy agreed that this was the case but said that there was some doubt as to whether this was a sound assumption as to the Soviet use of their ICBMs. The President replied that the presentation assumed that we are trying to destroy the will of the Soviet Union to fight. If in the first thirty hours of the nuclear exchange the US succeeded in accomplishing the degree of devastation in the Soviet Union that had been outlined in this morning's presentation, we would already have accomplished our purpose of destroying the will of the Soviet Union to fight. One could not go on to argue that we must require a 100 percent pulverization of the Soviet Union. There was obviously a limit – a human limit – to the devastation which human beings could endure.]

Secretary McElroy expressed his agreement to the action recommended by Mr Gray and the President brought the meeting to a conclusion with an expression of warm congratulations to General Thomas and his associates and also a welcome to General Hickey who would be taking over henceforth from General Thomas.

The National Security Council:

a. Noted and discussed the Annual Report for 1958 of the Net Evaluation Subcommittee, pursuant to NSC 5816, as presented orally by the Director and other members of the Subcommittee Staff.

b. Noted the President's request for an appraisal of the relative merits, from the point of view of effective deterrence, of alternative retaliatory efforts directed toward: (1) Primarily a military target system, or (2) an optimum mix of a combined military-urban industrial target system. Such an appraisal is to take into account the requirements of a counter-force capacity and whether such a counter-force capacity would be adequate for (1) or (2) above and vice versa. The Secretary of Defense, the Chairman, Joint Chiefs of Staff, and the Special Assistant to the President for National Security Affairs are to determine the best means of defining and accomplishing such an appraisal, relating it as necessary to the current review of NSC 5410/1 and the interests of the Department of State and other Executive agencies.

NOTE: The action in b above, as approved by the President, subsequently transmitted to the Secretary of Defense, the Chairman, Joint Chiefs of Staff, and the Special Assistant to the President for National Security Affairs for appropriate implementation.

December 31, 1958

This classified memorandum covers discussions concerning the decision to "preauthorize" certain commanders to use nuclear weapons on their own initiative, within certain guidelines, without previous communication from the President. The memo re-emphasizes that nuclear weapons are preauthorized for use against any major Soviet or Chinese attack, whether that attack is nuclear or conventional in nature. Eisenhower, in turn, emphasized that any such use of nuclear weapons would be strictly limited to the immediate defense of the attacked American forces in the face of a serious danger to US security, saying that he did not want an incident such as the torpedoing of an American aircraft carrier to lead to nuclear escalation.

Legally, all American nuclear weapons belong to the Atomic Energy Commission, and are only released to Department of Defense custody when an attack is ordered. The memo, therefore, also discusses the process of deploying nuclear weapons overseas, making them immediately available for local commanders in case of attack.

The locations of these nuclear weapon caches are censored from this report, but we know from other sources that American nuclear bombs were stored in Spain, Italy, Morocco and Britain during various periods of the Cold War. Nuclear intermediate range missiles were also deployed during this period in Italy and Turkey.

MEMORANDUM OF CONFERENCE WITH THE PRESIDENT
December 19, 1958 - 2:30 PM

The purpose of this meeting was to present for the President's approval the joint defense/AEC proposal for dispersal of atomic weapons. (State had concurred.) Various items of discussion came out during the presentation. Essentially, these were:

a. Custody of atomic weapons, specifically that the military commanders be authorized to act as an agent of the AEC in maintaining custody of atomic weapons.

b. [censored]

c. Means of safeguarding dispersed atomic weapons in the event of limited or general war.

d. Relationship of the AEC with the Joint Congressional Committee on Atomic Energy in operational matters.

In further discussion, the President stressed certain points of particular interest. He queried how well protected our weapons are overseas, and Mr Quarles said they have the same protective arrangements as here. The President added that he had the feeling there was increasing lack of control on these weapons, and emphasized that there must be no carelessness in their custody. General Twining pointed out the need to balance conflicting considerations: while dispersal undoubtedly lessens control, if the weapons are not locally available to commanders in an emergency they may not arrive in time. The President commented that, as to anti-aircraft and anti-submarine weapons, he did not have too much reservation; when it comes to increasing the number of large weapons that are dispersed, he wanted very careful review of protective arrangements.

[censored]

He said his thinking was that the United States may not be able to carry out more than one sortie from this area, because fields could well be immediately destroyed. He asked as to the Defense thinking on this matter, indicating that while enough weapons to arm the planes that are stationed there could logically be kept on hand, one must ask why we could not send the other B-47s planned for straight from the United States with weapons aboard. The defense members said they would study this matter further.

The President approved the dispersal plan as presented by Admiral Parker. However, he desired that he be briefed at a later date on the planning by which this dispersion scheme has been calculated in order to afford optimum economy and usefulness of our national stockpile. (Scheduled for January 5, 1959.)

At this point Admiral parker and Colonel Schinz departed and Mr Lay joined the group.

The group then presented a letter for the President's approval entitled "Instructions for the Expenditure of Nuclear Weapons in Accordance With the Presidential Authorization dated May 22, 1957." Mr Gray brought the President up to date on this subject by reminding him that the matter had been discussed this last September in Newport, at which time Mr Gray had presented a version of these instructions agreed between Department of State and Department of Defense. At that time the President had raised certain questions. Mr Gray stated that the language had been agreed but had at that time been too broad in that it allowed [*a commander to*] attack any element of Sino-Soviet forces, without restriction. He pointed out the revised language in this letter states in relation to retaliatory missions, [*"An authorizing commander....may also order expenditure of nuclear weapons against elements of the attacking force in the Soviet Union, but only when an attack has been launched against the Continental United States as authenticated through prescribed procedures as approved by the President." (Section "B", paragraph 4a2).*]

In regard to this language, the President questioned the status of China, pointing out that only the Soviet Union has been mentioned.

(At this time word was received that the ATLAS satellite was transmitting the President's voice over the radio.)

Mr Quarles, in answer to the President's question, stated that this limitation does not preclude an attack on China.

The President then asked whether these instructions were confined to a situation in which the enemy used nuclear weapons. Mr Gray responded to this by pointing out that they apply to any attack, nuclear or non-nuclear, which threatens to destroy US forces overseas. He pointed out, however, that it requires a clear situation [*in which Presidential authority cannot be obtained.*] Mr Quarles affirmed this statement adding that pursuit into any territory as necessary is permitted except into the USSR, unless [*the commander knows*] there has been an attack on the US—in which case pursuit into the USSR is authorized.

The President expressed his concern by citing the example in which an enemy submarine shoots two torpedoes into a carrier. In this case, does the commander suddenly decide that he must destroy targets on land in order to assure the safety of the rest of the force? In other words, he points out there is an infinite variety of conditions possible. To this, Mr Quarles answered that this letter sets forth principles only and that each commander will receive separate instructions, each set to be specifically approved by the President.

The President continued to stress the point of degree of retaliation. He cited the case of China. There he felt we might hit bases which threaten US forces and would not go so far as to hit Chungking with big weapons. Mr Gray said that retaliation would be only sufficient to eliminate the local threat of Sino-Soviet forces.

The President continued to express doubt on the degree of response, citing the USS PANAY incident of 1937 as a case of attack on a portion of a US force. This type of incident is exactly what he does not want parlayed into a major attack on our fleet. (Mr Murphy gave as an example the necessity to strike [censored] in the event of an action in Korea.) The President let this subject pass, however, with Mr Quarles' assurance that this letter sets forth principles only and that the implementing instructions will deal with these contingencies specifically.

The discussion then turned to [*the level of command to which the authority to expend nuclear weapons should be delegated. Mr Gray pointed out that the authority is delegated to the commanders in chief of unified and specified commands only. This may be sub-delegated to the level of field armies, numbered fleets, numbered air forces, and task forces of like size. However, in order to so sub-delegate,*] permission must be granted by the Joint Chiefs of Staff, with Presidential approval in each case. Such instructions will go to the unified commanders sealed.

[*The President here cited as an example the Seventh Army in Europe. He does not feel that authority to expend atomic weapons should be delegated to such a command, which is a portion of US forces in Europe. To Mr Gray's statement that the Seventh Army represents an individual case which would have to be dealt with individually, the President then questioned the wisdom of designating the field army level of command. Instead, he considers it preferable to state simply that all exceptions to the policy of delegating only to unified and like commanders be brought to the President for approval. He and Mr Herter agreed that it is most important that word of any delegation from the President be withheld from our allies. It is in the US interest to maintain the atmosphere that all authority stays with the President without delegation.]*

Mr Gray pointed out that if this letter is approved, it should be typed in three copies, one of which should be addressed to the Defense Department, one to the State Department, and one retained in the President's files. To this the President did not respond, but stated that he would like to retain this letter for further examination.

Mr Quarles pointed out that the Secretary of Defense and the Joint Chiefs of Staff would be seeing the President on Monday, December 22, and it could be discussed further at that time. This the President approved.

(It was later decided to hold off on this discussion in order to give the President time to study the paper.)

August 17, 1959

By mid-1959, the US nuclear arsenal had grown to such a level that it was becoming necessary to coordinate any retaliatory attack to reach the most effective targets. As a result, the military recommended that a Single Integrated Operations Plan (SIOP) be produced, that would serve as the master plan for nuclear warfare. Since it was assumed that worldwide communications networks would be knocked out early in any attack, the SIOP would allow nuclear weapons to be pre-sited and then launched against preplanned targets as soon as the order came for counter-attack, without the need for continuous communication with the President.

This classified memo reveals some of the discussion concerning the process of selecting and prioritizing the targets in the Soviet Bloc that would be hit under such a coordinated plan.

The memo reveals some details about US war planning. It is noted that some 2,400 locations in the Soviet Bloc were targeted. The discussion revolved around the options of either launching a pre-emptive first-strike against the USSR, or of a retaliatory strike against the Soviet Union after a Russian attack. In the event of an American first-strike, the primary targets would be the Soviet ICBMs and bomber bases. In 1959, however, the US had no spy satellite capability, and therefore could not be sure that an American first-strike would eliminate the Soviet nuclear capability. In a retaliatory strike, on the other hand, there would be no point in hitting the empty Soviet nuclear bases, so the full weight of the American response would be targeted at urban areas and industrial targets.

NOTE BY THE SECRETARIES TO THE JOINT CHIEFS OF STAFF ON TARGET COORDINATION AND ASSOCIATED PROBLEMS

The enclosed memorandum by the Chairman, Joint Chiefs of Staff, dated 17 August 1959, is circulated for information.

MEMORANDUM FOR THE SECRETARY OF DEFENSE

Subject: Target Coordination and Associated Problems

1. On 28 July 1959, at the Armed Forces Policy Council meeting, you asked for my views on procedures for coordination of atomic strike plans. This memorandum presents, for your information, a resume of what we are currently doing and a discussion of controversial issues which must be resolved in order to improve our effectiveness. If the Joint Chiefs of Staff are unable to reach agreement on any aspect of this problem area, you will be advised.

2. Target coordination and associated problems have received more and more attention during the past few years not because of unacceptable weaknesses in our present position—but, rather, because of the impact of decisions in this area on future Service programs and on the allocation of resources available to the Department of Defense. We do have weaknesses in our system today, and these weaknesses should be eliminated as rapidly as possible. However, the major impact of our current examination of this problem will be on future posture and future capability, and we must expect that attitudes and judgments on these issues will be somewhat influenced by the budgetary implications.

BACKGROUND

3. Before 1952 there were so few atomic weapons in the stockpile and such limited capability outside the Air Force that coordination presented no significant difficulties. Early in 1952, as the stockpile became larger, and delivery capability of other than Air Force forces increased, the Joint Chiefs of Staff set up machinery to coordinate atomic targeting. Two types of procedures evolved: planning coordination and operational coordination.

4. Planning coordination stems from the requirement by the Joint Chiefs of Staff that commanders develop and dove-tail with other commanders the individual strike plans which are spelled out in their atomic annexes, which are prepared in support of the JSOP. Up to the present time, this initial coordination of plans between commanders has been somewhat spotty. It is rather good between some commands; inadequate between others. Following individual

coordination between commands, the plans are further coordinated at conferences at which all commanders are represented.

5. Prior to 1955 this coordination was accomplished at conferences held at SAC. Since 1955, this coordination has taken place at World-Wide Coordination Conferences (WWCC's) held at the Pentagon. The last two of these were monitored by a senior member of the Joint Staff and the next conference is scheduled to be monitored by J-3. This is in line with the new operational responsibilities of the Joint Chiefs of Staff.

6. Following the World-Wide Coordination Conferences, the plans are submitted to the Joint Chiefs of Staff for review and approval, at which time the Joint Staff reviews each plan and the combined plans as a whole.

7. So far I have been dealing only with planning coordination. To effect operational coordination the Joint Chiefs of Staff have established Joint War Room Annexes (Pentagon and Fort Ritchie) and the Joint Coordination Centers (JCC's) [*located in the United Kingdom and in Hawaii.*] These centers screen all atomic strike plans, and, based on targets and routes thereto, identify potential conflict situations. Actual conflicts develop only when actual strike timing is made known. Representatives of the commands, permanently stationed at the JCC's, are charged with monitoring execution of the plans and resolving conflicts as they develop. Communications exist so that recommendations on conflicts which cannot be resolved can be referred to the Joint Chiefs of Staff, and agreed resolutions can be flashed to commanders for implementation. Joint exercises are held periodically to test the effectiveness and exercise the procedures of this system. The last of these exercises, DICE CUP, was held between 27 February and 2 March of this year. While these exercises have resulted in some improvements, they have also defined more clearly certain fundamental weaknesses in current procedures.

8. The procedures outlined above are elaborate, well-established and sophisticated systems which over the years have effected a substantial measure of target coordination. Out of a total of about 2,400 targets, something over 300, or about 13%, have been labeled "duplications". Whether or not these are in fact duplications is a matter of judgment entailing such considerations as the degree of destruction required on a target, the reaction time of the various forces, the attrition of delivery vehicles, and other operational factors. Furthermore, an overlap in scheduling because two or more

commands consider the destruction of a single target essential to the accomplishment of their missions does not necessarily mean that there will, in fact, be a duplication in execution. Once it has been determined that a target has been neutralized or destroyed the procedure is that messages will be dispatched to preclude a second and unnecessary attack. However, an elaborate world-wide communications system is required to effect the coordination. In maneuvers and exercises communications frequently lag too far behind. Under combat conditions the system would undoubtedly be degraded and might function with considerably reduced effectiveness.

9. From our experience in this area to date, we can derive at least one fundamental principle. This principle is that atomic operations must be pre-planned for automatic execution to the maximum extent possible and with minimum reliance on post-H-hour communications. However, with respect to the Joint Coordination Centers, I believe that we should continue their functioning even if we make other changes which will be discussed hereinafter. The Joint Coordination Centers are an extremely useful maneuver tool. Even if they never functioned in war, during exercises they isolate problem areas and develop valuable data which is fed back into our operational plans.

10. From our experience to date, I have also arrived at the conclusion that not much more progress can be achieved under the present arrangements for target coordination. Some minor improvements can, of course, be made, but any significant progress will require fundamental changes in our present system. Some of these changes should be made immediately; action on others may be deferred without serious consequences.

ACTIONS CURRENTLY IN PROGRESS

11. In addition to the routine staffing of atomic annexes as described in the preceding paragraphs, two actions are now in process which may contribute toward improvement. These are:

    a. The "Optimum Mix Study" being conducted by General Hickey's staff, due date 31 October 1959.

    b. JCS study of procedural arrangements for target system analysis and war gaming.

UNDERLYING ISSUES

12. Having described procedures currently in effect, and noted additional actions in process, we should now examine the underlying

issues. In terms of these issues, the problem breaks down into three categories. These categories are:

a. The process of targeting which leads directly to consideration of force adequacy.

b. The development of integrated operational plans.

c. The question of operational control of the strike forces involved.

13. In the past there have been basic differences of viewpoint within the Joint Chiefs of Staff on all three of these categories. Unfortunately, it is not possible to resolve the issues by mathematics or precise techniques. Diagnostic studies and mathematical treatment can provide inputs which assist in tackling these problems—but such analytical work cannot produce a definitive answer. Ultimately, military and executive judgment must be exercised in determining specific policies and programs.

14. The resolution of the underlying issues calls for command decision, and we will never make much more progress in this area until decisions are made and enforced. In order to isolate the specific decisions, which in my judgment are required, I will treat with each category of the problem in some detail.

THE PROCESS OF TARGETING

15. The process of targeting is the most complicated of all the issues. It involves specific sub-issues and problems which are discussed in the following paragraphs.

16. The first problem is - how many and what kind of targets should be destroyed? The area of disagreement here is exceedingly wide. Opinions vary possibly by a factor of ten. The real question is— what constitutes an adequate deterrent and an effective counter-force if deterrence fails? What should our targeting philosophy be? Should we plan only for the destruction of population centers and control centers? Or should we keep in being a strong counter-force capability? What constitutes an "optimum mix" of targets of various categories?

17. Those who propose a basically population center target system for the future insist that it will be an impossible task to neutralize the Soviet ICBM system; that we will not know where the missiles are located and, even if we did know, we would never strike the first blow—hence the Soviet missiles would be on the way before we could counter-attack. On the other hand, if we were to strike certain urban and control centers, the Soviets would be incapable of prosecuting the war, and the United States would emerge in top. Therefore, according

to this line of thinking, it is a waste of money to build a strategic delivery system capable of attacking more than a few hundred targets.

18. Those who propose a strong counter-force capability insist that we must develop the necessary Intelligence; that it will be easier to destroy a missile before it is launched than after; that the Soviets will not be able to launch anything like 100% of their missiles in the first salvo; that, in any case, we must destroy the Soviet capability to re-attack in order to minimize damage to the United States; that a force geared to a few hundred targets cannot survive a surprise attack in strength and thus would not provide a deterrent to Soviet aggression; and that we will have no strength in foreign policy if we lose the capability for pre-emptive action based on strategic Intelligence.

19. My own judgment on this issue is influenced somewhat by our past experience and by my estimate of Soviet philosophy. We have developed a strategic capability to launch, under good to optimum conditions, possibly 2,000 to 4,000 strategic weapons with manned aircraft, and we have, thus far, deterred general war. Soviet military doctrine is based on the Principle of Mass, and I believe that the Soviets will respect only a very powerful force. Further, I believe that they will attempt, over the next several years, to augment their present force of about 1,000 medium and heavy jet bombers with a limited number of manned bombers of advanced design and with an ICBM force numbered in four figures. We have developed our present long-range strategic force during a period of relative Soviet weakness. I would see no logic in allowing our own strategic force to decline in power. Moreover, I consider that the necessity of prevailing in general war is of such import that any error in judgment should be on the safe side. I, therefore, lean to the heavy side on this issue.

20. From previous experience and study I have always believed that we should adopt a policy along the following lines:

Policy. We should continue to develop and keep up-to-date a target system for strategic attack which includes:

(1) The critical components of Soviet long-range nuclear delivery capability.

(2) Governmental and military control centers.

(3) War-sustaining resources.

(4) Population centers.

21. On completion of General Hickey's study we may have more definite information on this subject. Once we have adopted a

targeting policy, such as the one above, or any other as finally determined by the Secretary of Defense, we will have made significant progress. The questions we next face are as follows:

a. who or what agency is going to apply this policy, develop the target system and keep it up-to-date?

b. what agency will review the target system for consistency with policy and give it the stamp of final approval?

22. My thinking on this is that the commander responsible for the strategic mission should take the initial steps to develop the national strategic target system—regardless of and without prejudice to what forces might attack what targets. For the development of this national strategic target system, the responsible commander should be provided with an approved targeting philosophy and guide lines. He will, of course, rely heavily on the work of the targeting section of the Air Intelligence staff and the analytical work which has been produced by such agencies as WSBG, DASA and Rand. Since any commander may be expected, at times, to err on the safe side in determining his requirements, higher level non-partisan review is obviously necessary. This kind of a higher level review, of the target system per se, is, initially, an Intelligence function. "Intelligence," in this initial review of the target system recommended by the commander, should determine if the system constitutes a suitable basis for further analysis. Is the target system in consonance with approved targeting policy? Will the system, if destroyed, accomplish the commander's mission as prescribed by the Joint Chiefs of Staff? Based on past experience and judgment, does the listing of targets appear excessive, insufficient, or generally in the ball park? In my judgment, this initial review is a Joint Staff (J-2) function. What J-2 should do here is to come out with one of the problem elements which is required in the succeeding steps of operational planning, operational analysis, and war gaming. The J-2 review of the commander's recommended target system should, of course, receive final review by the Joint Chiefs of Staff before the succeeding steps are taken.

DEVELOPMENT OF INTEGRATED OPERATIONAL PLANS

23. The next major issue with respect to targeting and associated problems involves both intelligence and operations. Once you have an approved target list for further analysis, the question arises as to how many bombs or missiles should be launched against each target. Here we get into the area of the "over kill" controversy. Operational

factors such as estimated attrition of the attacking force, weapon yield, CEP, level of destruction required, and surface versus airburst weapons enter into this aspect of the problem. Do we want a 10% probability of 10% destruction, or a 90% probability of 90% destruction, or something in between? Should we surface burst, which gives a higher level of local destruction and fall-out but requires more bombs, or should we air burst? These are complicated problems and the answers are not the same for the various categories of targets. The geography of the problem is also important because it affects friendly or neutral populations. However, in general, it can be stated that the Army and Navy favor a lower level of destruction while the Air Force favors a higher level of destruction. The Air Force favors a higher level of destruction because of their experience that it is almost always cheaper to destroy a target in the initial attack, even if it requires more force, than to have to re-attack the same target.

24. Fortunately, this aspect of the problem can be better handled by analytical and mathematical techniques than can the other aspects of the problem. However, handling this aspect of the problem goes beyond the Intelligence function of targeting. It requires that there be developed an outline operational plan which provides a general plan of attack, to include timing and the characteristics of delivery vehicles and weapons. Working with the operational plan, it is possible to apply war gaming techniques to shed some light on the question of how many bombs or missiles should be launched against the various elements of the strategic target system.

25. In the past and at the present time commands have been involved in the planned attack of the strategic target system. Hence, the agencies which have conducted war games have had no single integrated operational plan with which to work. They have had to piece together the operational plans of the field commanders and utilize the results of World-Wide Coordination Conferences as a basis for war gaming. One of the problems, then, is: do we need a single integrated operational plan for the strategic attack? In my judgment we do need such a plan. Since CINCSAC is assigned the major portion of forces responsible for the strategic mission, I would think that he should be charged with the responsibility for developing such a plan. His plan should, of course, be reviewed by the Joint Chiefs of Staff.

26. In the development of this integrated operational plan we would have to face up to two questions now and one at a later date.

a. The two questions for immediate decision would be:

(1) should any force without an all-weather capability be allocated strategic targets?

(2) should the aircraft carrier forces be taken off strategic targets because of uncertainty as to their location at the outbreak of general war?

b. The additional problem, not requiring immediate decision but continuing attention, is where does POLARIS fit into this scheme of things?

c. With respect to the question of all-weather delivery capability, I would strongly recommend that vital strategic targets, such as enemy long-range nuclear delivery capability and control centers, be assigned only to forces having all-weather capability.

d. With respect to the aircraft carrier forces, the following factors and arrangements should be considered:

(1) In order to provide maximum security to the fleet, it should not be tied down to an area limited by the requirement to remain within aircraft range of pre-selected targets. The fleet should be free to exploit its inherent mobility. In addition, the usefulness of the carrier forces in limited war situations should not be degraded by the requirement to remain on station, on a continuing basis, in order to cover targets of vital strategic importance.

(2) These conclusions suggest that the carrier forces should not be assigned H-hour responsibility for any pre-planned strategic targets.

(3) Possibly the carrier forces should be considered as having three primary functions:

One: As a strategic reserve for follow-up attack as required.

Two: As a mobile limited war force.

Three: As an element of a unified commander's forces, when on station, with target responsibilities in support of the local commander's plans—but not to include any targets on the national strategic target list.

e. With respect to the POLARIS submarine force, I would leave this force under naval control until a proven weapon system has developed. If the POLARIS submarine force develops a significant combat capability (in terms of reliability and weight of effort which can be delivered on target), we may then find that a Unified Strategic Command is required. Such a command eventually might have subordinate component commands for aircraft, for land-based missiles and for sea-based missiles. If a Unified Strategic Command is not established eventually, as a minimum, the targets to be attacked by POLARIS and the timing of the attack should be derived from a single integrated operating plan. I therefore believe that an appropriate nucleus of Naval officers should be assigned at an early date to CINCSAC's operational planning staff. For the immediate future these officers would assist in the development of an integrated operational plan, and they would constitute a nucleus of Naval personnel if later decision were made to establish a Unified Strategic Command.

27. Assuming that for the immediate future we are to take no action on the proposal for the establishment of a Unified Strategic Command, but assuming that we do take action to develop a single integrated operational plan, we would then be in a position to do more effective operational analysis and war gaming, and these exercises could be conducted under varying assumptions.

28. War gaming does two principle things:

a. It provides additional information which tends to validate, invalidate, or modify a target system; and

b. It indicates the feasibility or infeasibility of the operations plan and the results which could be expected from execution of the plan.

29. The policy direction of this type of war gaming should be above Service or command level. There is no capability within the Joint Staff at the present time for this kind of analysis and war gaming. It has been done in the past by Rand, by SAC, by the Air Staff Plans and Intelligence organization, and by the NESC (which relies heavily for support on the Services and DASA). The Joint Chiefs of Staff are currently considering methods by which this type of war gaming could be performed for them. It has been suggested that DASA might perform the function, or that it might be performed by the Air Battle Analysis Division of the Directorate of Plans, Air Staff. Under either solution, the JCS organization should provide the policy guidance and terms of reference for each analytical study or war game which is conducted. The agency making the study for the JCS would not make policy—but would provide electronic computers and trained personnel for doing the mechanical job of analysis. Wherever this function is assigned, the Joint Chiefs of Staff need a war gaming capability which is responsive to Joint Chiefs of Staff policy control. This does not require a large new agency. It does require decision as to what existing agency will do this work.

The Question of Operational Control of the Strike Forces Involved

30. Up to this point, this memorandum has been focused entirely on resolving the issues associated with the national strategic target system. However, when we get into the question of operational control we must broaden the problem, to include an examination of employment of atomic weapons by unified commanders having an area responsibility. These commanders traditionally have insisted that certain strategic targets were of such importance to accomplishment of their local missions that they should have the responsibility for seeing that they were neutralized or destroyed. To eliminate duplication in targeting brought about by this situation the following decision is required: As a general policy, targets on the national strategic target system list will not be included as H-hour objectives of the forces of unified commanders, and forces will not be justified nor programmed for such attack.

31. However, the local area commander has a legitimate concern and responsibility with respect to enemy military forces and installations. There may be one or several strategic targets interspersed in the same geographic area. The problem is therefore one of possible mutual interference, not on a single target basis, but on an area basis.

32. Assuming that the series of decisions which I have outlined were taken, the question of operational control of the various strike forces and the problem of avoiding mutual interference would be greatly simplified. They would be greatly simplified because mutual interference resulting from two or more commands targeting the same objective for H-hour attack would be largely eliminated. We would have an approved national strategic target list and a single integrated operational plan for strategic attack. These documents would provide a sound basis for the necessary coordination of the operational plans of local commanders with CINCSAC's plan. Potential conflicts could be worked out between the commanders concerned by analysis of routes to and from target, by agreement on timing, and by transfers of targets between commands as dictated by good judgment. Conflicts not reconcilable between commanders would have to be solved by the Joint Chiefs of Staff, but this would be a manageable problem against the background of policy decisions which I have discussed.

33. In my judgment, we should resolve the issues which I have discussed as soon as possible. To that end, I am circulating a copy of this memorandum to the Joint Chiefs of Staff.

NF Twining
Chairman
Joint Chiefs of Staff

February 19, 1960

This classified memorandum continues the previous discussion concerning targeting priorities for the SIOP.

By this time, the Pentagon had settled on a mix of military and civilian targets. It was decided that a "cities-only" targeting strategy would not be sufficient, while a "military-targets-only" strategy would be unworkable since the US didn't have reconnaissance capability to locate all the Russian ICBM sites. Therefore, the plan settled on an "optimum mix" of both civilian and military targets.

The Pentagon also estimated that only 15% of US manned bombers would survive to reach their targets, which gave added importance to ICBMs and led to new emphasis on the Polaris submarine-launched missile already in development.

The SIOP went into effect in 1960. It envisioned, in response to any attack on the US or Western Europe, a single massive series of attacks against targets throughout the Communist Bloc, including Russia, China and the East European nations, with the intent of destroying them completely as functional societies.

MEMORANDUM FOR THE DIRECTOR, JOINT STAFF
SUBJECT: Appraisal of Relative Merits, From the Point of View of Effective Deterrence, of Alternative Retaliatory Efforts

1. The Joint Chiefs of Staff have reviewed the Hickey study and have discussed it with the Secretary of Defense on several occasions.

2. The Joint Chiefs of Staff are in agreement that the concept of the "optimum mix" target system is sound, and that the order of magnitude of the target system appears to be reasonable, within the scope and time frame of the study.

3. However, the Service Chiefs have requested that I briefly mention certain observations which they have on the conclusions of the study.

4. General Lemnitzer has made the following major observations:

a. The conclusions of the study are predicated on the assumption that our defenses will be capable of containing a Soviet attack on the Continental United States to the extent that we will survive as a viable nation. An adequate air and missile defense, both active and passive, is therefore absolutely essential in order that we may have the residual relative superiority necessary to prevail if the deterrent fails.

b. The problem of locating and destroying enemy ICBM sites is a major factor bearing on the conclusions. This problem requires further study.

c. The relatively small number of bomb release line high-yield weapons required to attack "optimum mix" target system indicates that we have reached, if not surpassed, the leveling off point for these weapons in our stockpile.

5. Admiral Burke has made the following major observations:

a. The study indicates that our current stockpile of high-yield weapons is adequate or even excessive if less vulnerable delivery systems were to be used.

b. For destruction of the basic target systems by bomber delivery, the percentage of aircraft in the national inventory that arrives on target is apparently only about 15%. This is of such concern as to suggest acceleration of programs for less vulnerable delivery systems.

c. The deterrent effect of forces required only for attack of the urban-industrial system is underrated.

d. The study concerned itself with a mix of targets but did not explore extensively a mix of weapons on targets. This requires further study.

e. With the exception of the POLARIS, the nuclear capable theater forces of CINCEUR, CINCPAC and CINCLANT were not employed in the war gaming attack of the "optimum mix" strategic target system. Employment of these forces would change the retaliatory force level required. Further studies on this aspect of the problem are required.

6. General White has made the following major observations:

a. The potential benefits of this valuable appraisal could be forfeited unless the term "optimum mix" is given the same meaning in our planning as it was given in the study. The study developed a target system consisting of a mix of vital military and important urban-industrial targets, including all vital strategic elements of the enemy's known nuclear offensive capability.

b. While General White has also expressed certain reservations regarding the specifics of the study, and does not share the reservations noted by General Lamnitzer and Admiral Burke, he has requested that they not be outlined here, since, in his opinion, none of those reservations has significant effect upon the major conclusions of the report, or upon the agreed Joint Chiefs of Staff recommendations with which I shall conclude my remarks.

7. Having summarized the major reservations and observations on this report, I would like to present my own views. It is my opinion that the appraisal is a commendably thorough and objective study. It was prepared by a qualified joint group which expended much time and effort to insure the accuracy or reasonableness of the factors which were used and the methodology which was employed. The study constitutes the best objective joint appraisal of strategic targeting and force requirements available at this time. I am confident that we can make significant progress in our planning if we use General Hickey's study until something better is developed. We have in this study a sound point of departure and we should accept its conclusions as a guide for present planning until it is superceded by an equally thorough and objective effort.

8. The most significant conclusions to be drawn from the study, in my judgment, are as follows:

One: A retaliatory force structure based on the destruction of an urban target system would not provide an adequate military posture.

Two: The strategic force level which we have developed is in the right ball park and does not appear excessive. Naturally, the composition of this force must change as the enemy's military target system changes and as our own technology provides improved methods of delivery. The appraisal reveals that strategic forces now programmed for 1963 will be more than adequate to attack an "optimum mix" target system of minimum size with a 75% assurance of one weapon arriving at each ground zero, but will be inadequate to provide a 90% assurance of one weapon on each ground zero.

Three: The present and planned composition of the atomic stockpile, particularly with respect to high-yield weapons, is also about right, and

Four: The study was reassuring to me in that this independent analysis generally substantiates current national planning with respect to targeting, the nuclear stockpile composition, and the level of strategic offensive forces required.

9. Taking note of the views of all concerned, the Joint Chiefs of Staff have reached agreement on certain recommendations. You will recall, Mr President, that in NSC Action 2009 you directed Mr Gray, the Secretary of Defense, and myself to arrange for the conduct of this study. We concur in the recommendations of the Joint Chiefs of Staff, which are as follows:

a. That the concept of the "optimum mix" target system be approved.

b. That the study be referred to the Joint Chiefs of Staff as a basis for planning.

c. That they be authorized to release a limited number of copies of the study to the Joint Chiefs of Staff and to the Service Planners.

April 26, 1960

This classified memo gives further details on the targeting criteria and the proposed destructive level to be delivered by the SIOP plan.

It was assumed that 75% of the weapons would reach their targets. Enough weapons would be sent to each target to give a 90% probability of moderate or severe damage.

The SIOP was intended to be a pre-planned program that, once put into motion, would roll on automatically without any need for communications, as each force package would launch at its pre-assigned target.

26 April 1960
MEMORANDUM BY THE DIRECTOR, JOINT STAFF FOR THE JOINT CHIEFS OF STAFF ON TARGET COORDINATION AND ASSOCIATED PROBLEMS

1. Reference is made to SM-340-60, a memorandum for the Director, Joint Staff, dated 11 April 1960, subject as above, in which the Joint Chiefs of Staff directed that the Joint Staff develop, as a matter of priority, a proposed policy upon which a strategic target system can be based.

2. Accordingly, a proposed statement of policy has been prepared for consideration by the Joint Chiefs of Staff and is attached as Enclosure "A" hereto.

3. The attached policy is completely consistent with and is in the nature of implementation of the decision on Study No. 209. Its approval is considered to be an essential prerequisite to the solution to many of the problems now confronting the Joint Chiefs of Staff.

4. Contingent upon approval by the Joint Chiefs of Staff of the policy set forth in Enclosure "A", timely implementation thereof requires that the next step be established and approved by the Joint Chiefs of Staff.

5. Accordingly, I recommend:

a. That the proposed policy in Enclosure "A" be approved.

b. That the policy in Enclosure "A" be incorporated in the forthcoming Atomic Annex to the JSCP.

c. That Enclosure "B" be approved.

6. It is recommended that copies of this paper NOT be forwarded to commanders of unified or specified commands.

7. In consonance with the provisions of JCS Memorandum of Policy No. 83, it is recommended that copies of this paper NOT be forwarded to US officers in NATO activities.

ENCLOSURE "A"
Draft
NATIONAL STRATEGIC TARGETING POLICY OF THE JOINT CHIEFS OF STAFF

1. <u>Intent</u>. The basic intent is to translate the guidance of Study 2009, and the President's decision thereon, into policy guidance at the national level for the development and attack of a National strategic Target List (NSTL).

2. <u>Concept</u>. The National Strategic Target List shall consist of an optimum mix of [censored   ] *in the Sino-Soviet Bloc.*] The effective attack of the targets on this list will provide sufficient destruction to achieve military impotency and economic paralysis which would preclude organized war effort on the part of [*the Sino-Soviet*] Bloc to the extent that, when coupled with the results of other essential military operations, will enable the Free World to prevail.

3. <u>Objectives</u>. The basic objective of this policy is to establish an over-all minimum task to be accomplished regardless of the conditions under which hostilities are initiated. The attack of the National Strategic Target List is considered to be a task, the accomplishment of which is of prime importance to our national survival. Specific objectives of the attack of the National Strategic

Target List are to destroy or neutralize [*the Sino-Soviet Bloc* [censored] centers of the [*Sino-Soviet Bloc*] to the extent that, when coupled with other essential military operations, it will paralyze the economy and render the [*Sino-Soviet Bloc*] incapable of continuing the war.

4. <u>Strike Priorities</u>. For the accomplishment of the attacks of the targets of the National Strategic Target List strike priorities will be as follows:

a. [First priority will be accorded to the destruction of Sino-Soviet Bloc [censored *] within the Sino-Soviet Bloc to the extent necessary to eliminate the threat of nuclear attacks on US and Allied forces and territories.*

b. Second priority will be accorded to the [censored *] to prevent over-running of large areas of US or Allied territory and to insure the maintenance of control of essential sea areas and the protection of vital communications.*

c. Third priority will be accorded to denying the use of [censored *] which can immediately and directly contribute to the enemy's capability to conduct initial military operations.*

5. <u>Supporting Targets</u>. It is recognized that the successful execution of attacks on the National Strategic Target List will require the concurrent attack by the commanders of certain additional targets, the destruction of which is essential to the accomplishment of the attacks of targets of the National Strategic Target List. Such targets are so-called Supporting Targets.

6. <u>Damage Criteria</u>. Plans and operations directed towards the attack of the National Strategic Target List will be based upon the damage criteria set forth below. In applying the damage criteria, account will be taken of cumulative damage effects.

   a. *Ninety percent probability of severe damage to* [censored]

   b. *Ninety percent probability of moderate damage to* [censored]

   c. *Ninety percent probability of destruction of 50 percent of industrial floor space* [censored]

   d. For other installations associated with National Strategic Target List the damage criteria are the prerogative of operational commanders, but will be no higher than 90 percent probability of severe damage.]

7. <u>Assurance</u>. Taking account of all pertinent operational factors, plans and requirements will be based upon [*achieving a minimum of seventy-five percent assurance of delivery at each bomb-release line*

(BRL)] of the necessary weapons to achieve the specified levels of damage to the various targets of the National Strategic Target List.

ENCLOSURE "B"
Draft
MEMORANDUM FOR THE DIRECTOR, JOINT STAFF
Subject: Implementation of Targeting Policy

1. In consonance with the policy set forth in Enclosure "A" to JCS 2056/149, the Joint Staff, with such assistance from the unified and specified commands, the Services, and other agencies as may be necessary, will, as a matter of priority, select for consideration by the Joint Chiefs of Staff, a proposed list of targets to be included in the National Strategic Target List.

2. Utilizing the targets selected in Annex "G" to Study 2009 as a basic starting point and modifying them as may be appropriate in the light of the most current intelligence available, a minimum number of targets will be selected for inclusion in the National Strategic Target List, which, if subjected to the damage levels envisaged in paragraph 6 of Enclosure "A" to JCS 2056/149 *[(Damage Criteria) would result in over-all damage to the Sino-Soviet Bloc war potential approximating that indicated]* in Annex "G" to Study 2009.

3. The list of targets selected will be submitted in such a manner as to indicate the proportions of the various elements of the *[Sino-Soviet Bloc]* war-making potential which are at risk in each target selected. These targets should be grouped geographically to facilitate target analysis and attack as complexes. Targets, the attack of which is necessary primarily for defense suppression and to facilitate penetration will not be included in the National Strategic Target List.

4. In addition, the Joint Staff will present to the Joint Chiefs of Staff for approval, an appropriate system for accomplishing additions, deletions, or other changes to the National Strategic Target List which may be necessary in light of current intelligence.

July 14, 1960
By 1960, the inability of the US to directly verify the numbers of Soviet ICBMs led to fears of a "missile gap", in which it was assumed that the USSR had a massive ICBM arsenal that could hit the United States. While the Distant Early Warning (DEW) line of radar installations would give sufficient warning time of Soviet bombers, Soviet ICBMs would be on target within half an hour of launch. It was therefore assumed that any Soviet attack would come in the form of ballistic missiles and not, as previously assumed, long-range bombers. This was a major change in nuclear warfare planning.

This detailed classified memo discusses some of the problems facing American defense preparations against Soviet ICBMs. A Ballistic Missile Early Warning System (BMEWS) would be constructed in the north polar regions (which Soviet ICBMs would pass over on their way to the US) to give a longer warning time of a Russian missile launch.

Discussion also centered around measures, including dispersal and the use of hardened underground "silos", to protect American ICBMs, allowing them to survive a Soviet first strike and still be available for retaliatory launches.

It was also discussed whether a "launch on warning" (in which American missiles would be launched immediately upon evidence of a

Soviet attack, to prevent them from being struck in their silos) posture should be taken. While nuclear bombers can be recalled while in flight, ICBMS are irrevocable once launched. Since even the BMEWS system would give only 15-20 minutes' warning, it was apparent that any nuclear response would only take place as Soviet warheads were actually detonating over their targets (a contingency known as "launch under attack").

Finally, attention was devoted to research into an anti-ballistic missile system (ABM) that could shoot down incoming warheads before they reached their targets.

DISCUSSION PAPER ON CONTINENTAL DEFENSE
I. Questions to which the paper is addressed
1. The advent of a ballistic missile era and of major Soviet capabilities to attack the United States with ballistic missiles dictates a reassessment of our continental defense policy. In the face of the increasing Soviet ballistic missile threat and the absence of foreseeable, effective anti-ballistic missile systems;

Question 1
Should US policy give increased emphasis to passive as compared with active measures for the protection of our retaliatory capability against ballistic missile attack? Moreover, if increased emphasis should be given to passive measures, what factors should be considered in determining those passive measures that would be most effective in the over-all continental defense effort?

Question 2
Should our air defense effort be reoriented so that, following an initial ballistic missile attack, it would retain a capability to cope with follow-on manned bombers and non-ballistic missiles?

Question 3
Should the United States revise its plans for survival of the military decision-making capability and its doctrine on response to attack and on response to warning of attack, in the light of decreased reaction time and in view of increasing US emphasis on retaliatory ballistic missile forces?

Question 4.
Should substantially increased emphasis now be given to protecting our population against fallout?

Question 5.

Are existing policies that provide for the continuity of essential wartime functions of the Federal Government in need of review?

Question 6.

Is there a clear need for vigorous research and development efforts to achieve a capability to destroy orbiting satellites and space vehicles?

II. SOVIET CAPABILITIES

2. The NIE notes that Soviet delivery systems for attack on the continental United States are changing importantly in character, and it implies the following periods:

a. The period is drawing to an end when the primary element in the threat to the United States is manned bombers—over one hundred unrefueled BEARs and refueled BISONs, possibly supplemented by refueled or one-way medium BADGERs, and by some short-range submarine-launched ballistic missiles.

b. The period of the early 1960's will represent a gradual transition from a largely bomber threat to one mainly composed of ICBMs supplemented by 100 BISON heavy bombers and possibly some refueled or one-way medium bombers, increased numbers of submarine-launched ballistic missiles, and possibly by cruise type missiles.

3. Critical characteristics of the changing threat are:

a. A maximum total travel time of about 30 minutes from launch of ICBMs compared to many hours for manned bombers (the above time for an average 5500 n.m. range.) Also, the inability to recall ICBMs once launched.

b. An ICBM accuracy and yield presently adequate to destroy unhardened installations with one or a very few missiles. The number of missiles required to destroy hardened targets will be reduced substantially over the coming period as accuracy, yield and reliability are improved. (Note: In the case of the "best" 1 January 1960 Soviet missile (__MT warhead, 3 n.m. CEP, and 75 percent reliability) 33 missiles would be required to give a 90 percent assurance of exceeding 100 psi at the target. In the case of the "best" mid-1963 Soviet missile (__MT warhead, 1.5 n.m. CEP, and 80 percent reliability), 8 missiles would be required. In the case of a "possible" 1965-1970 missile with a __MT warhead, 1.0 n.m. CEP, and 75 to 85 percent reliability, only 4 missiles would be required. See NIE 11-8-60 and NIE 11-2-59. Data for the blanks are being furnished by a separate memorandum.

c. The development of improved ICBMs, with a solid or storable liquid propellant and all-inertial guidance by 1965; also during the 1965-1970 period there is expected to be refinement of guidance systems, improved warheads and decoys, and possibly drastically reduced radar reflection which might permit avoidance of detection even in the Ballistic Missile Early Warning System (BMEWS) beam.

4. There are additional technological possibilities which the Soviets may pursue, including:

a. High velocity, flat trajectory ICBMs with trajectories under the planned cover of BMEWS.

b. Advanced supersonic and later hypersonic cruise or glide vehicles, manned or unmanned, for possible weapons delivery (including air-to-surface missiles of increased range, speed and accuracy) as well as reconnaissance.

c. ICBMs launched from unexpected locations or following unexpected directions of flight, e.g., ICBMs traveling from the USSR around the South Polar region, thereby avoiding the three presently-planned BMEWS radars.

d. Satellite based weapons systems for use against ballistic missiles and other targets, as well as for reconnaissance, communications, and jamming.

III. US CURRENT POLICIES, CAPABILITIES AND RELATED FACTORS

A. Defense Against Manned Bombers and Aerodynamic Missiles

5. In the era in which the dominant threat was that of mass Soviet bomber attack, sufficient warning of a mass bomber attack was considered achievable to permit the launching of a significant portion of our strategic bomber force before it could be destroyed on the ground. The several hours available were sufficient for alerting the military forces, for the evaluation and decision-making process by key officials, and for transmission of the necessary communications. In addition, evacuation and relocation could reasonably provide continuity of government and contribute to protection of the civil population.

6. Reasonably reliable early warning, combined with limited bomber speeds, made it possible to plan a continental defense in depth on the assumption that greater attrition could be effected by employing a series of "active" defense elements in succession against

an initial mass bomber attack. Predominant emphasis was placed on active defense measures to provide the protection of our counter-offense forces and our civilian population. (Note: In accordance with accepted practice, the term "active defense" is used in reference to those measures that involve an attempt to physically incapacitate or destroy a threatening objective; e.g., interceptor aircraft, surface-to-air missiles, anti-missile missile systems. The term "passive defense" embraces all other means of defense; e.g., warning and response to warning (including the launch of recallable aircraft), dispersal, mobility, hardening.) Initial early warning permitted preparations to be made to launch the counter-offense forces; "area" coverage was provided by interceptor aircraft; and a "point" defense of potential targets was achieved using shorter range surface-to-air missiles.

7. An integral part of the protection of the SAC retaliatory forces in this era has been the Positive Control Doctrine that permitted the launching of our bombers even on receipt of equivocal warning. At a later time the bombers either receive a "go-ahead" signal or they must return to base. (The ability to recall a retaliatory force to its base is referred to throughout this paper as the "recallable" characteristic.) There is every reason to believe that this tactic can be employed in such a way as to provide a high level of confidence that some portion of the bomber force can avoid destruction on the ground.

8. The tactical warning system has weaknesses, particularly the lower detection probabilities at very low and very high altitudes, and the possibility of "end runs", as for example, by small numbers of aircraft on one-way missions.

9. The logical extension of the means of defense against manned bombers, including long-range manned interceptors and interceptor missiles, could extend the coverage beyond the continental limits of the United States. However, because of the changing nature of the threat, the once-planned programs to provide for major growth and extension of the defenses against this threat have been largely discontinued or cut back. These included the long-range interceptor F-108, the replacement AEW aircraft, the Canadian CF-105, the full continental coverage of SAGE, the Super Combat Center Program, Bomarc-B and NIKE-HERCULES.

B. Defense Against Ballistic Missiles

10. The three general aspects of defense against ballistic missiles, namely early warning, active and passive measures, are somewhat analogous to those of defense against manned bombers. However, the

means of accomplishment and the projected performance are vastly different.

Early Warning of Ballistic Missiles

11. It is expected that the Ballistic Missile Early Warning System (BMEWS) will provide some warning capability in September 1960, when Site No. 1 is scheduled to become operational. This capability will be increased when Site No. 2 is scheduled to become operational. This system is planned for completion in 1963 and should then be capable of providing some 15 minutes of warning against a large-scale missile attack arriving over great circle trajectories from Soviet areas. The portion of the SAC bomber force that is maintained on a 15-minute ground alert basis can, because of inherent recallable characteristics, be launched in response to BMEWS warning or such other warning as may become available.

12. An additional means, now in the research and development stage, showing promise of supplementing or extending BMEWS warning, is the satellite-borne infrared detection system (MIDAS). Other possibilities include aircraft-borne infrared detectors and over-the-horizon radars. (NOTE: MIDAS is expected to sense the launching of large boosters anywhere in the world with an average warning time of about 25 minutes. An operational system might be achieved as early as 1963. To date, there has been no successful system feasibility trial. Infrared detectors carried in very high altitude aircraft patrolling the Soviet perimeter could detect launches from a substantial area of Russia and China with an initial detection of about 25 minutes before impact on US targets. A number of over-the-horizon radar techniques have been proposed or are under study. One of these, TEPEE, will undergo full-scale feasibility trials this year. The concept is attractive because of anticipated low cost, ease of installations, and possible early availability, if the technique proves feasible.)

13. A bomb alarm system is currently being installed to provide notification of actual nuclear explosions occurring in the vicinity of retaliatory force bases. Successful operations of this system would make it possible to launch alert forces from surviving bases if the dispersion interval between initial impacting missiles and those for the other bases is sufficient.

Passive Defense Against Ballistic Missiles

14. While elements of the SAC alert bomber force could be airborne or could be launched on receipt of early warning because they are "recallable", ballistic missiles are "irrecallable". It is

questionable whether US response doctrine will permit the launch of "irrecallable" ballistic missiles solely on the basis of information received from a warning system. There are, however, a number of passive measures that can be employed to protect the US retaliatory missile forces; e.g., dispersal, mobility, shelter or hardening, and concealment.

15. <u>Dispersal</u>: By physically dispersing our retaliatory weapons at a large number of sites, each remote from the other, it may be possible to confront a potential attacker with a situation in which he does not possess a sufficient number of attacking weapons to permit him to calculate with high confidence his ability to destroy all such installations before an unacceptably large number of weapons are launched in retaliation. The relative advantages of dispersal can be calculated on the basis of reasonable estimates of the enemy's strike capability.

16. The present distribution of SAC bomber bases was made to achieve dispersal in the era of threat of manned bomber attack. The number is so small as to provide protection, by dispersal alone, only in the very early part of the era of ballistic missile threat. Current plans call for dispersal of a significant portion of the "fixed" US missile installations.

17. <u>Mobility</u>. This technique combines the advantages of dispersal with those that result from either continual or intermittent motion of the retaliatory weapons. By such means it is possible to deny a potential aggressor the ability to predict the physical location of all retaliatory weapons. For example, a limited capability to mount an airborne alert in periods of international tensions is being provided; Polaris is a mobile system; and current plans call for part of the Minuteman force to be rail-mobile.

18. <u>Hardening</u>. This concept involves providing the retaliatory weapon with a protective shell in order to decrease its physical vulnerability. A portion of the US retaliatory missile force will be located in hardened sites. There is no hardening program for manned bombers. It should be noted that the true "hardness" of a missile system is limited to the extent to which existing types of communications can be hardened. Hardening can also be used to protect the civil and military population from direct weapons effects as well as from radioactive fallout. The relative costs and effectiveness of such measures have been extensively studied. The case for increased emphasis on fallout shelter is considered in Question No. 4.

19. <u>Concealment</u>. It is possible, as in the case of the POLARIS submarine, to couple mobility with concealment and thereby decrease weapon vulnerability over that achieved by mobility alone. In the case of MINUTEMAN, it may be possible to couple mobility and hardening with concealment. In general, however, it is extremely difficult to conceal fixed military installations on the North American continent.

Active Defense Against Ballistic Missiles

20. Nike-Zeus is the major active defense system against ballistic missiles now under research and development. It is to be a terminal area intercept system in that it must be physically located in the target area in order to intercept a ballistic missile in its terminal phase. The Nike-Zeus system would be soft (2-3 psi), and it could be saturated by feasible attacks. The system probably could be decoyed by relatively simple techniques. The maximum radius of coverage would be about 75 miles and this radius might be reduced to about 15 miles in the presence of reasonably effective decoys.

21. A system test is scheduled in the Pacific in 1962. If production were begun now, the earliest date on which an initial operational deployment could be achieved would be approximately 4 years. The cost of an operational deployment of 70 batteries at 27 defense complexes by the end of FY 1968 would be about $9 billion. No program has been approved for the production of an operational Nike-Zeus.

22. In addition to Nike-Zeus, advanced research into techniques and components for active anti-ballistic missile defense is underway at about $100 million a year primarily under Project Defender. At this time, no operational system based on this program appears feasible within the next 10 years barring unforeseen technological "break throughs".

C. Defense Against Satellite Systems

23. Currently the United States has a limited capability to detect satellites that pass over the United States. By fully exploiting our existing and planned high-power radars, it would be possible to determine orbits at altitudes up to about 400 miles in a low-density environment within a week or so after launch.

24. It appears feasible to develop a system which would detect and determine the orbit, within 12 hours after launch, of all satellites that pass over the United States with altitudes up to 3,000 miles. This system should have a reasonable traffic-handling capacity.

25. Studies are underway on the feasibility of satellite inspection and destruction systems. Research and development to achieve a co-orbital capability appears promising. It appears that, with our present knowledge of bomb fragmentation and kill mechanism, the development of a destruction capacity for such a system poses no critical technical problems.

IV. DISCUSSION OF QUESTIONS

Question 1: Should US policy give increased emphasis to passive as compared with active measures for the protection of our retaliatory capability against ballistic missile attack? Moreover, if increased emphasis should be given to passive measures, what factors should be considered in determining those passive measures that would be most effective in the over-all continental defense effort?

26. As previously indicated, the United States will not have an "active" anti-ballistic missile capability within the next 5 years, and in the 1965-1970 period the best that could be achieved would consist of a Nike-Zeus type system with minor improvements. Therefore, for the next 5-10 years, protection of the land-based retaliatory forces against Soviet missile attack must depend on early warning and an appropriate response thereto, coupled with such passive measures as will increase the ability of these forces to survive or will increase the Soviet force requirements for launching an attack. (It should be noted that for the next few years, the United States will not have assurance of obtaining early warning against ballistic missile attack.)

27. The vulnerability of SAC bombers to ballistic missile attack might be decreased by dispersing these aircraft to a number of existing airfields. However, this advantage has to be weighed against costs and possible degradation of operational readiness resulting from the adverse effects on command and control, ground support, maintenance and manning. Provision is also being made for a capability to mount an airborne alert of a portion of the SAC bomber force in periods of international tension. The extent of, and the benefits accruing from, such an airborne alert should, however, be weighed against its cost and against the adverse effects on ground support, maintenance and manning.

28. The dispersal of retaliatory weapons can impose unacceptably large force requirements on a potential attacker. However, in considering particular dispersal programs, account needs to be taken of their possible effects in increasing wartime hazards to the civil population. Dispersal of military aircraft to civilian airfields serving

large cities could, for example, result in an increased level of damage to the civil population and the industrial base if an aggressor chose to attack all these targets. Similarly, dispersal of missile bases could either increase or decrease the danger to the civil population, depending upon their location. Therefore, dispersed retaliatory installations should be located as far as possible from centers of population.

29. Hardening adds to our deterrent posture since, to produce a given level of damage, a larger number of weapons must be employed against a hard target than would be required against a soft target. Although it is conceivable that hardening could result in an increased hazard to the civil population in the vicinity of a hardened target under attack, an enemy could, with the same total number of weapons required to destroy a hard site, target a larger number of soft installations and cities and the over-all damage to the civil population might be still greater.

30. Mobility of the retaliatory force would greatly complicate the problems of the aggressor without necessarily increasing the hazard to the civilian population. Mobility at sea might have the advantage of drawing fire against retaliatory forces away from continental United states.

31. An extensive study has been conducted by the Weapons System Evaluation Group in the Department of Defense to ascertain the cost effectiveness of the Nike-Zeus system. Based on the conclusions of this study, it would appear to be less costly and far more effective to increase the probability of survival of US retaliatory forces by deploying additional retaliatory missiles in hardened sites than to attempt the protection of a lesser number of missiles with a Nike-Zeus anti-ICBM system. According to this study, this conclusion appears to be valid, even if it is assumed that there exists some, as yet undiscovered, adequate decoy discrimination techniques. The study further indicates that the disparity in cost/effectiveness would be still greater if the comparison were made between Nike-Zeus and the deployment of additional mobile missile forces.

32. In view of this situation, there is a clear need to revise that portion of existing policy for Continental Defense which places predominant emphasis upon measures to improve our active defenses as compared with—but not to the exclusion of—passive defense measures. Such revision should not prejudice continuation of those active defense measures that can significantly contribute to the

protection of our effective nuclear retaliatory power; e.g., active elements of the air defense system. Moreover, a vigorous research and development program directed toward achieving an effective active defense against ballistic missiles continues to be required. However, since it is questionable whether any adequate AICBM system could be developed and deployed within the next 10 years, it seems imperative that recognition be given in policy to the necessity for increased emphasis on passive measures for the protection of our retaliatory capability.

33. It should be noted that the measures to provide for passive defense of the retaliatory forces are interrelated with the characteristics of the various retaliatory weapons systems themselves. Accordingly, the vulnerabilities and response characteristics of retaliatory weapons should be considered among the other factors in determination of the "mix" of the retaliatory forces.

Question 2: Should our air defense effort be reoriented so that, following an initial ballistic missile attack, it would retain a capability to cope with follow-on manned bombers and non-ballistic missiles?

34. The present air defense system would be of questionable value following a missile attack. This results primarily from the fact that the present "active" elements of the system are almost totally dependent on the existence of a highly centralized system of close control. The "hardening" of vital elements of this control system, i.e., the Super Combat Center Program, would not provide a solution to the problem of vulnerability. The system could not be made operational until the United States is well into the missile era at a time when the Soviets could be expected to possess a large number of ICBMs. Even assuming that the centers could be hardened, there are practical limitations on achievable hardness for vital communication links. The "soft" data inputs, i.e., the radars, and the "soft" air defense weapons currently in use would also be seriously degraded by a missile attack. Finally, an air defense system designed primarily for defense in depth against an initial mass bomber attack is not equally suited to a period when the initial attack would be by ballistic missiles. In the latter situation, the air defense system needs to be designed primarily to cope with follow-on bomber attack.

35. It would, therefore, seem desirable to consider modification of the existing air defense system in such a way that, even after absorbing substantial damage from a ballistic missile attack, sufficient capability would remain to deny the enemy unopposed access to

continental US airspace. If practicable, over-all system vulnerability could be decreased by relocating those SAGE Direction Centers and interceptor squadrons that are now located at SAC bases. Some fraction of the manned interceptors could be provided with improved radars and fire control equipment so that they could function effectively after ground control ceased to exist. If the existing manual control capability were retained in standby status, instead of being eliminated as SAGE Sectors become operative, other manned interceptors could be employed for air defense after SAGE centers were destroyed.

36. This discussion suggests the need for a reexamination of present air defense concepts to take into account the necessity for retaining a capability to cope with follow-on attacks by manned bombers and non-ballistic missiles, following an initial ballistic missile attack. (Defense and JCS consider that this matter is constantly under study in the Department of Defense.)

Question 3: Should the United States revise its plans for survival of the military decision-making capability and its doctrine on response to attack and on response to warning of an attack, in the light of decreased reaction time and in view of increasing US emphasis on retaliatory ballistic missile forces?

37. The US retaliatory capability depends on its ability to survive until the decision to counterattack. In order to protect fully our ability to use the retaliatory capability, Continental Defense plans and programs must ensure the survival of the decision-making machinery and the means of communication of the decision to the surviving retaliatory forces, in addition to providing for the survival of an adequate number of the delivery vehicles.

38. The existing capability to provide early warning of mass bomber attack appears to be adequate. Even though the probability of initial mass bomber attack is decreasing with time, the United States must maintain this early warning capability in a high state of operational effectiveness so long as the Soviets possess a significant long-range bomber force. This tends to inhibit Soviet employment of these weapons. It should be realized, however, that our early warning system can be avoided by a bomber attack of small scale. The desirability of expending resources for improvement of the present system to provide early warning against a small number of aircraft must be weighed against the relative probability of such an attack and

against the effect of such an attack on the over-all retaliatory capability of the United States.

39. Thus, in an era of threat of manned bomber attack, without the ballistic missile threat, the available tactical early warning provides adequate time for decision-making and launch of retaliatory forces. Equivocal early warning could serve as the basis for launching the "recallable" SAC alert forces and for the initiation of the attack decision process. Decision-making officials could be alerted and placed in contact with one another either by assembly or by pre-arranged communications so that initial warning information and subsequent developments could be evaluated and a decision made in time to permit positive strike instruction to go out to the SAC bomber force already on its way and out of danger of destruction on its home bases. Even under conditions of enemy avoidance of the early warning lines, the tactical warning interval provided by the contiguous zone, and the combat zone elements, and the travel times of enemy aircraft in getting to deep interior SAC bases, appears sufficient to permit the saving of adequate bomber retaliatory forces and the decision-making process.

40. The United States does not today possess a capability to obtain early warning of a ballistic missile attack. However, a capability is being achieved by a high-priority program—BMEWS—as indicated in Section III-B. It is evident, therefore, that some capability to provide 15-minute warning of mass ICBM attack will soon be available and that this may later be extended to as much as 25 minutes.

41. Thus, with the advent of ballistic missile threat, the achievable total warning interval becomes severely limited. This limited warning time is adequate to permit launch of the recallable SAC alert bombers, thereby preventing their destruction on the ground. It is inadequate to permit the decision to release aircraft and missiles to targets prior to the impact of enemy missiles on the United States. Therefore, the decision-making process and the means for the communication of the decision to the strike forces must survive the initial missile onslaught.

42. Until such time as BMEWS can be expected to provide a 15-minute warning interval of missile attack, the limited initial Soviet ICBM capability might destroy the seat of government and an increasing fraction of the retaliatory forces. The only indication of attack would be provided by the planned bomb alarm system. The number of SAC bombers on ground alert saved under such conditions depends critically on currently unknown factors including the

dispersion in the arrival time of the Soviet missiles, the number of missiles actually arriving, and their accuracy in hitting particular targets.

43. As our US-based retaliatory capability becomes predominantly ICBMs we tend to lose the benefit of the recallable feature of manned aircraft. It is, of course, essential that the United States avoid the possibility of irrecallable launching of strike forces based on the erroneous conclusion that an attack is under way. It appears questionable that BMEWS or any other warning system can produce such high confidence early warning as to result in a US decision to launch irrecallable retaliatory missiles before bombs have detonated. Therefore, a reliable bomb alarm system is essential to provide early positive information of actual missile hits.

44. Nonetheless, tactical warning of attack can be extremely important during the period when our SAC retaliatory forces consist largely of bombers and of fixed vulnerable missiles that require a significant "count-down" period. Although the planned BMEWS can provide valuable time for launching SAC bombers and for bringing these missiles to an adequate state of readiness for firing, this warning will be of little value unless bombers can be launched and missiles can be fired before they are themselves destroyed. Currently CinCNORAD is charged with the responsibility for evaluating all warning information in order to determine whether an attack is underway and for transmitting this information to Washington DC to initiate the decision-making process. It is questionable whether 15-25 minutes of warning time will be adequate to: (a) apprise the necessary officials of the situation; (b) permit a decision that sufficient evidence is received that an attack has actually occurred; and (c) communicate a decision to undertake retaliatory strikes. There is no assurance at present that, following the detonation of the missiles in the initial attack, there will remain a capability to authorize the use of and employ effectively those retaliatory weapons that may have survived.

45. It appears that an a priori response doctrine would increase the probability that our surviving missiles could be launched and our manned bombers released to target even though the initial attack destroyed the seat of government and other vital links of the planned system for command and control. An a priori response doctrine might be one that permitted the launch of the surviving missiles by subordinate commanders in the event more than a given number of the missile and bomber bases actually received hostile missile hits.

Technically, the information that this had occurred could be provided by a bomb alarm system.

46. On the other hand, we should not rely exclusively on an a priori response doctrine that would permit decentralized decisions to attack the Soviet Union. The range of possible circumstances of outbreak of a thermonuclear war is so large and complex that all possible important eventualities cannot be foreseen and provided for by doctrine. We should preserve for ourselves, if at all possible, the option of more than one retaliatory response. For example, if there is a reason to believe that the Soviets have not spent their entire force in the initial attack—and they may not in order to be able to blackmail us—it is believed by some that we may wish to have the option of altering our retaliatory attack, or we may find it to our advantage to hold our forces in reserve to use them as a threat, to conclude the war, or to deter follow-up attacks.

47. It has become increasingly evident that we must achieve a survivable system of command. It is also recognized that, as missile yield and accuracy improve, hardness alone cannot provide the desired level of survivability for the command posts. A combination of hardness and achievable active missile defense may prove more effective. In connection with the problem of how we can effectively obtain a "decision time" adequate for the missile age, it would be desirable—depending on the outcome of currently-planned field tests of Nike-Zeus—to consider the possibility of employing a limited number of AICBM weapons for point defense of two or three vital centers of command.

48. In sum, there is need for a thorough study of capabilities, plans and programs to ensure the survival of the decision-making machinery and of reliable means of communication of the decision to the surviving retaliatory forces on land, at sea, and in the air, within the time dimensions of a surprise ballistic missile attack. As an essential part of this study, attention should be given to the preparation of a response doctrine that is not dependent on the survival of the seat of government and other vital links of the planned system for command and control. (Defense and JCS consider that these matters are constantly under study in the Department of Defense.)

Question 4: Should substantially increased emphasis now be given to protecting our population against fallout?

49. Existing policy for the protection of the population against radioactive fallout is stated in NSC Action No. 1842-d. This action approves the "concept of fallout shelter" on the basis that "improvements in active defense can give reasonable promise, together with fallout shelters, of limiting estimated civilian casualties, in the event of nuclear attack on the United States, to a level which will permit the United States to survive as a nation and will in no case be greater than a similar casualty ratio in the USSR." Since it appears that an effective active defense against ballistic missile attack cannot be expected within the next ten years (Note: See paragraphs 20-22), it seems advisable to re-examine this policy to determine whether substantially increased emphasis should be given to fallout shelters.

50. The extreme vulnerability of populations to fallout has been shown in various studies. (Note: WSEG Report No. 45 includes a study of the effect of various enemy targeting doctrines, attack levels and fallout shelters on the total resulting casualties in the United states based on present population patterns (casualties from indirect effects such as disease, starvation, genetic effects, etc, are excluded.) Conclusions of this study follow:

A. Weapons delivered uniformly at random over the entire US (the results of such an attack resemble those for an attack with major emphasis on retaliatory bases):

Millions of deaths:

	TOTAL YIELD IN MEGATONS		
	1000	2000	5000
Without shelters	58	99	162
With shelters	7	14	45

B. Weapons delivered in proportion to the population:

TOTAL YIELD IN MEGATONS			
	1000	2000	5000
Without shelters	97	130	160
With shelters	27	49	86

C. Targeting to maximize population fatalities:

TOTAL YIELD IN MEGATONS			
	1000	2000	5000
Without shelters	106	140	171
With shelters	41	61	92

Fallout shelters appear to be far more effective than any foreseeable anti-ICBM system for protecting the population against the effects of a nuclear attack. (NOTE: The following estimates of deaths from WSEG Report No. 45 indicate the relative efficacy of a perfect 75 n.m. anti-ICBM system and a fallout shelter program in protecting the population against the effects of nuclear attack in which weapons are delivered uniformly over the United States (the results resemble those for an attack with major emphasis on US retaliatory bases):

Millions of deaths:

	TOTAL YIELD IN MEGATONS		
	1000	2000	5000
No shelters, 75 n.m. perfect AICBM	32(18%)	68(38%)	126(70%)
Shelters, no AICBM	7(14%)	14(8%)	45(25%)
No shelters, no AICBM	54(30%)	97(54%)	162(90%)

Even if NIKE-ZEUS were made operational, it would have a kill altitude as low as 40,000 feet and a range of effectiveness as low as 15 miles. Kill at such low altitudes, especially if the high-yield enemy warhead were also to detonate, would severely damage the exposed population and structures and the active defenses themselves. (NOTE: A Department of the Army study shows that for Soviet attacks of 200-400 warheads with no undiscriminated decoys, a $10 billion NIKE-ZEUS program would limit direct damage to 54 metropolitan areas to between 16% and 26%.) Active protection from blast and other direct effects of nuclear attack would be of little over-all advantage if the persons saved from death by blast and fire were subsequently to die from fallout.

51. Present policy calls for a "low-key" approach to shelter promotion, but in the absence of increased emphasis by the federal Government it appears unlikely that a comprehensive shelter system will be completed in the near future. A recent survey by the House Committee on Government Operations indicated that only 1,565 shelters had been built in the United States during the last two years. This count is probably incomplete, but the implications of the survey are not seriously questioned.

52. Additional factors involved in this situation are exceedingly complex and difficult to grapple with objectively because most of them are based on considerations of public psychology, both here and abroad. In 1958, when the present concept was adopted, it was

deemed important that the concept be carried out without (a) creating public over-confidence in shelters or a public passive defense psychology; (b) causing Congressional and public reactions prejudicial to higher priority national security programs; (c) losing the support of our allies or causing them to adopt neutralism; or (d) presenting the posture of the United States as that of a nation preoccupied with preparations for war.

53. Some believe that there was no clear determination in 1958 as to whether a more vigorous approach to shelter-building would have these deleterious effects, and there appears to be no evidence which would place the matter beyond debate at the present time. It is clear, however, that the matter of the national and international psychology is important to a resolution of this issue, and an attempt will therefore be made in the following paragraphs to clarify the alternative ways of looking at the problem.

54. Proponents of a substantially increased emphasis on fallout shelters regard provision of such shelters for the civilian population as necessary, both to ensure the continuance of a positive support for other national security programs, and to deter the enemy from actions which might lead to war. The importance of this argument goes far beyond the question of fallout shelters. It is a question involving the national psychology and our ability and willingness to react in a positive way to the tensions of the coming decade. The lack of an effective civil defense has, so far, not been a handicap in the conduct of foreign affairs. This lack has, at least in part, been compensated for by the general feeling that our deterrent capability was overwhelming, and by the prospect that an active system of ballistic missile defense might eliminate the need for shelters. The basis of both compensating effects appears to be fading.

55. Proponents believe a determined effort to provide fallout protection, as a meaningful and positive response to the threat, would be interpreted as an indication of the national will to "see it through", whereas any less effort would receive the opposite interpretation. There has been some indecision from NATO sources that our Allies would for that reason welcome a decision by the United States to build shelters. Proponents feel that this could be done on other than a "crash" basis as an act of hysteria, and point out that shelter-building in Europe has not resulted in panic.

56. Proponents argue that the effect on a potential enemy of a US decision to place a substantially increased emphasis on fallout shelters

is also uncertain. Assurance of the survival of a larger part of the US civilian population might have essentially no effect on an enemy's calculations, but there is reason to believe that it would, since Soviet military planning provides for the contingency of a protracted war following the initial nuclear exchange. Shelter for the population would greatly enhance our ability to support a limited military effort after absorbing a nuclear attack, and the enemy might well believe that this would prevent him from achieving world domination.

57. Deterrence implies a hoped-for state-of-mind on the part of a potential aggressor that results from his estimate of our ability to retaliate effectively and our willingness to do so. Proponents believe that, in the absence of effective means to protect the population, our will to retaliate may be suspect. As we move into a period in which nuclear blackmail becomes, at least implicitly, an increasingly important factor in international diplomacy, one may question whether public support for taking of necessary risks in foreign policy will continue to be as strong and constant unless measures for population protection are taken.

58. Opponents of a substantially increased emphasis place a different interpretation on the same factual situation. They feel that substantially increased emphasis on a shelter program above and beyond the present low-key approach would be viewed outside the Executive Branch of the Government as a "crash" program and as indicative of a dramatic re-assessment of the likelihood of nuclear war. They also believe that giving new emphasis to a shelter program would be inconsistent with the efforts to achieve agreements with the Soviet Union on arms control and a nuclear test ban.

59. Opponents contend that the growing doubts among some of our NATO allies as to US intentions might be intensified if the United States were to launch what appeared to be a "crash" program for the creation of a comprehensive shelter system, and that our problems would be aggravated in maintaining a friendly attitude among neutral nations in less-developed areas in the face of Soviet charges of war-mongering. They also believe that initiation of a "crash" shelter program by the United States could well create fears in the Soviet Union that the United States intended to attack when the program was complete, and might cause the USSR to initiate general war before the shelters could be built.

60. Opponents believe that the US determination to respond to a Soviet nuclear attack or threat of attack, rather than to submit to

Soviet blackmail, would not be materially affected by the degree of fallout protection available. They contend that since many millions of casualties would be expected even if shelters were available, the US decision in any given circumstances would be the same regardless of whether a comprehensive shelter system existed.

61. Opponents of shelter-building are convinced that if substantially increased emphasis were to be given to shelters, the Executive Branch would be compelled to make major changes in other national security policies. Although recognizing that it is difficult to foretell the pressures which might result from an alarmed public opinion, this group feels that congress could well be forced to curtail sharply foreign economic assistance and programs for increased contact with the USSR while at the same time there would be accentuated demand for major increase in other military programs, thus further emphasizing the posture of a nation preoccupied with preparations for war.

62. Those who believe that a low-key approach should be retained contend that, so long as even with shelters the probable number of casualties would be in the range estimated by current studies, preponderant efforts should continue to be concentrated in deterring war. They contend that whatever resources are available are better used for such purposes, including strengthening the retaliatory capability, protecting the retaliatory capability, strengthening allied military capabilities, increasing limited war capabilities and employing non-military security measure such as economic and technical assistance, exchange and information programs.

63. Regardless of the resolution of this question, it appears that consideration should be given to protecting selected military personnel and installations as part of the over-all defense of retaliatory capability discussed in Question 1, and of the air defense capability discussed in Question 2.

64. In addition, there is a third group who feel that considerable increase in emphasis is possible within the essential concepts of the policy laid down in NSC 5807/2. They believe that it is too early to say, on the basis of experience, that the present policy will not result in significant shelter building. Those who hold this third view point out that the policy approved by the President in 1958 contemplated appropriations of the order of $100 million spread over the first three years. Actually, Congressional action has reduced appropriations in Fiscal Year 1959 to $2,075,000; in 1960 to $5,474,000; and it appears

that less than $5 million will be available in 1961—a total for three years of only $12 million. In addition, Federal leadership has been lagging in many important areas—construction of shelters in new public buildings has so far been limited to a laboratory building of the Bureau of Standards in Boulder, Colorado, and this was not specifically approved by Congress. No start has yet been made on installation of fallout shelter in existing Federal buildings, and the military has not installed fallout shelters in either base construction or Military Dependents' Housing.

65. Those who support the third position calling for more vigorous prosecutions of present policy note that editorial and public reaction has been generally favorable. A recent Gallup poll indicated that 38 percent of the population would be willing to build fallout shelters costing up to $500 at their own expense. This, and the many letters being received by OCDM and state and local civil defense offices indicate the possibility that the program may be catching on. A concerted effort to obtain congressional backing for appropriations support of the order originally contemplated is needed before the conclusion can be reached that the policy currently in effect is inadequate. There is room for much more Federal example and much more public information effort before there is any slight danger of violating the "low key" injunction of current policy guidance.

Question 5. Are existing policies that provide for the continuity of essential wartime functions of the Federal Government in need of review?

66. Present concepts to assure the operational capability of the Federal Government in the event of attack involve three essential elements:

a. Hardened, dispersed control centers with communications: Of the 17 emergency control centers in the relocation arc, only three offer any special protection against blast or radioactive fallout. As a consequence, nearly all civilian agencies plan to concentrate selected staffs at the OCDM relocation site, which in net effect creates a lucrative target near Washington DC. Even if all the facilities were fully protected and operational as planned, it would still be possible for a large part of the existing Federal Government to be destroyed in an initial missile attack.

b. relocation of senior officials: Planning for the relocation of civil and military elements of the Federal Government continues to assume a degree of warning time more appropriate to the manned-bomber era than to the missile age. Under the Joint Emergency Evacuation Plan, about 50 of the top civilian officials could be airlifted to emergency sites within 40 minutes after alert. But several hours of effective warning would be required for evacuation of thousands of subordinate officials with emergency assignments. There is also the assumption that civilian employees will leave their families upon warning of enemy attack and repair to their designated relocation sites.

c. The cadre concept: The inability of senior officials to survive an attack on the Seat of Government might place the Federal problems for the conduct of the war and post-attack survival in the hands of a small number of employees of limited high-level executive experience, lacking in electoral or appropriate authority, and unknown to the public-at-large.

67. There is now a possibility that a situation could arise in which the responsibility for making decisions would be in doubt for an indefinite time. While this possibility exists, it should by no means be regarded as a certainty which renders useless present arrangements. There is always the possibility of strategic warning. But even without strategic warning, a large part of both the civilian and military officials would be capable of reacting intelligently in a deteriorating situation under pre-arranged succession plans, within limited fields of competence.

68. It is noted that there is no clear agreement as to the decisions that would be required of policy-making officials of the Federal Government during the attack and survival period.

69. Present planning for the continuity of the essential functions of the Government should be restudied in relation to (a) the reduced time available for the implementation of such plans, (b) the unlikelihood of the survival of many key Government officials, and (c) the disruption of communications and the widespread destruction immediately following the attack. In this connection, among the possibilities that would need to be studied are: strengthening the cadre to include more high-level officials; increasing the number of hardened dispersal sites beyond the number planned; use of airborne and seaborne command posts; greater pre-arrangement for emergency delegation of authority; greater decentralization of Government functions; greater dispersal of high-level officials and their staffs; an enlarged Presidential succession roster; better shelter protection in Washington for the President and Vice President;

providing hardened facilities within present headquarters buildings and a concept of in-place operations; and greater emphasis on the alternate headquarters concept.

Question 6. Is there a clear need for vigorous research and development efforts to achieve a capability to destroy orbiting satellites and space vehicles?

70. Present policy provides for "a vigorous research and development" program in support of continental defense and specifies a number of areas "of particular importance", including "defense against satellites and space vehicles". (NSC5802/1, paragraph 12)

71. Since satellite-based bombing systems would probably be less accurate, less reliable and more costly and vulnerable than land-based ballistic missiles, it is questionable whether the current threat of space-based military systems warrants US emphasis on defensive measures. This seems clear even though a possible advantage to the USSR would accrue from the psychological effects and the resulting blackmail potential a space-based threat might have on the United States and its allies. Moreover, it is questionable whether US activity in this field, especially of demonstration of kill capability, would be consistent with US policy and proposals for the peaceful uses of outer space.

72. On the other hand, we must anticipate a marked increase in the exploitation of space for military purposes. The United States, for example, is already proceeding with plans to orbit satellites for reconnaissance, navigation, early warning and communications. While USSR efforts to achieve space-based systems will probably depend more upon their view of Soviet requirements than on limitation of capability, the Soviets have a technical capability to implement similar plans in the very near future. Therefore, it appears desirable that the United States continue research and development efforts in order to achieve a thorough technical background and a defensive capability in the event the USSR achieves an offensive capability.

73. At the present time, research and development is underway to explore the feasibility of obtaining a co-orbital capability; i.e., placing a satellite in close proximity to, and in the same orbit with, an existing satellite. Such a capability would permit the passive inspection; e.g., close-up visual observation and survey with special detectors of suspicious satellites. Such a capability would also permit the

destruction or disabling of errant US satellites as, for example, one which is inadvertently jamming important radio frequency bands, The development of a co-orbital capability appears promising and desirable. With present knowledge of fragmentation and kill mechanism techniques, it appears that the development of a destruction capability for such a system poses no critical technical problems.

74. Therefore, while it appears desirable to pursue research and development efforts in this area, it is agreed that it would be unwise to undertake a test of such a system without specific Presidential approval.

January 18, 1961

In 1961, the original SIOP was modified. The SIOP had been designed as a single and sudden attack, to be launched either as an American first strike in response to a Soviet invasion, or as an American retaliation to a Russian first strike using nuclear weapons. Since the plan was pre-planned and was designed to be carried out automatically once it was ordered into action, it was rigidly fixed, and no part of it could be changed without affecting all the rest. It therefore treated the entire Communist Bloc as one monolithic entity, which would all be struck at once, regardless of the situation under which the war was started.

By the end if his administration, President Eisenhower was beginning to become uncomfortable with the rigidity of the SIOP, and began exploring ways to make it more flexible. Under SIOP, for instance, the People's Republic of China was to be attacked with nuclear weapons whether it had participated in an attack on the US or not – Eisenhower wanted to revise the plans to allow for the subtraction of particular countries like China. The new modified plan would be known as SIOP-62.

This classified memo examines the proposed SIOP-62. It reveals some interesting details about the American war plan. About 3400 nuclear weapons would be used globally in the SIOP, of which 1450 were to come from forces that were placed on alert to protect them from a Soviet initial strike. Each target was assigned multiple weapons to insure that at least one would give an accurate hit, and the highest-priority targets were assigned enough weapons to give a 97% probability of destruction. To increase the damage, each weapon was to be detonated at low altitude—which also increased the amount of radioactive fallout that would be produced.

REPORT OF PRELIMINARY REVIEW OF SIOP-62
A. JCS 987018 DTG 092127Z DEC
B. JCS 539220 DTG 070009Z
1. Reference B

Requested initial submission of recommendations required by Ref A by 20 Jan.

2. My preliminary review of SIOP-62 confirms doubts in my mind as to the validity of several planning factors which were used in the development of the plan. I think we can produce a better one based on more reasonable planning input factors.

3. Damage criteria.

a. The criteria furnished in JCS guidance for SIOP-62 were responsible for producing such a large number of DGZs. In thinking about this, I re-examined the photographs of damage which was inflicted on Hiroshima by a 17KT air burst. This exercise revealed the extremes to which we have gone in our plans during the past 15 years. While I can conceive that severe damage as currently defined may not be necessary in respect to Soviet atomic delivery capabilities, I cannot do so when I think of striking major government controls. Here is an example where, in my opinion, damage criteria applied to one type of target should not be applied against another type. Adopting graduated damage criteria for different types of targets would permit changing DGZs to take full advantage of co-location of target elements in an area which can be damaged by a single detonation. I believe we can obtain our objectives by doing less damage and using fewer forces and weapons.

b. In the case of *[industrial floor space* [censored   ] the criteria used for SIOP-62 did not permit selectivity as to critical industries and did not encourage taking into account collateral damage caused by other weapons effects. Only blast effects were considered by the JSTPS. Other effects such as heat, fire and radiation should be used when drawing up damage criteria for the SIOP.

4. Constraints.

a. Upon reaching an incapacitation threshold of an individual, small additional exposure to radiation may cause death and as a minimum, will increase recovery time. While the magnitude of the radiation effects resulting from the enemy's use of nuclear weapons is unknown, we do know that the center of the area covered by residual radiation is down-wind from the detonation point. This means to us in PACOM that off-continent winds aloft may cause us to be more concerned about residual radiation damage resulting from our own weapons than those of the enemy. Nevertheless, when we consider that worldwide about 1450 weapons are programmed by alert forces and about 3400 weapons by all of the committed forces, we realize that our weapons can be a hazard to ourselves as well as to our enemy.

b. The procedure used by JSTPS of using the single largest weapon yield on a given DGZ for constraint computation is not satisfactory, particularly in view of the high damage criteria which were used. These criteria caused the height of burst to be lowered and several weapons to be programmed against each DGZ to meet the desired assurance. In the case of programming multiple attacks for high assurances we expect on a random probability basis that more than one weapon will be delivered most of the time. This should be taken into account when computing probable fallout on our own forces and on our friends.

5. Assurance

As pointed out during the conference at Omaha, an assurance of 97 percent was planned on high priority targets because no base survivability factor has been developed. In other words, the high methodology of applying an assurance factor should be refined. More important, however, is the necessity for determining whether or not a base survivability factor can actually be developed.

6. Weather Factor

I do not quarrel with the factor itself nor the manner in which it was derived. My position while SIOP-62 was being developed was that the weather factor should not be applied as an across-the-board weapons system degradation factor. I took the position during the planning cycle that the factor should be applied to non all-weather aircraft which are in the alert force because they are required to launch upon receipt of a random Go signal. However, I did not agree that the same factor should be applied to the follow-on forces whose launch time is flexible within a range of 4-5 hours. My view on this subject was not changed, and I hope it will be reconsidered when developing guidance for the next SIOP. The problem is one of determining the probability of non all-weather aircraft survival until such time as they can launch under conditions where they can identify visually their target. A point which we wish to reiterate is that our forces out on the WESTPAC line can operate for some five (5) hours before SAC arrives on the scene and thus before there is an interference and coordination problem. We have a leeway of 5 hours and will adjust our launches within this leeway to achieve much higher probability of visually sighting the target than that derived from using the overall night/bad weather factor. We think a factor approximating 85 percent instead of 49 percent is proper for application to our follow-on forces.

7. Target weighting system

Targets must be ranked to insure conformance with JCS guidance. This means that a target weighting system must be used. The JSTPS has just distributed a target weighting system manual which is described as being an internal JSTPS procedural manual. It is noted that point values contained in the manual differ from those contained in the National Strategic Target Data Base (NSTDB) published 12 Oct 1960 which was used in the development of SIOP-62. We are reviewing this manual and intend to comment on it because of the effect procedures will have on developing SIOP. I would have appreciated the opportunity to have previewed the manual concurrently as it was being developed.

8. War gaming

a. I am proceeding with the development of a two-sided war game of the friendly forces operating in the PACOM primary area of interest. By this means, I propose to identify the significance of the variables under my control in providing maximum target damage with minimum attrition, of necessity, much effort will be expended in further exploring those factors discussed above. Subsequent study of the gaming results should significantly fix the contribution of each variable of primary concern.

b. In the near future I plan to send a team to the Washington area and JSTPS to determine the extent of comparable activities in those areas, with a view toward exchanging ideas and procedures which might be of mutual benefit.

c. Notwithstanding my plans to game SIOP-62, for the long haul I believe we should give consideration to the establishment of a central war gaming facility for use by JCS, JSTPS as well as the unified and specified commanders in gaming their plans. It is possible that such a facility could be an extension of present equipments currently used by

NESC, and should be close to Washington where use can be made of bomb damage assessment computers. Further, the facility should contain sufficient equipment to provide adequate accommodation to users specified above. This suggestion is made in recognition of the millions of dollars required to establish duplicative war gaming staffs. If a central facility were established, machines, programmers, technicians and administrative personnel would serve all users. Operations analysts in staffs of commanders concerned could determine types of programs and inputs and utilize central facility to produce war game conclusions.

9. Organization of JSTPS

I realize that the JSTPS was hastily assembled and organized last August under the pressure of having to produce the NSTL and SIOP by Dec 60. As a consequence, some organization and realignment of billets within the JSTPS is probably warranted and desirable in light of experience gained thus far. Although I have no specific recommendations regarding the organization of the JSTPS to make at this time, the following are the principles which I think should apply:

a. Since JSTPS is an agency of the JCS, its organization and manning should approximate that of a JCS staff directorate, with due regard to the problem with which it is concerned and the duties for which it is responsible to the JCS and the SECDEF.

b. JSTPS personnel should not be assigned responsibility outside JSTPS.

c. Service representation in the JSTPS should be equitable, particularly in key billet assignment.

May 1961

This report is part of the official classified history of the Joint Strategic Target Planning Staff (JSTPS) which drew up the SIOP nuclear war plan. It gives a very detailed account of how and why the SIOP was produced.

Coordination problems in nuclear planning began early, as the Navy began deploying its own aircraft capable of delivering nuclear weapons, which sometimes conflicted with SAC planning. The introduction of the ballistic missile submarine gave the Navy a force of strategic nuclear weapons. Inter-service rivalry than kicked in, as both the Air Force and the Navy drew up their own strategic target lists, which often duplicated each other. This overlap made the need to coordinate targeting and planning overwhelming. The result was SIOP and its successor, SIOP-62.

The SIOP was directed at a mix of Soviet nuclear forces, government and command centers, and urban areas. Originally, some 4,000 preliminary targets were selected; this was narrowed down to a number of Desired Ground Zeros (DGZs) which made up the actual target list.

The SIOP included only those nuclear weapons that were actually available for use at the time of planning, including the B-52 and F-100 aircraft and the Atlas ICBM. By assigning a reliability figure for each weapon delivery system, the plan was able to calculate how many weapons needed to be sent to each target to assure its destruction. Detailed schedules and mission plans were then worked out, and each strike unit was given the information related to its own particular target.

HISTORY OF THE JOINT STRATEGIC TARGET PLANNING STAFF; BACKGROUND AND PREPARATION OF SIOP-62

Preface

This document is the initial installment in the continued History of the Joint Strategic Target Planning Staff. It is concerned first with the development of problems in strategic target planning during the 1950's and the evolution of plans for the integration of the activities of the various commands into one plan; second with the organization of the Joint Strategic Target Planning Staff at Headquarters SAC; and third with the preparation of the first Single Integrated Operational Plan. In the preparation of this history the historian did research in JSTPS files at Headquarters SAC and in the files of the Joint Chiefs of Staff in Washington. Documents indicated as exhibits (Ex) are on file in the History and Research Division, Directorate of Information, Headquarters SAC.

Background

Secretary of Defense Thomas Gates' decision of 16 August 1960 to establish a joint staff at Headquarters Strategic air Command (SAC) under the direction of Commander in Chief, SAC, brought together for the first time all elements of the armed services with a strategic nuclear capability into one integrated operational plan. Secretary Gates considered the decision the most important he had made in seven years in the Pentagon. Perhaps the magnitude of this action can be better appreciated after a review of the history of planning and coordination activities for the strategic nuclear offensive between 1952 and 1960.

Between the end of World War II and the beginning of the Korean War, SAC had a virtual monopoly on the means of delivering atomic weapons. The Joint Chiefs of Staff (JCS) drew SAC forces under its direct operational control in 1946 and strengthened these bonds in subsequent years by preventing usurpation of control of SAC forces by theater commanders. Therefore, during these years no coordination problems existed in planning and executing the atomic offensive, but by the early 1950's the situation was changing because of a proliferation of weapons and delivery vehicles.

The United States Navy announced in 1952 that all of its new attack planes were capable of carrying tactical atomic bombs, and that it had on hand aircraft capable of delivering large bombs. Newly activated tactical units in Europe and the Far East also became able to deliver small weapons. Indeed, the Secretary of the Air Force, Thomas

K Finletter, announced that "nearly all" USAF combat aircraft were being modified to carry them. The time was also rapidly approaching when the Soviet Union would become a major atomic power. It exploded an atomic device in 1949, and a year later USAF credited Russia with already having a "formidable long range air force" which by 1952 could cover all of the United States.

To meet this increased Soviet threat the JCS acted to gain more direct control of the nation's expanding atomic force. In March 1952 an ad hoc committee of that group examined existing procedures for control and coordination of atomic operations and recommended centralizing them for maximum bombing effect and minimum interference between forces. The JCS agreed and established facilities for lateral coordination of planning called Joint Coordination Centers (JCC) in Europe and the Far East (Buckinghamshire, United Kingdom, and Pershing Heights, Tokyo, Japan). They were war room facilities for receipt, compilation, display, review, coordination, and relay of information concerning the plans and operations of atomic forces for the benefit of the unified and specified commanders concerned and the JCS (in Europe, Commander in Chief Naval Forces Eastern Atlantic and Mediterranean CINCEAM, Commander in Chief United States Forces Europe CINCEUR, and the Commander in Chief Strategic Air Command CINCSAC, and in the Far East, Commander in Chief Pacific CINCPAC, Commander in Chief Alaska CINCAL, and CINCSAC). This was operational coordination, that is, it took place after hostilities began.

Early exercises of the Joint Coordination Centers disclosed a requirement for pre-hostilities coordination of commanders' atomic plans. Accordingly in 1954, the JCS asked each appropriate commander to submit an atomic annex, i.e., a target list, to his war plan and to coordinate it with theater commanders and CINCSAC. In 1955 SAC was directed to act as host for a conference of appropriate commanders to determine a methodology or "modus operandi" for defeat of communist air power. This conference failed to agree on anything except the requirement for periodic coordination of atomic war plans. With JCS approval these conclaves became known as World-Wide Coordination Conferences (WWCC). They were held each subsequent year through 1958. Plans coordinated at these conferences and approved by the JCS were pre-positioned with the Joint Coordination enters for operational coordination required by an exercise or the initiation of hostilities. The total coordination activity pre- and post-hostility, was known as the atomic coordination machinery.

How successful was this machinery? The magnitude of the problem probably can be appreciated best by recalling the complex problems of generation, launch, mutual support, and maximum bombing involved in preparing a single command's strike plan. These factors were manageable because the work went on within the framework of a common doctrine. When coordination between commands with different concepts, doctrines, traditions, and techniques was attempted, the problems became formidable. On the positive side, world-wide conferences did enable commanders to appreciate more fully each others capabilities, tasks, objectives, and plans. Target lists, forces, and strike timing were discussed and compared. Some conflicts were avoided. Yet the defects of the program were clearly more evident than its successes, at least to SAC. The conferences did not solve targeting conflicts; for example, in the 1957 and 1958 meetings duplications and triplications (two or more commands delivering weapons to the same targets) were not significantly reduced. Neither did they achieve mutual support or unity of strategic effort among the JCS commanders. At the JCCs, operational coordination procedures depended upon a highly sophisticated communications system. During peacetime exercises the communications time lag between sending and receipt of messages tended to increase causing a backlog; under combat conditions the system's efficiency would be greatly reduced. In each of the exercises of the JCC machinery from 1958 through 1960 over 200 time over target (TOT) conflicts highlighted the degree of conflict in existing execution plans. In wartime, with disrupted communications, this could result in needless loss of aircraft and crew. A comparison of target lists and some conflict resolution were the net gains in four years of coordination effort. General NF Twining, Chairman of the JCS, believed one fundamental principle had evolved from these coordination activities: "Atomic operations must be pre-planned for automatic execution to the maximum extent possible and with minimum reliance on post-H-hour communications."

<u>The Search for More Effective Coordination</u>

The Defense Reorganization Act of 1958 (Public Law 85-599), passed by Congress on 23 July 1958, seemed to open new vistas for better coordination of the strategic offensive. President Eisenhower, in outlining his plan to the Congress, emphasized "the vital necessity of complete unity in our strategic planning and basic operational direction." It was necessary that the Secretary of Defense and the Joint Chiefs have the authority to take action in these matters. The Air Force, traditionally in favor of integration along functional lines, supported the President's program, as did the Army. The Navy was less enthusiastic.

Armed with increased authority over the development and operation of new weapon systems given him by the reorganization act, the Secretary of Defense, then Neil McElroy, examined plans for the new Fleet Ballistic Missile, or Polaris, then in development. In December 1958 he asked the Joint Chiefs for their views on the future employment of the system.

As spokesman for the Air Force, General Thomas D White advocated creation of a unified US Strategic Command, to encompass subordinate units from the Air Force (heavy and medium bombers and intermediate and intercontinental ballistic missiles) and the Navy Polaris. With approval of the JCS, the CINCSAC would develop the organization so it could be functional by the time Polaris became operational. Strategic Air Command personnel would be integrated with those of the participating services and assigned to the new headquarters. General White believed a unified strategic command provided the organizational structure best suited for developing maximum atomic offensive plans.

The Army, Navy and Marine Corps were in general opposition to the Air Force plan. Admiral Arleigh Burke, Chief of Naval Operations, objected to integrating all strategic weapons systems into a single command and recommended rejection of the Air Force position. The Navy had earlier asked that Polaris be assigned to Commander in Chief, Atlantic (CINCLANT) and eventually to United States Commander in Chief, Europe (USCINCEur) and Commander in Chief, Pacific (CINCPac). Admiral Burke saw little need for change; in his opinion coordination had been working well since the 1958 Reorganization Act and integration of Polaris into the fleet would pose no targeting problems. Assignments of all weapons to a single command, on the other hand, "would disrupt and alter the US defense organization." Authority already existed in the JCS to prevent undesirable duplications in strategic targeting, planning, and weapons employment and the CNO believed it should remain there. The Army generally agreed with the Navy, but it believed the entire investigation was premature. It would assign Polaris to the fleet and examine its command structure later when it had become a proven system. The Marine Corps favored making the JCS responsible for selection of targets, after which the unified commanders would assign them to attack forces. It feared assignment of targets to one commander would create a "monolithic" structure to control aircraft and land and fleet missiles which would have great coordination problems and be vulnerable if communications were destroyed.

As a result of this disagreement, a split decision paper was presented to the SecDef. Although General White reported Mr McElroy did not believe a decision on command arrangements was urgent because the system would not become operational until late in 1960, there was no doubt that the Secretary intended to press for improvement of target coordination procedures. In late July, following an EWO briefing at Headquarters SAC for the SecDef and members of the JCS, he requested the Chairman present his views on this problem.

In his reply, General Twining reviewed the history of coordination to date and concluded "not much more progress can be achieved under the present arrangements". He rejected modifications to the existing machinery, advocating instead "fundamental changes" to the system. The problem divided into three categories; (1) targeting policy, (2) development of integrated operational plans, and (3) control of strike forces. Regarding the first, he inclined toward the Air Force counter force philosophy, believing the target system should include (in order of priority) long range nuclear delivery capability, government and military control centers, war making resources, and population centers. After adoption of a targeting policy, in the Chairman's opinion the commander responsible for the strategic mission should develop a national strategic targeting system or list subject to review by J-2 (Intelligence). On the second question, he believed an integrated operational plan was definitely needed. He would charge CINCSAC with its development. Naval carriers would not be assigned any pre-planned strategic targets, but when Polaris developed a significant operational capability it would be brought into the integrated plan. On the third issue, the Chairman reasoned that if the above actions were taken the question of operational control and problems of mutual interference would be "simplified". The promulgation of a national strategic target list (NSTL) and a single integrated operational plan (SIOP) would, in General Twining's words, "provide a sound basis for necessary coordination of operational plans of local commanders with CINCSAC's plan." Only after decisions were made, in the form of a command decision, and enforced, there would be no progress in the area of target coordination.

At the time he presented his views to the SecDef, the Chairman sought the positions of the services on the issues of targeting coordination by requesting answers to 18 questions. Initially, an interservice ad hoc committee prepared a reply to the questions. Later, each service individually prepared their answers. As in the issue of command and control of Polaris, a wide divergence of opinion existed between the services. But no further action was taken on the matter during 1959, awaiting the completion of Study 2009, an optimum target system for general war being prepared for Presidential approval.

Secretary McElroy also left office in December 1959; and the task of resolving the target coordination problem fell to his successor, Thomas S Gates. The new SecDef gave early indications that he intended to take action. On 20 January he told the Joint Chiefs that he wished to discuss SM-171-59 (the split decision Polaris paper) at their convenience. Events during the early spring provided fresh evidence that action was needed. Representatives to a coordination conference at Supreme Headquarters Allied Powers, Europe (SHAPE) agreed that targeting of a wide variety of weapons without a waste of resources was "far beyond the capability of coordination conferences." The senior representative of CINCEur and CINCSAC stated in their memo to the JCS: "With the increased number of weapons and their diversified utilization, it appears that an efficient application of the force can only be accomplished by a single authority."

Meanwhile, the issue remained stalled at the roadblock of conflicting service positions. On 6 May General Twining advised the Secretary that the Chiefs could not agree on a response to the 18 questions; their individual views were forwarded. After a two-day discussion in the middle of June in which the service positions were freely discussed with the new Secretary, the Joint Staff prepared a paper expanding on differences in the areas of policy, target detection, and planning and coordination. The Joint Chiefs were in agreement that a basic targeting policy was needed to translate guidance contained in Study 2009 and the President's decision on the study into workable instructions for unified and specified commanders, and that guidance was needed for selection of targets in a national target list, but they differed on what that policy should be. General Twining felt the elements of this diversity arose, partially at least, from endemic conceptual differences. He urged that the JCS not wait for a "perfect solution". To fit action to the word, he proposed a national strategic targeting policy. Service positions went to the SecDef as SM-696-60 on 20 July 1960.

On 16 August 1960, after over a year of consideration by the JCS and two Secretaries of Defense, the issues of command and control of strategic systems and strategic targeting became the subject of a SecDef decision. It was a clear compromise, indorsing neither the Air Force position favoring a unified command, nor the Navy position that existing JCS machinery could do the work. Recognized by Secretary Gates was CINCSAC's extensive experience in strategic planning. The individual designated as CINCSAC, acting as the agent of the JCS, would collect at Headquarters SAC a team of experts from all services to prepare a plan for all US forces committed to the initial strategic strike effort. CINCSAC's duties as Director of Strategic Target Planning (DSTP) were an additional and separate responsibility. On 18 August Secretary Gates assigned as General Power's deputy Rear Admiral (subsequently promoted to Vice Admiral) Edward N Parker, an expert in nuclear weapons and former head of the Defense Atomic Support Agency.

ORGANIZATION

General Power began immediately to gather his inter-service staff at Headquarters SAC. Actions to bring in new people and organize and train them in SAC methods proceeded at a brisk pace and they constituted the organization's main problems during the early formulative months. Time for preparation of the first plan was short; the SecDef wanted it done by early December.

The organization was kept as small as possible, with maximum participation of the existing SAC staff, but all services participated in all aspects of planning. Commands involved (SACEUR, CINCLANT, CINCPac, CINCal, and CINCNELM) were requested to send representatives to a 24 August meeting at Offutt AFB to discuss organization and manning. Three days later a proposed organizational structure to perform the main work assigned, i.e., preparation of a National Strategic Target List (NSTL) and a Single Integrated Operational Plan (SIOP), was prepared and forwarded to the JCS.

The organization was divided into two general categories. The first was the Office of the Director. General Power, in his capacity as Director of Strategic Target Planning, had as his mission to:

a. Organize a Joint Strategic Target Planning Staff consisting of personnel from the various services possessing the required skills to perform the targeting and planning functions.

b. Develop and maintain the NSTL and the SIOP for attack of the targets on the NSTL.

c. Submit the NSTL and the SIOP to the Joint Chiefs of Staff for review and approval, highlighting points of difference which he resolved during the preparation of the NSTL and the SIOP.

Also assigned to this office was a deputy, who assumed the responsibilities of the Director in his absence and acted as his principle assistant and advisor on JSTPS activities, and one representative each from the Army, Navy, Marine Corps, and Air Force. These service representatives served as a personal staff for the director and his deputy, represented their services in policy matters, and performed a liaison function. They were not in the command channel. Representatives from unified and specified commands supplying forces to the SIOP and a JCS liaison group were also attached to the staff. The CINC representatives (the number assigned was at the discretion of their commander) participated in the preparation of the SIOP and NSTL. They were not integrated into the staff, but were directly responsible to their respective commanders. A JCS liaison group, an integral part of the Joint Staff, JCS, assisted the DSTP in interpreting JCS guidance and informed the JCS and the services of progress in the preparation of the NSTL and SIOP. The CINC and service representatives served as a Policy Committee under the chairmanship of the deputy director. This committee reviewed and approved policy; disagreements went to the director for the final decision. Also part of the Office of the Director was the Secretariat, responsible for administration and personnel supervision. The second category consisted of the two production units of the Target Staff—the National Strategic Target List Division and the Single Integrated Operational Plan Division—which took their names from the work they performed.

The initial Joint Table of Distribution (JTD) of 269 spaces requested for the organization was divided as follows: SAC resources – 140 officers, 57 airmen, and 22 civilians; Army – 10 officers; Navy – 29 officers; Air Force – 8 officers; and Marine Corps – 3 officers.

On 1 September 1960 the JCS approved the proposed organization, officially designating it the Joint Strategic Target Planning Agency (JSTPA) (on 29 September 1960 the JCS redesignated the organization as the Joint Strategic Target Planning Staff), and the initial Joint Table of Distrbution (JTD) consisting of 50 military spaces to be added to the 197 SAC military personnel working in related areas. In one change, the JCS stipulated that the deputy chief of the SIOP Division be a Navy officer in the grade of rear admiral or captain.

Subsequently, as a result of the survey made of the NSTL Division's intelligence structure and the intelligence support agencies of SAC Headquarters, at the Chief of Naval Operation's request, the Deputy Director of JSTPS requested 69 additional military spaces, which with the exception of 5 airmen from the Air Force were to be furnished by the Navy and Army. Forty of these were to be assigned to Headquarters SAC Intelligence functions and 29 to the JSTPS. After review, the JCS approved the interim augmentation of 29 military personnel and 3 civilian spaces, but disapproved the additional 40.

The organization to prepare the first NSTL and SIOP was assembled in haste because the SecDef had ordered the two documents completed by 14 December 1960. Emphasis had been placed on acquiring the best people from the services to do the job; not much analysis had been made of existing capability within the SAC staff. But with completion of the initial NSTL and SIOP the organization could be adapted for the future, i.e., the work of keeping the documents current. General Power recommended a reduction; the non-SAC authorization would be reduced from 83 to 75 spaces and SAC personnel in a dual function status would be cut from 219 to 111. He also asked that the number of permanent representatives of the CINCs be held to a minimum.

The Army and Navy did not agree. The Chief of Naval Operations did not think it adequately represented all services at all levels, but favored the Air Force. Because the duties of the NSTL Division concerned primarily intelligence and target selection, in the Navy's opinion all services should be equally represented. Neither did Admiral Burke favor the proposal to reduce the number of the CINC representatives, preferring instead to leave their appointment to the discretion of the commander concerned. Injecting a new feature, the CNO recommended creation of an intelligence panel, with representatives from the CINCs, the services, the Joint Staff, and the

Central Intelligence Agency, "to provide the broadest and most expert intelligent base which can be achieved to support the SIOP." The Army did not think the proposed manning met the criteria of a joint staff, nor did it agree with maintaining SAC officers with two jobs in key positions, except for the DSTP. It recommended equal representation among services in the NSTL Division and proportional representation (based on committed forces) in the SIOP Division.

The DSTP argued that existing JCS guidance for creation of joint staffs did not provide precedent for assignment of joint staff responsibilities to a specified command. He defended the JTD as representing his interpretation of JCS guidance: it was the most economical, made the most efficient use of space and technical equipment, and most adhered to the composition of forces and weapons assigned to the plan. He had not used forces submitted to the plan as a basis for representation; if he had the Navy and Marine Corps would have been reduced by one-half. In the document 14 key positions out of 34 were identified as Army, Navy, or Marine Corps (41 percent). Although the DSTP had no requirement for an intelligence panel, he welcomed the addition of one intelligence officer from each of the CINCs to monitor SIOP intelligence, and he agreed to the addition of 10 personnel to provide "confidence" and coordination of intelligence by unified and specified commanders.

After considering the new proposal and the above comments by the services, the new SecDef, Robert S McNamara, notified General Power that he had "complied fully" with directives issued by Secretary Gates, but that he should realign the JTD using the following guidance:

a. Persons occupying key positions in the NSTL Division of JSTPS will be assigned no other duties.

b. Key positions in the NSTL Division will be filled by the best qualified officers regardless of their service affiliation.

c. Key positions in the SIOP Division will be filled by service representatives essentially in proportion to the forces each service provides for the execution of the SIOP.

d. The JSTPS should be organized so as to receive, evaluate and utilize pertinent intelligence from all available resources. However, no 'Joint Intelligence Review Panel' appears necessary.

The revised JTD submitted 27 April 1961 was essentially the same basic organization as proposed in January: 34 key positions and a total of 186 military and civilian personnel. Sixteen positions in the

NSTL Division, however, were identified as "no service specified"; the best qualified would be chosen for these posts irrespective of service. In the DSTP's opinion, the guiding principle of the JSTPS organization was "that of service representation proportional to the service forces involved". The organization as submitted was approved by the JCS on 14 June.

Preparation of SIOP-62

General Power, in his capacity as DSTP, was guided by the National Strategic Targeting and Attack Policy (NSTAP), a JCS document which formed the core of this nation's strategic strike planning. [*Specific objectives of this policy were to destroy or neutralize Sino-Soviet Bloc strategic strike forces and major military and government control centers, and to strike urban-industrial centers to achieve the level of destruction indicated in Study 2009.*] These objectives were to be accomplished by integrating strategic forces and directing them against a minimum list of targets. The first task of the JSTPS after its organization was to determine what targets were to be attacked. On 18 August General Power directed his Directorate of Intelligence to prepare a preliminary target list. At the initial meeting of the Staff six days later Intelligence presented a working list, known as the National Strategic Target Data Base (NSTDB) of about [*4,000 targets. (NOTE: From this list a team of experts from NSTL Division and the CINCs eventually prepared the final list.) A Steering Committee headed by Admiral Parker insured that the targeting needs of all the CINCs were satisfied. General Power wanted the final list to include only targets which had been positively identified and located.*]

Basic to the preparation of the NSTL was the NSTDB, a compilation of [*Sino-Soviet targets of strategic significance*] representing the combined knowledge of US intelligence sources. By a process of refinement the highest priority targets in this target data base eventually comprised the NSTL. After assigning a relative worth to the targets in the base by means of a target weighing system, the process of developing desired ground zeros (DGZs) began.

[censored   ] [*considering the number of*] [censored   ] [*weapons available, which could accomplish objectives set down in the NSTAP, was thus developed. Upon completion of the SIOP this list contained*] [censored   ]

Concurrent with work on the target system, personnel of the SIOP Division and CINC representatives analyzed capabilities of forces submitted by the CINCs preparatory to applying these forces to the target system. Only forces and capabilities existing in December 1960 were considered in the SIOP-62. Reliability planning factors for each weapon system were also determined and submitted to the Policy Committee for approval.

In the middle of September 1960 work began on applying weapon systems gathered by the SIOP Division to the DGZs prepared by NSTL Division. *The target system was divided into two parts —[censored] Coordinating [censored] (NOTE: This was a force of 874 delivery systems, 1447 weapons [censored] (NOTE: Consisting of 1464 aircraft and missiles and 1976 weapons [censored] strikes was difficult because of the great variety of delivery systems and weapons targeted. For example, forces available consisted of such divergent systems as the B-52, the F-100, and the ATLAS and the Mace;* [censored] *Detailed source data sheets were prepared on each sortie. They contained information on* [censored] *After further detailed flight planning, the complete source data program was run through SAC's 704 computer to* [censored] *Task force commanders received only those sheets directly related to their mission. At the tactical unit, strike timing for individual sorties was extracted from the timing sheets and integrated into the individual combat mission folders.*

After the work of applying committed forces to targets was completed, damage assessed, and necessary refinements and adjustments made, the NSTL was produced. It was a list of all National Strategic Target Data Base in stallations to be attacked in the SIOP. These targets fell into [censored]

On 1 December 1960 the SecDef, JCS, commanders of unified and specified commands committing forces to the SIOP, and other high ranking military and civilian leaders, 32 in all, gathered at Headquarters SAC for briefings on SIOP-62. Presented were the NSTL; operational concepts; enemy defenses; force application; assessment of sortie success, damage and casualties; and dissents to the plan.

The complete SIOP-62 was a detailed plan of what targets were to be attacked, by what forces, and in what manner during the initial strategic attack [*against the Sino-Soviet Bloc*]. It superceded any conflicting guidance contained in the Joint Strategic capabilities Plan. Eight annexes represented the key portions of the plan: intelligence, responsibilities and command relationships, atomic, concept of operations, coordinating instructions, strike timing, communications, and administrative procedures. [*The JCS, acting under orders from the President, reserved the prerogative of putting the plan into effect. Its mission was to:*

a. Destroy or neutralize the Sino-Soviet strategic nuclear capability and primary military and government controls of major importance.

b. Attack the major urban-industrial centers of the Sino-Soviet Bloc to the extent necessary to paralyze the economy and render the Sino-Soviet Bloc incapable of continuing the war.

[censored   ]

Disagreements with certain SIOP-62 planning factors were presented at the briefing by CINCLant's senior representative to the JCS, Rear Admiral JJ Hyland. Although they had earlier been resolved by the DSTP, by JCS direction they were presented as part of the SecDef briefing. First, Admiral Hyland objected to what he called the [censored   ]

[censored   ]

The DSTP's decision of 31 October 1960 had placed the [censored   ] The SIOP-62 was approved without major change by the JCS, SecDef, and the President on 2 December to be effective 1 April 1961. The plan went into effect on that date.

<u>Summary</u>

The Single Integrated Opertional Plan for 1962 represented a unique advancement in war planning. Prior to its development, atomic targeting was coordinated after the fact, handicapping mutual support and economy of force. After lengthy consideration of the issue by the JCS produced no unanimity of opinion, the Chairman proposed a national strategic targeting policy. The Secretary of Defense accepted this plan and directed it be used as guidance by CINCSAC in his new capacity as Director of Strategic Target Planning. In his decision of 16 August 1960, the Secretary decided a strategic command was not needed, but neither did he think target planning could be done within existing JCS capabilities. He created the Joint Strategic Target Planning Staff, responsible to the JCS, but located at Headquarters SAC. The JSTPS replaced the World-Wide Coordination Conference method of planning coordination, [*although operational coordination was still required in the* [censored   ] Working with a short deadline, a nucleus of SAC officers, assisted by officers of other services assigned to the new organization, produced the first NSTL and SIOP in less than four months. As expected, the process was not completed without differences arising from diverse service concepts, but they did not interfere with submission of the final plan to the SecDef on 1 December and its acceptance at that time. The JSTPS was not a panacea for all the problems of nuclear strike coordination, but it was a beginning, a foundation for future development.

September 5, 1961

This is a classified memo to General Maxwell Taylor, military advisor to President Kennedy, which discusses the US planning in the event that the Berlin Crisis (the blockade of West Berlin by the Soviet Union and the construction of the Berlin Wall, followed by the American-led Berlin Airlift) led to a nuclear war.

From the memo, we learn that the US was capable of launching its alert force of 1500 nuclear weapons in one hour, and could launch its entire nuclear force of 3400 weapons within 28 hours. The SAC alert force of bombers were to be sent out first, since they were recallable if the attack turned out to be a false alarm or a misinterpretation. American nuclear forces were to be directed at 3729 total targets. Since many of these targets were located together, there were 1077 "Desired Ground Zero's" at which nuclear weapons were to be targeted – 480 of these were assigned to the alert forces. Every nation in the Sino-Soviet Bloc was to be targeted.

The memo also raises a question that was not explicitly asked in previous documents: should the US launch a surprise nuclear first strike against the USSR (referred to as a "minimum-warning attack")? In all its nuclear planning, the US was deliberately ambiguous about the option of a first strike, and all of the planning was done without specifying which side would launch first.

We also learn that the SIOP-62 was essentially an all-or-nothing plan – once set in motion, all the nuclear weapons would be used in one automatically-unfolding massive attack which would completely destroy the

Soviet Union and China as functioning societies. The number of warheads that were actually launched was limited only by the amount of time available before a Soviet strike hit the US and destroyed our missiles and airbases. The alert force of one-third of SAC's bombers, carrying half of the available nuclear bombs, would be sent in the first wave to attack primary targets, with subsequent waves sent to lesser targets. The ICBMs would not be launched until after an attack had been confirmed. The US had 189 ballistic missiles available, of which 79 were Atlas ICBMs, 80 were the new Polaris submarine missiles, and 30 were intermediate-range Jupiter missiles based in Turkey and Italy. In both the US and the USSR, the vast majority of the potential strike force consisted of bombers. Each delivery vehicle (whether ICMB or bomber) was assigned a particular planned "time over target" to insure that the detonation of one nuclear weapon would not interfere with the trajectory of any others also assigned to that target.

A total of 295 "urban-industrial complexes" were targeted inside the USSR, and 199 of these were to be struck by the first wave of alert forces. It was expected that if the alert forces alone were able to strike, the attack would kill 37% of the entire population of the USSR and 55% of its urban residents, while an attack by the full American nuclear force would kill 54% of all Soviet citizens, including 71% of all urban dwellers — in the first 72 hours. However, the Pentagon concluded, even in the event of a US first strike, the Soviet retaliation could still kill as many as 3-7% of the US population. American planners expected a minimum of 16 million deaths in the US from a Soviet first strike.

There was no flexibility or alternate plans for smaller attacks on a limited set of targets, such as a limited strike solely on Soviet missile sites and avoiding Soviet cities. The lack of flexibility in the SIOP-62 led the Kennedy Administration to propose a new revised plan, to be known as SIOP-63.

MEMORANDUM FOR GENERAL MAXWELL TAYLOR, MILITARY REPRESENTATIVE TO THE PRESIDENT

SUBJECT: Strategic Air Planning and Berlin

1. The plan which now determines the use of our strategic striking power in the event of war is SIOP-62. This plan, prepared well before the present Berlin crisis, is built around two concepts that may well be inappropriate to the current situation. First, the plan is essentially a second-strike plan, which envisages a response to an attack on us, the size of which depends essentially on the amount of warning of enemy attack we receive. The minimum warning assumed is one hour: this suffices to generate the alert force of nearly 900 vehicles carrying

almost 1500 weapons. In 28 hours, the full force of some 2300 vehicles carrying about 3400 weapons can be launched. Second, the plan calls for strikes against a single set of targets, the "optimum-mix" of Sino-Soviet air and missile bases, and cities, and the various force generation options determine how far down the list the targets are struck, and the degree of their coverage by more than one weapon to assure achievement of planned damage levels. The single target list embodies the notion of "massive retaliation", the threat of which is expected to deter attack. At least two sets of circumstances that seem likely to arise in the context of the struggle over Berlin suggest the need for supplementary and alternative plans. The first is the problem raised by a false alarm, whether arising from a deliberate feint or a misinterpretation of events, that results first in the launching of SAC and then a decision to recall it at the positive control line. The second is the broader question of whether we might wish to strike first, and thus how appropriate both the target list and the operational concept of the SIOP are in that case.

2. If the present state of tension over Berlin persists over a period of months, it is likely that, at some point, a Soviet action will appear to threaten an attack on the United States with sufficient likelihood and imminence to cause us to launch SAC, and initiate the SIOP. After some lapse of time, we may conclude that we had been wrong, and, under the positive control arrangements, recall the force. There is, roughly, a six-hour interval between bases and the positive control line for aircraft in the first wave. After recall and return to base, that part of the force which had been launched would require a stand-down of about eight hours before it was again ready for launch. Thus, there would be a significant degradation of our capability for a short period of time after such a false alarm. How large it was would depend on how much time had elapsed when the recall was ordered. If the full six hours had elapsed, not only would the alert force (one-third of the vehicles carrying nearly one-half the weapons and a higher proportion of the megatonnage) have reached the neighborhood of the control line, but another 22% of the full force would already have been launched.

Further, in the nature of the SIOP, that part of the force which was still in reserve might not be ready to attack an appropriate set of targets, since their initially assigned targets would have been chosen under the assumption that the vehicles in question were part of the follow-on force, coming after the targets assigned to the first wave had already been attacked. These consequences of a false alarm suggest two dangers; first, the value to the Soviets of a feint; second, the danger that we will have a tendency to refuse to interpret any alarm as a false alarm, once the force has been launched, since the temporary degradation of our striking capacity on a recall may be unacceptable in the situation which provoked the alarm.

3. The second and broader question is whether a second-strike plan of massive retaliation is appropriate to our current position. Our military contingency plans for Berlin call for a number of ground force actions of increasing scope and magnitude. Their basic aim is to force the Soviets to withdraw the impediments to our access to West Berlin which have called them forth. Implicitly, they rest on the expectation that the Soviets will not respond, at least to the earlier steps, by initiating general war. If each increase in the scale of our action is met by a corresponding and always dominating increase in the Soviet response, we will clearly be forced at some point to move from local to general action. Is the SIOP the appropriate form of this action? If the SIOP were executed as planned, the alert force would be expected (in the statistical sense) to kill 37& of the population of the Soviet Union (including 55% of the urban population) and the full force 54% (including 71% of the urban population), and the two forces, respectively, to destroy 75% and 82% of the buildings, as measured by floor space. (Further, there is reason to believe that these figures are underestimated; the casualties, for example, include only those of the first 72 hours.) Is this really an appropriate next step after the repulse of a three-division attack across the zonal border between East and West Germany? Will the President be ready to take it? The force of these questions is underlined by the consideration that the scale and nature of the SIOP are such as inevitably to alert the Soviets to its initiation, and that all [censored] Thus Soviet retaliation is inevitable; and most probably, it will be directed against our cities and those of our European Allies.

What is required in these circumstances is something quite different. We should be prepared to initiate general war by our own first strike, but one planned for this occasion, rather than planned to implement a strategy of massive retaliation. We should seek the smallest possible list of targets, focusing on the long-range striking capacity of the Soviets, and avoiding, as much as possible, casualties and damage in Soviet civil society. We should maintain in reserve a considerable fraction of our own strategic striking power; this will deter the Soviets from using their surviving forces against our cities; our efforts to minimize Soviet civilian damage will also make such abstention more attractive to them, as well as minimizing the reserve forces, except insofar as aircraft return and can be recycled into operation.

4. Two recommendations for action follow from this discussion: both in the realm of inquiry, initially.

a. CINSAC should be asked, in the appropriate fashion, to examine the impact of a false alarm—i.e., one that results in the launch and then the recall of the force—on his plans in the context of the current situation, and to make whatever changes in his plans that the examination indicates. In making this examination, CINCSAC should be urged to examine targeting, as well as operational aspects of the problem, since the questions involved go not only to how the operational plans can be modified so as to minimize the degradation of capability consequent on a false alarm, but also, what might be done in the way of programming alternate targets for various segments of the force, so that the remaining capability can always be brought to bear in the most useful way.

b. The Joint Chiefs, the Director, Strategic Target Planning, and CINCSAC should be asked, in the appropriate fashion, to consider the preparation of alternatives to SIOP-62 for the use of our strategic striking power in the context of Berlin contingency planning. In so doing, they should be asked to give special attention to planning first strike attacks at Soviet long-range striking power, and planned so as to minimize casualties and damage to the Soviet, and to reduce the maximum extent possible both Soviet capabilities and Soviet incentives to strike a retaliatory blow at American and Allied cities.

It is clear that much of the concrete planning involved in both of these activities overlaps, and therefore there is an advantage in combining the two requests.

5. To indicate in a crude and sketchy way that plans of the type called for in 4b may be feasible, Annex A is attached. This sketches some of the elements of such an operation. Annex B, by contrast, provides a summary of SIOP-62. Annex C is a draft request for the planning study described in 4b, so drafted as to be sent out either by yourself or the President.

ANNEX A: AN ALTERNATIVE TO SIOP-62

The current crisis over Berlin makes it desirable for the United States to consider how it would use its strategic striking power in response to a major reverse on the ground in Western Europe. In this situation, we may well wish to assume the initiative in beginning general war. Is there a plan which offers the prospect of a more effective and less frightful operation than SIOP-62? It seems reasonably clear what objectives we would like to achieve under the postulated circumstances. These objectives would be to destroy the long-range nuclear offensive capabilities of the Soviet Union; to limit or avoid damage to the United States and its Allies; to limit damage to the Soviet Union compatible with the achievement of the military objective; and to have capabilities in reserve available to press home the attack, if necessary, to dissuade the Soviets from using any residual forces against the US and Allied cities.

Achievement of these objectives would obviously require up-to-date, complete information about the target system, and an attack so delivered and coordinated as to prevent the enemy from launching his vehicles. The task looks imposing considering that the target system lies in an area covering millions of square miles. In principle, the ICBM would be the ideal vehicle for attack because of its speed and the predictability of its arrival on target. However, the United States will have only 189 ballistic missiles available over the next eight or nine months. Of these 80 will be Polaris and 30 Jupiter. The reliability of our missiles will be low, their accuracy uncertain, and the problems of achieving simultaneity on target formidable. These factors would appear to rule out the ballistic missile as a candidate for a minimum-warning attack at the present time.

We are left, then, with the bombers, and particularly with the B-47s and B-52s, and overseas-based or carrier-based aircraft. But the bombers are not looked upon as the instruments for a minimum-warning attack for a number of reasons. The very smallest target system is usually calculated as around 150 DGZs, and even then there is a question as to whether all the Soviet ICBM sites have been included. Enemy early warning systems represent a hazard and there are the enemy defenses which must be penetrated. The problem of getting the requisite combat radius with the bomber and yet recovering it looks difficult. So do the problems of coordination. Working back from the DGZs to the number of aircraft required for the mission usually results in an answer of mass; and mass means a high probability that the enemy will detect the raid in time to launch some or all of his force. But does mass really have to be the answer to the problem?

Consider first the size of the target system. There are three types of targets which it seems essential to destroy in the first wave of an attack. They are the home and staging bases of the Soviet heavy and medium bombers, and the ICBM sites. Let us suppose, for purposes of calculation, that the number of DGZs in these three categories is as follows:

Home Bases   46
Staging Bases   26
ICBM Sites   16
Total DGZs   88

By this estimate, if we destroy a total of 88 DGZs, we will have eliminated or paralyzed the nuclear threat to the United States sufficiently to permit follow-on attacks for mop-up purposes or for the elimination of other targets—such as bomber-capable airfields and nuclear storage sites—which might provide the basis for a later attack on the United States, and IRBM bases which threaten Europe.

Let us make four other assumptions, namely that;

[censored]

2. One third of the 62 DGZs--or 21 points—are closely enough located to 21 other points so that one-third of the bombers assigned to the raid can hit two targets within a time of twenty minutes.

3. A majority of the bombers on the raid can carry four [censored] bombs.

4. All targets are soft-vulnerable, to, at most, [censored]

With these assumptions, we must get a minimum of 41 bombers into the Soviet airspace and over their initial targets with no more than 15 minutes between the first and last bomb-drop. One hour thereafter we want to cover the staging bases and to have brought in the first of our follow-on forces.

The key to the raid, of course, is represented by the 41 bombers. This is a relatively small number, but it does not allow for some kind of attrition en route, and it certainly does not by itself explain how the aircraft are to arrive undetected over their initial targets.

Two other assumptions are required. The first is that there will be an attrition en route of 25%, making for 55 aircraft that will penetrate Soviet airspace. The second assumption is that these aircraft can fan out and penetrate undetected at low altitude at a number of different points on the Soviet early warning perimeter, then bomb and withdraw at low altitude.

In sum, the success of the raid would seem to depend upon small numbers, dispersal, and low-altitude penetration. If something on the order of 41 aircraft were involved in the attack, and all their weapons were dropped, this would involve a total of [censored] bombs per aircraft [censored] all weapons should be airburst against the soft Soviet target system, mortalities in the Soviet Union would result primarily from blast and thermal effects rather than fallout. Given the locations of the targets, and assuming there are no gross errors in the bombing, mortalities from the initial raid might be less than 1,000,000 and probably not much more than 500,000.

Two questions immediately arise about this concept. How valid are the assumptions, and do we possess the capability and skill to execute such a raid? Answers cannot be obtained without the most careful and detailed operational studies and exercises. But there are numerous reasons for believing that the assumptions are reasonable, that we have the wherewithal to execute the raid, and that, while a wide range of outcomes is possible, we have a fair probability of achieving a substantial measure of success.

Consider first assumptions about the target system. Available information suggests that Soviet heavy and medium bombers are normally located on a maximum of 46 bases, and that there are 26 bases through which they could stage in order to fly missions against the US. The bulk of the heavy bombers appears to be based to the south; the Badgers are deployed on the western and eastern frontiers. As a consequence, they are somewhat difficult to get at, but they are mal-deployed for offensive action and might conceivably be kept out of the war by elimination of the northern staging bases. All targets are soft. Moreover, the home bases are so located that at least one-third of the attacking bombers could hit two targets within a period of 15 minutes (a distance of about 110 miles if the bombers are traveling at 450 knots).

An estimate of the number of ICBM sites that would have to be attacked in the near future is rather difficult to make. At the moment, it seems safe to say that there are at most 8 missile sites (of which 4 can be targeted now) and allow 2 aiming points for each site. This totals 16 DGZs for the ICBM system. [censored] They constitute 25 aiming points, mostly near the western borders of the Soviet Union. One way of dealing with them is to assign them as follow-on targets, immediately after the first wave; assigned to long-range fighters based in Europe and carrier-based naval aircraft.

Alternatively, it can be assumed that the threat of follow-on attack on Soviet cities by our reserve forces, accompanied by an explicit message to that effect, might be sufficient to deter Soviet retaliation against Allied cities in Europe.

There are three uncertainties about the numbers that have been mentioned. There could be more or fewer ICBM and MRBM sites. Depending on the circumstances, the heavy and medium bombers could be disposed to a larger system of bases and some of them could be airborne with bombs on board. Finally, missile-launching submarines could be in port, in transit, or on station and able to make their entry into the war. In short, a raid involving 41 bombers could be too large or too small; and some enemy forces could conceivably escape regardless of the skill with which the raid were executed. Last-minute intelligence might well be able to reduce some of these uncertainties.

A second major assumption is that there will be a maximum en route attrition of 25%. This figure is intended to allow for aborts and for the hazards of low-level penetration. The supposition is that there would be no losses to enemy air defenses. The figure is quite arbitrary and requires examination. However, NIE 11-3-61 (11 July 1961) states that below about [censored] the Soviet air defense "would lose most of its effectiveness. At present, the USSR has little capability for active defense against very low altitude attacks." Careful planning of mission profiles might enable the bombers to evade such defenses.

[censored] target system is counterbalanced by the danger of making the size of the raid too large. What constitutes the appropriate scale of attack must therefore be a matter of careful study and evaluation.

The problems of designing and scheduling follow-on attacks are also substantial. The follow-ons represent the means of destroying targets not hit in the first wave and increasing the assurance of success against the initial targets. Among the most important targets for the follow-ons are the [censored] but again, the urgency is counter-balanced by the importance of not giving warning of the initial attack. Several possible ways of getting around this dilemma may be available: the airborne alert aircraft, and A3Ds and A4Ds of the 6th fleet, and the fighter-bombers in Europe. Their numbers, targeting, scheduling and recall possibilities would have to be examined in detail before determining whether or not they could be programmed effectively without giving away the attack.

Clearly, there are risks here, but there are opportunities as well. Since the US would have the initiative, there are many steps it could take to reduce the consequences of partial success or failure, and to exercise control over Soviet behavior. Once bombs have fallen in the Soviet Union, air defenses can be alerted and reinforced. Civil defense measures can be instituted. Most important of all, very large strategic offensive capabilities can be generated. In these circumstances—if we are hitting selected military targets in the Soviet Union, and doing so in a discriminating manner—we should be able to communicate two things to Krushchev: first, that we intend to concentrate on military targets unless he is foolish enough to hit our cities; secondly, that we are prepared to withhold the bulk of our forces from the offensive (although we may continue to overfly them), provided that he accepts our terms.

A wide range of outcomes is possible from initiating such an attack. The raid could be recalled before any damage is done. Detection might occur during penetration and enable the bulk of the Soviet force to launch. A partial success might be achieved. The initial attack might be a complete success, but planning and execution of the follow-on attacks might fail. Without further work, it is difficult to say what degree of success might be achieved, and with what degree of confidence. However, the choice may not be between "go" and "no go"; it may be between "go" and SIOP-62. Compared with SIOP-62, the small-scale, minimum-warning attack—coupled with carefully-timed and executed follow-on raids—has distinct advantages. In conclusion, it may be well to enumerate the principle ones.

1. Recall: [censored   ]
2. Minimum Warning: [censored   ]
3. Reduction in Soviet Long-Range Capabilities: [censored   ]
4. Control: [censored   ]

APPENDIX TO ANNEX A

Attempts to assess the damage to the US that might result from a minimum-warning attack on the Soviet Union must deal with a large number of uncertainties. This appendix will discuss the uncertainties and offer rough calculations on the possible range of consequences.

1. It is not clear exactly what is the structure of the Soviet long-range offensive force or what would constitute its nuclear armament. Of major uncertainty is the number of bombers assigned to the strategic mission and the bomb loads they could carry. However, it

seems reasonable to believe that the capability of the full force lies somewhere between 1000 and 2000 megatons. One typical set of assumptions would result in the following totals:

Vehicle	Number	Weapon Yield	Number per Vehicle	Total Megatons
Bison	80	1 MT	4	320
Bear	40	1 MT	4	160
Badger	400	1 MT	2	800
ICBM	52	7 MT	1	364
				1644 MT

Whatever the merit of this particular assignment, it indicates how important the bomber remains to the weight of the Soviet offensive (in this case contributing more than 75% of the megatonnage), and how critical it is to keep as much as possible of the bomber force out of the war.

2. Given these capabilities, there are a number of variables which would affect the amount of damage done to the US. The most important of these variables are:

a. The number of Soviet vehicles and weapons surviving the minimum-warning attack, penetrating US defenses, and hitting their targets. This number could vary from zero to something approximating the full force.

b. The numbers and types of targets attacked. The Soviets might have a targeting philosophy similar to our own and aim at an "optimum mix". They might have a city target system, or they might concentrate on military targets. If their command-control is as vulnerable as our own, and if their strike plans are as automatic, considerable disruption in their weapon assignments could occur, depending on the degree of success attached to the US attack. Some of their targets might go untouched; others might be killed several times over. The range of possibilities is very wide.

c. The numbers and yields of weapons per target. The damage to the US, particularly if the attacks go against urban areas, is very sensitive to these factors.

d. The height of burst of the weapons. The mortalities in the US are quite heavily dependent on the mix of air-bursts and ground-bursts that the Soviets choose for their weapons. Fallout can add few or many to the casualty list.

e. The civil defenses available and the uses made of them by the US population. For the short-term, presumably, the US will have, at best, an improvised shelter program. Nevertheless, even improvised shelters—if sensibly used—could bring about a sharp reduction in the mortalities from fallout.

3. A major uncertainty having to do with the outcome of a minimum-warning attack is the degree to which the US can influence Soviet retaliatory choices. In principle, there are several possibilities open to us. We can indicate in peacetime that, despite our abhorrence of nuclear warfare, we intend to use nuclear weapons against strictly military objectives—unless, of course, the enemy initiates a counter-city campaign. We can also show the dramatic difference between military and urban-industrial campaigns in terms of mortalities and industrial damage. Should we initiate a minimum-warning attack, there are, as already suggested, a series of actions we can take to affect Soviet response. We can:

a. Confine our initial attack to a small number of military targets, airburst weapons wherever feasible, and keep Soviet mortalities low. Russian cities would then stand as hostages to our follow-on attacks.
b. Communicate to the Soviet government what we have done; that we have large forces on their way which can hit military or civil targets—depending on Soviet retaliation (if any); that we are prepared to offer reasonable terms in return for a cessation of hostilities; that, meanwhile, we shall overfly and do reconnaissance over the Soviet Union.

c. Design and launch our follow-on attacks so that they can hit military or civil targets, or refrain from bombing at all.
d. Point out that any effort by the Soviets to retaliate against European cities or try to seize Western Europe as hostage can only lead to an intensification of our attacks and the probable destruction of Russian communications and logistics.

In short, we can offer the Soviets powerful incentives to use whatever residual forces they command in a sensible manner. Whether these incentives would be powerful and timely enough remains a matter of speculation.

Charts I and II are intended to give a rough approximation of the range of mortalities that the US might suffer from various weights and types of Soviet retaliation:

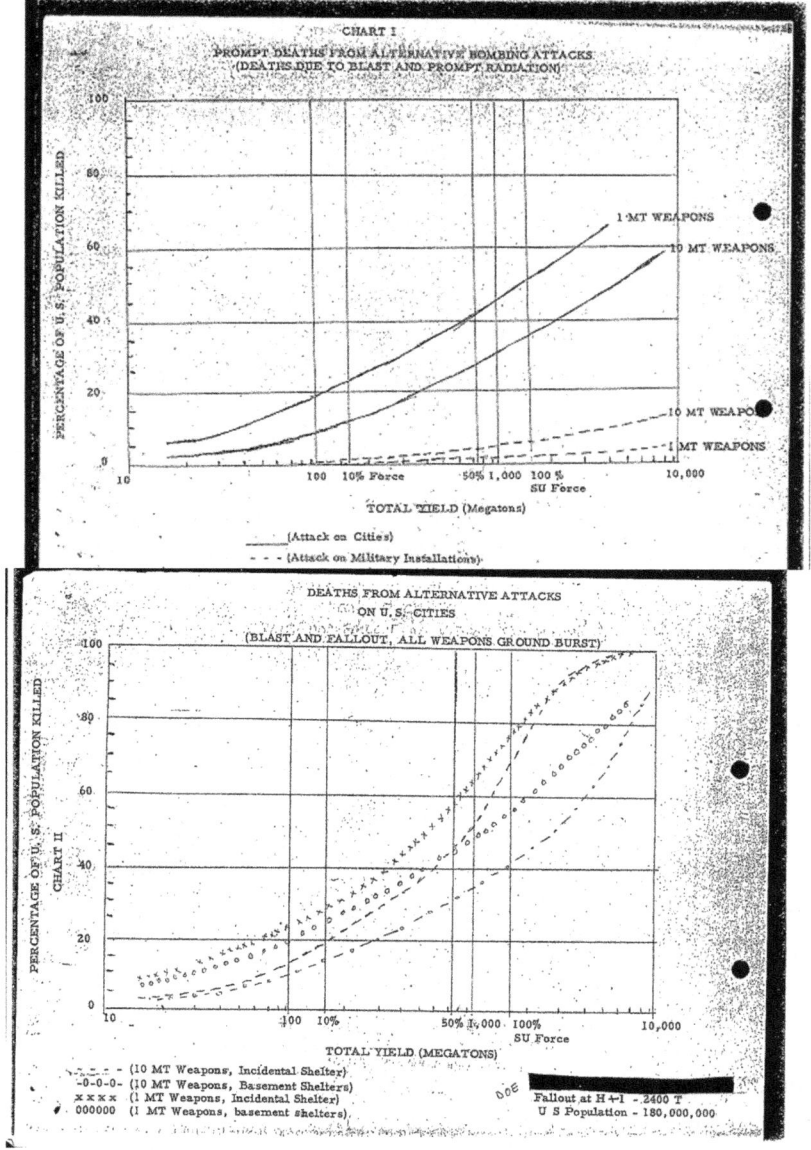

Attention should be drawn to the lower end of the scale for the cases where the Soviets retaliate against cities. The number of mortalities that the US suffers where only a few megatons are involved, while small percentage-wise — between three and seven percent — can range between 5,000,000 and 13,000,000. This is because New York and Chicago, with their great concentrations of people, can be virtually wiped out by a small number of high-yield weapons. In thermonuclear warfare, people are easy to kill.

The charts show ordinates corresponding to the full megatonnage calculated above, 50% and 10%, to give some indication of the results of the range of success or failure of the first attack.

ANNEX B
SIOP-62 AN APPRECIATION

The Single Integrated Operational Plan is the war plan which directs the bulk of US and Allied atomic strike forces in the event of general war with the Sino-Soviet Bloc. The origins of SIOP-62 lie in Study #2009 of the Net Evaluation Subcommittee. The study developed a single list of targets, known as the "optimum mix", and indicated what levels of damage could be accomplished against the target system with varying levels of assurance and capabilities. President Eisenhower approved of the target list and selected the damage and assurance criteria to be used in operational planning.

On 19 August 1960, the JCS issued the National Strategic Targeting and Attack Policy (NSTAP) as guidance for the planning staffs of the unified and specified commanders. Since NESC #2009 had considered the initial attack only, the NSTAP and SIOP-62 are similarly concerned and do not provide for follow-on attacks. The NSTAP laid down two objectives for the planners: (1) to destroy or neutralize the Sino-Soviet Bloc strategic nuclear capability and government controls of major importance; (2) to attack the major urban-industrial centers of the Sino-Soviet Bloc in order to achieve the general level of destruction selected by the President from NESC #2009.

With this guidance, the Director of Strategic Target Planning (DSTP), assisted by a joint staff in Omaha, established a National Strategic Target List (NSTL), determined the priorities to be given to these targets, and drew up a plan for a coordinated attack on the target system by major US and Allied atomic strike forces. SIOP-62 resulted from this effort and became effective 1 April 1961. Unless changed, it will remain in effect until 1 July 1962 when SIOP 63 is scheduled to supercede it.

SIOP-62 starts from the premise that a single operational plan suffices for the atomic strike forces regardless of the circumstances in which a general war might be initiated. The target list is constant and the only question at issue is how much of the list can be destroyed with what degree of assurance. Consequently, the list is broken into two parts: a minimum NSTL containing 2220 primary objective targets, together with 835 active defense installations which must be hit in order to reach the primary objectives; and the full NSTL, which contains 3729 targets. Since many of these targets are co-located, and can be destroyed by a single weapon of sufficiently high yield, the actual number of Desired Ground Zeroes (DGZs) in SIOP-62 adds up to 1077.

The target list is assigned a total value of approximately 5,000,000 points; each target is allocated a certain number of points according to its importance: DGZs are then "optimized" to destroy the maximum number of targets within a given complex; and finally, the most important DGZs are assigned to those forces which have the highest probability of surviving and destroying the targets. [censored] In other words, the optimum mix determines what targets should be attacked and when they should be attacked.

Table 1 illustrates in a rough way the targets that are attacked and the relative importance that is attached to them. The Alert Force is assigned 480 DGZs; the full force, as stated, would cover 1077 DGZs. All countries in the Sino-Soviet Bloc are represented on the target list, but the Soviet Union contains the bulk of the targets. As one example, General Power points out (in JCSM-406-61, appendix A) that "four SAC alert sorties (11 weapons) are targeted in [censored] However, he goes on to say that they "may be withheld at any time prior to launch of the SAC alert force on a calculated risk basis."

The requirements set by President Eisenhower, based on NESC Study #2009, was that the atomic strike forces have a capability to achieve a 75% assurance of inflicting [censored] severe damage to enemy nuclear delivery capabilities and military and government controls. Similarly, there was to be a 75% assurance of inflicting [censored] severe damage to the industrial floor space of the Soviet Union and China. A variety of techniques are used to achieve this amount of destruction with the requisite level of confidence. The maximum number of vehicles is launched consistent with the amount of warning received and the readiness of the force. Routes of all vehicles are coordinated, and time over target (TOT) is carefully controlled. The major tactics used to penetrate enemy defenses are:

[censored]

TOP SECRET

Table 1

Targets and their Assignment*

Type of Target	Total Targets	Alert Force Targets
1. Nuclear Threat to the U.S.		
Airfields with nuclear storage and primary staging bases	76	76
Nuclear storage sites	68	68
Missile sites and storage, ICBMs**	4	4
[censored]	218	166
	6	6
Missile sites, MRBM**	1	1
Missile storage, MRBM	29	26
Naval Bases		
[censored]	88	56
	5	5
	369	217
	11	11
Naval Base, Surface	80	72
	29	26
V. Urban-Industrial Complexes at Risk		
USSR	295	199
China	78	49
VI. Government Control Centers		
USSR and China	126	118

* Although this table is based on a JCS document, it does not represent the full target list. For example, 835 active defense installations are omitted.

** These numbers undoubtedly will change or already have changed.

- 3 -

TOP SECRET

In order to deliver the requisite damage to target with the desired assurance, a system of cross-targeting is employed. Different types of vehicles, launched from a variety of bases, are scheduled against a particular target. Thus, a Jupiter, a Titan, and 3-B52s are programmed against [censored]

A number of degradation factors are used in order to determine the probability that a weapon will reach a given bomb release line

(BRL) and detonate on target. [censored] Table II indicates some of the probabilities that have been obtained with respect to SIOP-62.

TOP SECRET

Table II

Some SIOP-62 Probabilities

Average Delivery Assurance	Vehicles
52.3%	SIOP missiles (including cruise missiles)
63.1%	All-weather aircraft
35.5%	Non-all-weather aircraft
56.8%	All SIOP weapons

Average DGZ Assurance (that one weapon will detonate on target)
87%

The delivery systems integrated into SIOP-62 total 2258 vehicles. They carry 3423 weapons with yields ranging from [censored] megatons. The Alert Force is programmed to deliver 1447 weapons with a total yield of [censored] The Full Force, with 3423 weapons, would deliver [censored] –assuming that the entire force got through to target. Tables III and IV show numbers and types of delivery vehicles, numbers and locations of bases from which they would be launched, and types of weapons to be employed.

TOP SECRET

Table III

SIOP Delivery Systems and Their Deployment

Type of Vehicle	Number	Location of Bases	Number
B-47	760	United States	
B-52	447		
B-58	32		
B-57	38		
B-66	17		
F-84-F	18		
F-100	221		
F-101	28		
Valiant	8		
Canberra	41		
AD	69	United Kingdom	
A3D	58		
A4D	168		
Polaris	80		
Atlas	58		
Titan	21	Germany	
Jupiter	30		
Snark	30		
Regulus	4		
Mace	54		
Matador	76		
	2258		

Massive Retaliation

Table IV

Weapon Variety in SIOP-62

Aircraft Delivery		Missile Delivery	
Type	Yield	Type	Yield
Mark 41		Titan	
Mark 39		Snark	
Mark 43		Atlas	
Mark 28		Jupiter	
Mark 5		Regulus	
Mark 7		Hound Dog	
Boar		Polaris	
Mark 105		Mace	
		Matador	

SIOP-62 contains 16 options. However, these options do not refer to alternative strategies but to the number of delivery vehicles that can be generated for launch at specified times after A-hour (time to begin force preparation). Thus, the alert force has zero generation time and represents Option 1. The full force can be generated with strategic warning of something over 28 hours. This represents Option 16. The alert force would be launched at an "optimum mix" of military and urban-industrial targets. Follow-on forces would attack additional targets together with the same targets scheduled for the alert force (in order to increase assurance of success). Table V shows the schedule of force generation.

Table V

Force Generation

Option	Time	Weapons	Delivery Systems	Total
1	0000		874	874
2	0100		70	
3	0200		57	
4	0300		232	
5	0400		46	
6	0500		50	
7	0600		65	1394
8	0700		54	
9	0800		91	
10	0900		51	
11	1000		80	
12	1200		97	
13	1400		75	1842
14	2000		193	
15	2800		209	
16	Strategic Warning		94	2338*

* This number is higher than the total shown in Table III. Although both numbers appear in the same paper, there is no explanation for the discrepancy.

132 *Massive Retaliation*

The actual flexibility in SIOP-62 consists essentially of the ability to withhold certain strikes from preplanned targets. [censored]

The outcome to be expected from implementation of SIOP-62 has been calculated to a certain degree for two cases: where the alert force gets off; and where the full force gets off. It should be noted that casualties and damage to the United States and its Allies customarily are not presented, although casualties in the United States alone (resulting from Soviet attacks) are expected to be 16,000,000 at a minimum. Tables VI, VII, VIII, IX and X show what might happen to the Sino-Soviet Bloc in the two cases mentioned above. Presumably the SIOP planning factors which provided the averages shown in Table II were used to obtain these results.

TOP SECRET

Table VI

Targets and their Destruction

Type of Target	Total Targets	Destroyed by Alert Force	Destroyed by Full Force
I. Nuclear Threat to the U.S.			
Airfields with nuclear storage and primary staging bases	76	76	76
Nuclear storage sites	68	56	68
Missile sites and storage, ICBM	4	4	4
[censored]	218	99	212
Missile sites, MRBM	6	1	6
Missile storage, MRBM	1	1	1
Naval Bases	29	20	28
[censored]	88	24	83
[censored]	5	5	5
[censored]	369	91	276
Naval Base, Surface	11	8	10
[censored]	80	15	56
[censored]	29	15	26
V. Urban-Industrial Complexes at Risk			
USSR	295	199	295
China	78	49	78
VI. Government-Control Centers			
USSR and China	126	85	121

[Table VII is censored]

~~TOP SECRET~~

Table VIII

SIOP Casualties

	Caused by	
	Alert Force	Full Force
	421,000	496,000
	258,000	308,000
	197,000	292,000
	4,200	214,000
	497,000	2,636,000
	1,300	58,000
	1,378,500**	4,004,000***

* These casualties result from strikes by SIOP-committed forces only.

** One percent of the ▮▮▮ population.

*** Four percent of the ▮▮▮ population.

~~TOP SECRET~~

Table IX

Damage to Sino-Soviet Bloc Civil Societies*

	Destroyed** by	
	Alert Force	Full Force
% Industrial floor space USSR	65	74
% Total floor space USSR	75	82
% Urban casualties*** USSR	55	71
% Rural casualties USSR	21	39
% Total casualties USSR	37	54
% Industrial floor space China	53	59
% Total floor space China	61	62
% Urban casualties China	41	53
% Rural casualties China	4	9
% Total casualties China	10	16

* Estimates based on the arrival of at least one weapon at each DGZ.

** Destroyed means damage to building or facilities which precludes production without essentially complete reconstruction of the installation. It connotes collapse or severe damage to all principal structures. A greater number of installations will receive lesser but significant damage which would require materials and effort before production could be resumed.

*** Casualties include fallout effects during the first 72 hours, with a 60% shielding factor.

[table X is censored]

The effort thus far has been to describe SIOP-62 and present official evaluations of the outcome of a general war should the SIOP be implemented. It may now be appropriate to underline several characteristics of the plan and briefly discuss the evaluations.

Although SIOP-62 possesses the potential of a limited amount of flexibility, it is actually an all-purpose plan designed for execution in its existing form regardless of the contingency that may arise. The rigidity of the plan, especially in regard to targeting, has a number of causes. Several of them are worth enumerating.

1. There is a widespread expectation among military planners that the Soviets, whether they strike first or second, will attack urban targets or some urban-military combination comparable to the "optimum mix" upon which SIOP-62 is postulated. Consequently there is no need to be especially selective about targets or discriminating in the US attack.

2. There is an equally widespread expectation that, regardless of the circumstances, the Soviets will manage to launch a number of weapons against the US. In other words, the US will never be able to achieve the combinations of surprise and complete destruction of the Soviet long-range nuclear capability; the Soviets will always execute either urban or optimum mix attacks; therefore the US must always attack a composite target system as exemplified by the SIOP-62. Nowhere is any real consideration given to the possibility that there may be an interaction between our targeting philosophy and that of the Soviet Union.

3. Accompanying these assumptions is the notion that prevailing in a general war means coming out relatively ahead of the enemy. As an example, if the US has lost 20% of its industrial capacity and 30% of its people, but the Sino-Soviet Bloc has lost 40% of its industrial capacity and 60% of its people, then the US, somehow or another, has won the war. In somewhat oblique fashion, the JCS express this philosophy in JCSM-430-61. As they put it: Diversion of US forces from other targets to military targets would reduce by relatively small percentage the effect on the Soviet civil society. If the diversion were highly pronounced, it could result in a failure to damage the war-supporting economies of the USSR and China to the extent necessary to render them incapable of further support of the war effort. This

latter condition was found by Study No. 2009 to be a shortcoming of attacking only military targets.

4. Finally, although this concern is rarely expressed, there is a growing fear that -- owing to the vulnerability of US strategic forces and our command-control – three consequences might flow from introducing any real flexibility into the SIOP. The first is that our offensive forces might be cut down to a very small fraction of heir prewar size by a well-executed surprise attack; hence our retaliation would hurt the Soviets only if directed against an urban or composite target system. The second is that a surprise attack might knock out the US command-control and leave our residual forces uncertain as to the plan they should execute. Existence of only one plan—SIOP-62— together with the elaborate system of cross-targeting, hopefully reduces the probability that the Soviets will escape unscathed from such an attack. A third consequence of great concern is that greater flexibility, introduced under these circumstances, will become widely known, will tempt the Soviets to attack, and thereby will weaken deterrence.

In addition to the rigidity inherent in SIOP-62, the plan depends very heavily for its success upon warning sufficient to launch the alert force. If sufficient warning is not received, it is conceivable that few, if any, US delivery vehicles would get off. Such a contingency is well within the bounds of possibility, especially with a growth of the Soviet ICBM force.

Finally, SIOP-62 is, to put it mildly, an extremely blunt instrument. Even in the case of strategic warning, the plan envisages using the force in such a way that the enemy has a high probability of receiving warning that a US attack is on the way. Penetration techniques, as noted, call for mass, countermeasures, and the development of corridors through which subsequent bombers can pass. These are brute force tactics which, in turn, make for almost certain fulfillment of the prophecy that the enemy will be able to launch some of his weapons, regardless of the circumstances.

The evaluation of the SIOP-62 contains a number of interesting features. The planning factors used to establish the assurance with which a weapon will reach the BRL are highly uncertain quantities. The averages, under some circumstances, could be much too high; under others, they may be much too low. Nowhere is a factor for base destruction in the US included. Consequently, however detailed and refined the calculations about damage to the Sino-Soviet Bloc, no great weight of confidence can be placed in them. Similarly, there must be large uncertainties about the level of damage that the US would suffer. In short, although the outcomes shown for SIOP-62 are of value, they are incomplete—not only because they play down the damage to the US, but also because they concentrate on one set of results rather than on a range.

ANNEX C
GENERAL WAR CONTINGENCY PLANNING AND BERLIN

The Berlin crisis, rising international tension, and the possibility that the United States may become engaged in direct conflict with the Soviet Union makes it imperative that we have general war plans—and particularly plans pertaining to the use of our strategic forces—which take account of the many ways in which general war may occur. One of the contingencies for which we must plan is the case where, as a result of major repulse to our conventional forces in Western Europe, the United States responds with a strategic attack against the Soviet Union itself. Review of SIOP-62 suggests that it need not be the only for such an attack. I therefore request, as a matter of the utmost urgency, that alternative plans be developed for a strategic attack upon the Soviet Union. I also request that such plans be evaluated for their effectiveness and that estimates be presented of the earliest date at which they could be instituted and implemented.

Certain objectives should be kept clearly in mind in the development of these plans. My desire is that the attack be concentrated on the smallest number of military targets compatible with the elimination of the Soviet intercontinental threat. The attack should be designed in such a way as to minimize damage to Soviet population, industry and governmental authority. It should also be designed so as to enhance the probability of minimizing damage to the population, industry and governmental authority of the United States and its European Allies. Unless adequate justification can be given for the inclusion of targets in other countries, the attack should be directed solely against targets within the Soviet Union. Finally, the attack should ensure that substantial forces be available for follow-on attacks.

Emphasis should be given to a minimum-warning attack with the smallest number of vehicles compatible with the decisive reduction of the enemy's strategic offensive capabilities. Combined missile-bomber strikes and bomber–only strikes should be analyzed. All plans should be based on the assumption either that a state of extreme tension exists between the United States and the Soviet Union, or that a local conflict has started between them. It should be assumed further that the strategic forces of both sides have been placed on a high alert, with the further possibility that overflights may be occurring over one or both countries.

The plans that are developed should be detailed and explicit in character. In particular, they should describe:
1. The target system
2. The desired ground zeros
3. Weapons assignments
4. Expected results, including:
a. Expected accuracies of delivered weapons
b. Expected damage per DGZ
c. Variations in expected damage resulting from variations in yield and height-of-burst of assigned weapons
5. Mission characteristics
6. Follow-on forces
7. Measures to reduce warning
8. Enemy air defenses. In this connection, particular attention should be given to attacks which do not depend for their effectiveness on the destruction of enemy air defenses
9. Optimum timing for execution of the plan
10. Pre-attack precautions
11. Overseas base requirements
12. US warning systems, air defenses, and civil defense measures

I request that each plan be accompanied by an evaluation of its expected effectiveness. Such an evaluation should include:

1. Soviet force survival
a. Numbers and types of Soviet strategic forces expected to survive the attack.
b. Confidence levels and uncertainties associated with these estimates.

2. Damage in the Soviet Union
a. Casualties and damage in the Soviet Union resulting from the attack, with varying assumptions about the level of Soviet civil defenses and the ability of the Russian population to make effective use of available shelter.

3. Warning given to the Soviets

a. Degree of warning (measured in time) that the Soviets might expect to receive of the attack.

b. Confidence levels and uncertainties associated with these estimates.

4. Damage in the United States

a. Casualties and damage in the United States, given varying assumptions about the size of the Soviet response, the targets in the United States to be hit, and the attrition that US defense could exact.

b. In this connection, consideration should be given to pre-attack and post-attack measures which might be taken in order to influence the nature of any Soviet reply.

5. Damage elsewhere

a. Casualties and damage in Allied countries resulting from the US attack and from possible Soviet responses.

b. Casualties and damage within the Sino-Soviet Bloc (the USSR excluded).

6. US follow-on forces

a. Estimates on numbers surviving

b. Readiness and ability to continue the attack

I request that, by 25 September 1961, a progress report on this project be presented to me, together with a preliminary estimate of the ability of US strategic forces actually to execute such plans.

B-36 nuclear bomber

B-52 nuclear bomber

B-61 nuclear bomb ready for loading

Atlas, the first operational American ICBM

Titan II nuclear missile in its hardened silo

Titan II at launch

Polaris missile being loaded into a nuclear submarine

Polaris missile at launch

Minuteman III ICBM in its silo

Minuteman III MIRV warheads

Minuteman III at launch

Poseidon missile launch from submarine

Proposed rail-mobile plan for the MX missile

MX Peacekeeper ICBM launch from silo

Soviet SS-9 ICBM on mobile launcher

Soviet SS-13

Soviet SS-14

Soviet DD-ST-85 SLBM on launch

Soviet SS-15

150 *Massive Retaliation*

Soviet SS-18 ICBM being loaded into its silo

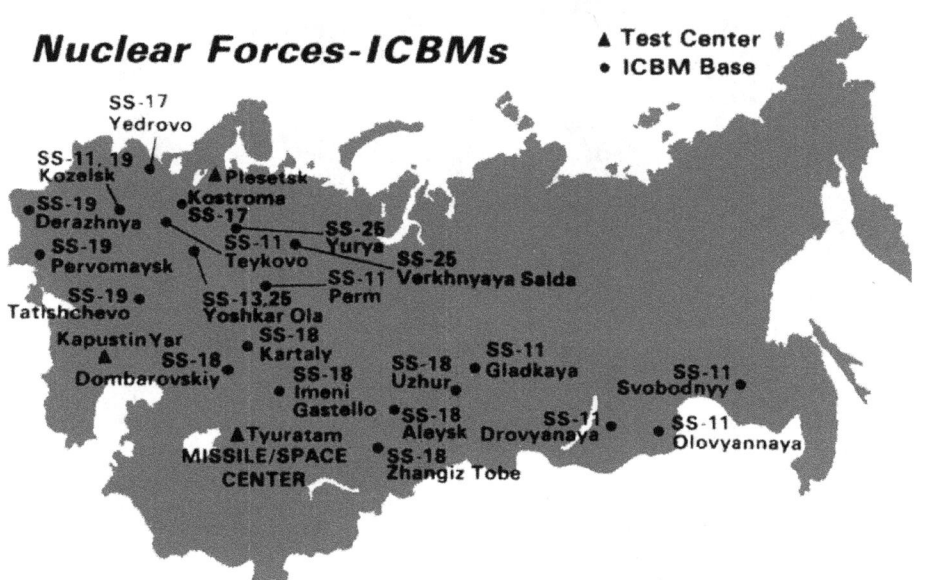

Soviet ICBM bases, 1980

Soviet "Blinder" nuclear bomber

Soviet "Backfire" nuclear bomber

August 29, 1964

This classified memo discusses the Minuteman ICBM program which was then in development, and which would be integrated into the SIOP-63 plans. The Minuteman was designed as a solid-fueled missile that could be launched within a short time, and was deployed in a specially-hardened underground "silo" for protection. A total of 590 "time urgent" targets were to be assigned to the missiles, to be struck during the first wave. Bombers would then be sent in to hit the lower-priority targets, and to place additional weapons on primary targets that had survived the first wave. The Minuteman was intended to move the US nuclear alert force away from bombers and towards missiles, which were more survivable in their silos than the bomber bases.

MEMORANDUM FOR THE SECRETARY OF DEFENSE

SUBJECT: Air Force Proposed changes to the tentative Force Guidance

This memorandum refers to my June 18, 1964 memorandum on this subject. General LeMay's comments are attached. The Air Force proposal regarding the AMSA, including studies and program change proposals, will be handled through separate correspondence.

There are three areas in your Tentative Force Guidance which I believe deserve specific comment. They concern the Strategic Retaliatory Forces, the Continental Air Defense Forces, and the Airlift

Forces. Although we believe that a larger force may be justified in the General Purpose Forces, we are not making a reclama at this time. Under the present program there will be opportunity to add to the force, should our additional studies further indicate the desirability of doing so. We are also making studies which may result in recommendations for a different mix of tactical fighters, including the addition of less expensive and less complex aircraft for missions such as close support under specialized circumstances.

With respect to the Strategic Retaliatory Forces, I believe that a 1200 Minuteman force represents a sensible minimum. None of the studies that I have reviewed have convinced me that we should reduce our position below this figure. The provision of one <u>on-launch reliable</u> Minuteman missile for each time-urgent target still seems to be a rational basis for sizing the force from the standpoint of both assured destruction and damage limitation. As shown in the attachment, the current requirement for known time-urgent targets is 1000 Minuteman missiles. Any growth in the number of targets and the minimum addition for contingencies would require a greater number than 1200 Minuteman missiles in 1970. <u>We support your objective of a balanced damage-limiting program; however, the cloudy future of the full fallout shelter program and the uncertainty regarding Nike X tend to emphasize the role of the Minuteman. Until these uncertainties can be resolved, it would appear prudent to place more, not less, reliance on the damage limiting value of the Minuteman</u>. I doubt that additional studies based on currently known facts will give us better answers for the requirements. In my opinion we should add an increment (per attachment) to our present 1000 missiles; therefore, 1200 Minuteman missiles would become our currently planned total. This will permit us to review the intelligence next year and make new decisions without loss of continuity of Minuteman installation.

With respect to the Continental Air Defense Forces, I think we should continue with the program in the manner proposed in my memorandum of July 27, 1963. At that time I agreed with you that it was premature to set any numerical level for a new interceptor force, but I was convinced that there be indications that the Russians were making serious efforts to deploy a manned bomber force with supersonic capability or with advance air-to-surface missiles. While the fact that the number of Blinders in the Russian inventory is greater than we had estimated is not in itself conclusive, it does convince me of the need to continue affirmative efforts in the direction of being able to deploy an interceptor force capable of coping with an improved and enlarged bomber threat. Since my specific proposals to meet this need involve details in the special projects area, I am forwarding them as a separate memorandum from this paper. Further, even a buy of a limited number of these new interceptors will provide a meaningful increment of operational capability for deployment either here or abroad. In addition we would acquire a capability to intercept, inspect and identify high altitude, high performance aircraft such as high altitude reconnaissance aircraft and supersonic transports.

I also recommend that you revise your intention to phase down our present interceptor force as sharply as you propose. Although the force is admittedly far from an ideal one and is of diminishing value, nonetheless, it does offer some degree of effectiveness in the light of the present Russian bomber threat.

Because of the relatively small cost, as the attachments show, it would seem to me worthwhile to leave the interceptor force at the present level pending decisions on the larger questions regarding Air Defense.

With respect to the Air Transport Force, I believe studies currently in progress will show clearly the advantages of including the CX-HLS which have already been indicated by preliminary studies. <u>Not only will this aircraft provide us the necessary outsize cargo capability, but equal or greater importance, it will provide us a higher degree of cost-effectiveness than any other transport.</u> For these reasons, I believe that your proposed Option B is the solution that we should adopt.

/s/ Eugene M Zuckert

<u>PROGRAM I – STRATEGIC RETALIATORY FORCES</u>

Some fundamental changes to the philosophy and forces contained in the Tentative Force Guidance are considered essential for the continued military effectiveness of US strategic forces.

Determination of the total Minuteman forces must be based on a range of parameters, where a change in any one will affect the end requirement. One consideration cited in the Tentative Force Guidance that I certainly support is the need for a balanced damage limiting program, e.g., strategic offense, air/missile defense and fallout shelters. However, as noted in recent studies, the effectiveness of a terminal missile defense is dependent on the offense, while the effectiveness of the offense is much less dependent on the terminal missile defense. Thus, improving the capability of the Minuteman force need not be delayed until decisions are made on the terminal missile defense system. Other major considerations are damage expectancy criteria, size and composition of the target system to be attacked by missiles, and the operational concept for reprogramming missiles for known failures.

The operational concept of reprogramming missiles for known failures is critical to the total forces required. Considering the eight stored targets capacity of the Minuteman and survivability of communications, it is not considered practical or possible to reprogram throughout the entire force. Assigning six targets to each flight of 10 missiles, and assuming a reprogrammable reliability of .70 will provide a high assurance (85%) that sufficient missiles will be available for each flight to cover its target. In addition, it can be expected 12% of the force will be available for reserve or the assured destruction requirements. This rationale provides for a reprogramming factor of 1.67 inventory missiles for each on-launch reliable missile assigned a war plan aiming point.

The median target list used in the OSD draft memorandum for the President, dated 6 December 1963, contained 80 bomber/staging bases, 130 tactical bases with a nuclear capability, 35 sub bases and 45 offensive controls. When currently confirmed missile sites, plus reported starts are added to these, the known time urgent total is around 600 (590). Using a reprogramming factor of 1.67 as developed in the preceding paragraph and assuming one on launch reliable missile per aim point, the current requirement for known time urgent targets is 1000 missiles. Prudence requires that 60-80 targets be added to the list for unknowns and possible Soviet missile deployments. This increases the requirement to some 1100 Minuteman. Based on DIA's estimates the Soviets will have 622 Missile Aiming Points by 1970. Adding the other time urgent targets increases the list to some 900 which would now require around 1500 Missiles (900 x 1.67).

Another major consideration in determining future force requirements is the projected qualitative characteristics of the weapon system. As CEPs of .17 to .40 nautical miles are predicted in the 1970 time period it appears prudent to use a criterion of programming one on-launch reliable missile against each time sensitive target. This tailors the force requirement to meet the low side of the threat (by numbers of missiles) for the early time period and provides the option of increasing missile capability for the later time period by qualitative improvements to the force.

Taking full consideration of the force previously approved by the Secretary of Defense and reaffirmed by the Joint Chiefs of Staff in JSOP-1969, the projected qualitative improvements to the Minuteman system in the early 1970's such as improved guidance and multiple independent re-entry vehicles (MIRVs) and in the interest of lessening the cost impact, a revised program (Tab A) has been developed for 1200 Minuteman force by end FY 69. Future objective force proposals will include recommendations for qualitative improvements to the Minuteman force.

Based on these considerations, it is recommended that a 1200 MM force be achieved in FY 69.

September 23, 1964

In 1964, President Lyndon Johnson made changes in the practice of "pre-authorizing" particular military commanders to use nuclear weapons under conditions where American forces faced an imminent Soviet threat, without communication with the President. This classified memo is a description of these changes. Under the procedures implemented by President Eisenhower, the use of nuclear weapons was authorized by military commanders if there was an imminent or actual attack and if communication with the President could not be established. President Johnson's order changed this by allowing use of nuclear weapons without prior communication with the President, under specific sets of circumstances. These included situations in which nuclear weapons would be exploded at sea or high in the atmosphere, where the damage to civilian populations was likely to be minimal.

MEMORANDUM FOR THE PRESIDENT
Re: Summary of the existing plans for emergency use of nuclear weapons

On March 26 you approved recommendations from McNamara and the Joint Chiefs to put into effect updated instructions for expenditure of nuclear weapons in emergency conditions.

This instruction covers four emergency situations. Two of them are essentially defensive and would allow the use of nuclear weapons only against military targets in the air or at sea. These are: 1. active defense against air and space nuclear attack on the US, and 2. naval and air action against an imminent seaborne missile attack on the US.

In these two cases the commanders could act without contacting the President if the necessary delay would make it impossible for them to prevent the imminent attack.

The other two cases are 1. retaliation to a nuclear attack on the US and 2. reply to a major assault on major US forces at sea or in foreign territory. In these two cases every effort to contact the President must be made (with the qualifying phrase in the second case: "every effort consistent with the preservation of his command"). The authorized retaliation for an attack on the US is a strategic attack on the Soviet Union. The authorized retaliation in the other case is against hostile forces but not repeat not against the Soviet Union itself.

The instructions reveal an interesting difference between situations in which nuclear weapons would do enormous civilian and industrial damage and situations in which they would be used in the upper atmosphere or on the high seas. In the latter cases commanders have latitude to decide that the delay in contacting the President would be excessive. This is in line with a belief which Eisenhower had that when the destructive force of nuclear weapons would hit only military forces, the decision on their use was a very much less serious matter. It is possible that we ought to take account of this distinction in anything we say in the next few days.

/s/ McG B

January 27, 1969

This memo lays out the script to be used in a slide show which served as a classified briefing for newly-elected President Nixon and his advisors which covered the contents of the SIOP as it existed in 1969 – known as SIOP-4. By this time, nuclear war planning had changed drastically since the SIOP-62 plan presented to President Kennedy. The US had a much larger number of ICBMs, some of which had Multiple Independently-targeted Re-entry Vehicles (MIRVs) which were multiple nuclear warheads that could each be directed to a different target, allowing a single missile to strike a number of different sites. The Soviet nuclear force had also changed during this time, from a predominantly bomber-based strategy to a rapidly-growing ICBM-based force which soon developed its own MIRV technology. The American ICBMs were based in hardened underground silos which allowed them to survive a first-strike and be available for retaliation; the Soviets focused more on mobile missile launchers, but also had a number of silos. In addition, both sides had a sizable number of submarine-launched missiles which were also largely invulnerable to a first strike by the other side. And the bomber forces from both sides were increasingly vulnerable to newer and better air defense systems such as radar-guided anti-aircraft missiles. SIOP-4 was designed to deal with all of these changes.

It was also designed to be more flexible than SIOP-62, and has five options with increasing degrees of severity. Presumably these include different options about whether to focus the strike on military targets, on urban targets, or various mixtures of both, and what proportion of the strikes are to be airbursts or groundbursts (which determines what the fallout levels will be). SIOP-4 also includes the option to withhold any strikes against particular nations — a recognition of the political and military split between the Soviet Union and Communist China.

SIOP BRIEFING FOR NIXON ADMINISTRATION
Vu-Graph XX-1 on (SIOP Header)

The purpose of this briefing is to acquaint you with the Joint Chiefs of Staff plan for conduct of general nuclear war if such should ever become necessary. The plan is called the Single Integrated Operational Plan or short title "SIOP". Since this is the fourth such war plan since inception of an integrated plan in 1961, it is known as SIOP 4. A major revision to the SIOP is published every six months so that the plan remains viable, flexible, and responsive to the dynamic enemy target system. In addition, interim changes are made throughout the life-time of each revision. This current plan became effective on 1 July 1966 and is now in its fifth major revision. Prior to the time of SIOP, each nuclear CINC had his own plan. As you can imagine, much duplication of effort and target conflicts were the result. So during the Eisenhower Administration the then Secretary of Defense, Thomas Gates, in 1960 decreed that these plans would be integrated into a single plan. Thus was born the Joint Strategic Target Planning Staff at Omaha to develop this plan.

Vu-Graph XX-1 off, XX-2 on
Agenda

The briefing will follow the agenda shown on this slide. (pause)

Vu-graph XX-2 off, SG-2 on (NSTAP)

Turning first to the National Strategic Targeting and Attack Policy for General War. This document is produced by the Joint Chiefs of Staff based upon inputs by the Joint Staff, the services, the Office of the Secretary of Defense, and the Commanders in Chief of the unified and specified commands. When approved by the Joint Chiefs of Staff, this document provides guidance to the Joint Strategic Target Planning Staff. The JSTPS is responsible for the development, publishing, and maintenance of the Single Integrated Operational Plan. The guidance stipulates that this will be a capabilities plan, which simply means a plan which employs designated US nuclear offensive forces of the Strategic Air Command, the Atlantic Command, Pacific Command and the US European Command for the purpose of conducting major strategic attacks against Soviet and Asian communist bloc target systems. Forces are committed for targeting purposes to the Director of Strategic Target Planning (who, in his dual capacity as CINCSAC, is currently General Holloway). However, operational control of these forces remains with the commander in chief concerned.

Vu-Graph SG-2 off, SG-3 on

Concept

The fundamental concept underlying the guidance is to maximize US power, to attain and maintain a strategic superiority which will lead to an early termination of the war on terms favorable to the United States and our Allies.

Vu-Graph SG-3 off, SG-4 on

Objective

The objective of the plan as stated in the guidance is simply this, as shown on the screen. (pause)

Vu-Graph SG-4 off, SG-5 on

Requirements

In order to attain this objective, military forces of the United States should be prepared to meet the requirements shown here. [censored] under all conditions of war initiation. In order that these requirements may be more clearly defined for the planner, they have been designated in the guidance as these three alphabetical tasks.

Vu-Graph SG-5 off, SG-6 on

Tasks

Task Alpha fulfills that requirement to [censored] Task Bravo [censored] lesser priority task. Attacks the residual military target [censored] In this case, [censored] Task Charlie is actually a two-pronged task which is designed to attack the [censored] and further to attack [censored] Under this category of [censored] are targets which functionally fall under Task Alpha or Bravo but which are located contiguous or adjacent to one of these [censored] if the effect of all the weapons targeted against a target would cause damage to [censored] then that [censored] is restrained so that it is attacked only when the [censored] is ordered executed.

Vu-Graph SG-6 off, XX-3 on

Target System

The next item on the agenda, sir, is the target system.

Vu-Graph XX-3 off, SG-7 on

NSTL

The National Strategic Target List is a document which is also developed by the Joint Strategic Target Planning Staff in conjunction with the Single Integrated Operational Plan. The NSTL, as it is called, is developed from the target data inventory provided by the Defense Intelligence Agency. It is compiled without regard to the quantity of forces that are available for employment in the Single Integrated Operational Plan. It identifies the targets by the tasks which we have just discussed, and it further indicates those which are programmed for attack in the SIOP.

Vu-Graph SG-7 off, SG-12 on

Task Summary

Currently this is a summary of these tasks contained in the NSTL. Shown across the top of the slide are the NSTL installations. On this side are those which are programmed for attack, both by installations and by Desired Ground Zeros or aiming points. These installations then are subject to attack or placed at risk out of the total number of NSTL installations for each of the three functional tasks. You will note that in the case of the Task Charlie [censored   ] targets, no installations appear since functionally they are contained either in Task Alpha or Task Bravo. The NSTAP directs in the case of the [censored   ] damage for the purpose of this plan, sir, is defined as that degree of damage which [censored   ] we see then that a total of [censored   ]

Vu-Graph SG-12 off, SG13 on

DGZ by country

This chart, sir, reflects the aiming points as they are laid out by country and by task. Across the top are the three functional tasks. Down the side are the countries which are targeted in the SIOP. It is significant to note that in the so-called [censored   ]

Vu-Graph SG-13 off, SG-14 on

Map

This is a map of the present target system showing the targets of USSR and the European and Communist dominated countries, as well as China [censored   ] As we can see from this chart the preponderance of targets are in the [censored   ]

Vu-Graph SG-14 off, SG-20 on

Forces header

Having discussed the target system briefly, sir, the next item on the agenda is a discussion of the SIOP forces available for execution of this plan.

Vu-Graph SG-20 off, SG-21 on

Forces

These forces are broken into two basic categories, the committed forces and the coordinated forces. Within the committed forces there is a further breakout of what are called the hard core forces which are comprised of the SAC bombers and missiles and all of the Polaris missile systems. These particular systems are irrevocably committed to the SIOP by the CINCs. In addition there are US theater forces which are committed to the SIOP by the Commanders in Chief concerned, and when so committed the SIOP is their first priority assignment. However, these forces may be subject to withdrawal by the Joint Chiefs of Staff for other contingency operations and may not necessarily be available for execution of the SIOP. When they are available and executed, however, they are targeted [censored   ] and, finally, they are used to [censored   ] Finally, sir, the [censored   ] these are the forces which are targeted [censored   ]

Vu-Graph SG-21 off, SG-24 on

Vehicles

The current delivery vehicles available for execution of the plan are shown here, divided by aircraft and ballistic missiles and further divided by the Commanders in Chief which have forces committed to and coordinated with the SIOP. I would point out, sir, that the block entitled [censored   ]—a total of [censored   ] aircraft and [censored   ] ballistic missiles are available for execution of this plan.

Vu-Graph SG-24 off, E-1 on

Execution

Turning now, sir, to the next agenda item—SIOP execution considerations.

Vu-graph E-1 off, SG-44 on

Procedures for execution

The procedures for the execution of the SIOP are as shown here. Of course, the President is the only one who may authorize execution of the SIOP and the release of nuclear weapons. The Joint Chiefs of Staff, as a corporate body, have these three specific tasks; [censored   ] designate country withholds [censored   ] the Joint Chiefs of Staff in arriving at these decisions make recommendations to the President regarding execution of the plan. Based then on this guidance, the Joint

Chiefs of Staff [censored   ] the Joint Staff, in the form of the National Military Command Center Operations Team, perform these specific functions: [censored   ]

Vu-Graph SG-44 off, E-2 on

Decisions

Six basic decisions are required for execution of the plan as shown on this screen. We will discuss each of these separately. To assist the Joint Chiefs of Staff and the President in making these decisions the Joint Chiefs of Staff Decisions Handbook, also known as the Black Book, has been published and is the one in front of you. These decisions are shown in page 11 under Tab A of the book. I will give you just a moment to look at these.

Vu-Graph E-2 off, E-3 on

Whether to execute

Turning to the first of these execution decisions—whether to execute. A thorough discussion on this particular item is found on page 15 under Tab A of the Black Book. This decision would be made when [censored   ] are also discussed in this section of the Black Book.

Vu-Graph E-3 off, E-7 on

Objectives

The selection of the objectives, or the tasks, is the next execution decision. A discussion of the attack to be executed are contained on Page 17 under Tab A of the Black Book. Obviously, the selection of these objectives will be dependent upon whether [censored   ] or whether we are [censored   ]

Vu-Graph E-7 off, E-8 on

Tasks

At this juncture, a brief review of the SIOP tasks is in order. The primary targeting objectives of each is underlined on this screen. The SIOP provides for an increasing [censored   ] which we can see more clearly in this next chart which is found at page 31 under Tab Bravo of your Black Book.

Vu-graph E-8 off, SG-18 on

Attack options

A brief explanation of the format of the attack option chart. Across the top, sir, are the three functional tasks which we have just reviewed. Down the side are the five attack option variations available for execution of the plan—[censored   ] following the chart in Tab B of your Black Book there are detailed discussions of the objectives, considerations, and favorable circumstances for employment of each of [censored] It is not our purpose today, sir, to discuss each of these separately. Generally speaking, however, if the US strategy is to [censored] However, it should be noted that there are still substantial casualties inflicted by a [censored]

Vu-Graph SG-18 off, E-16 on

[censored]

Turning now, sir, to the next decision: whether or not to [censored] If you will, sir, please refer back now to Page 19 under Tab A of your Black Book where a discussion of this item is contained. The National Strategic Targeting and Attack Policy affords the capability to [censored]

Vu-Graph E-16 off, E-17 on

[censored]

The next decision, sir, regards whether or not to attack [censored] A discussion of this decision is found at Page 21 under Tab A of the Black Book. This package provides the [censored]

Vu-Graph E-17 off, K-2 on

Country withholds

This brings us, sir, to our next of the basic decisions—whether or not to withhold any of the countries targeted in the SIOP. This decision is discussed on Page 23 under Tab A of the Black Book. In addition, very detailed information is available on each of these countries as far as [censored] These are all contained in Tab E to the Black Book which we will not discuss in detail during this briefing. The SIOP provides for [censored]

Vu-Graph K-2 off.

In concluding the discussion on the [censored] is found on Page 25 under Tab A. The decision as to [censored]

Also contained in the Black Book in front of you, sir, are some other important chapters. [censored] Since this should be the subject for a separate briefing, the intelligence discussion will not be held today. We would, however, like to discuss briefly some of the items under Tab C regarding various means of improving our defense posture.

Vu-Graph C-3 on

JCS A-Hour

One of these is the declaration of an A-Hour or alert hour by the Joint Chiefs of Staff. [censored] The advantage to be gained here is obvious because the [censored]

Vu-Graph C-3 off, S-1 on

SEAGA

Another means of improving our readiness posture and ensuring survivability of the force is implementation of the Selective Employment of Air and Ground Alert, more commonly called "SEAGA", which is a SAC concept. This concept uses the unclassified name of "Giant Lance", and when implemented currently can mount [censored] They are targeted primarily against [censored] When this plan is fully implemented, these [censored] shown on the chart.

Vu-Graph S-1 off, S-8 on

Map

The [censored] A discussion of "SEAGA" is also contained in the Black Book.

Vu-Graph S-8 off, P-2 on

Positive Control Launch

Still another means of insuring survivability of the forces is the SAC Positive Control Launch. [censored]

Sir, that completes discussion of the Black Book.

Vu-graph P-2 off

Before we leave the Black Book, sir, a word of caution is in order. This document contains SIOP-ESI material, which is defined as "Extremely Sensitive Information". A compromise or disclosure to unauthorized persons not on the access list could cause exceptionally grave danger to the United States. Stringent controls have been established by the Joint Chiefs of Staff, in compliance with the letter and intent of Executive Order 10501, to insure that only those persons having a need-to-know are granted access to ESI documents and briefings, Normally, your (executive) (security) officer can advise you who is, or who is not, cleared for access to ESI information.

There is one other item associated with execution, however, which we feel that you should be aware of, and that is the [censored]

Vu-Graph 2 on

CINCs

Shown on this chart are the five additional commanders in chief [censored]

Vu-Graph SG-50 on

Conclusion

In summary, our discussion today concludes that the SIOP is an extremely flexible and responsive nuclear strike plan in spite of the fact that the entire target base is now programmed for attack. Procedures for execution are straight-forward and in themselves are neither new or unusually complicated. It is in the decision-making process, the evaluation and selection of the many attack responses available, wherein the problem becomes complex. Choices are wide and may be made on [censored   ] In a crisis mounted over a period of time it should be possible to eliminate early some of the alternatives, such as whether or not to attack particular countries. In a long drawn out crisis, with highly intensified force readiness on one or both sides, it may even be possible to eliminate from further consideration some of the attack options. But in a sudden emergency, with little or no warning, all of these considerations must be entertained and discussed with the President (pause) and perhaps in no more than a very few minutes. Sir, that concludes my briefing. I will be happy to answer any questions.

February 1, 1969

This classified memo gives a brief overview of the strategic nuclear situation as it stood in 1969. It discusses the relative nuclear forces of the US and the Soviet Union, the introduction of MIRV warheads, and planned anti-ballistic missile (ABM) systems.

At this point, ICBMs made up the vast majority of US nuclear forces, with 1054 land-based ICBMs, 656 submarine-launched missiles varied by 41 Polaris subs, and only 300 strategic bombers. When the deployment of new ICBMs with MIRV warheads was complete in the early 70's, the US expected to have about 5800 nuclear warheads on its missile force. The Soviets were expected to have available a force of 1500 ICBMs and a few hundred MRBMs – they were actively expanding their missile submarine fleet and were estimated to be about four years away from deploying their own MIRV weapons.

As the number of ICBMs and warheads grew on both sides, nuclear strategy began to change. In their hardened silos and the elusive submarines, the missiles were virtually invulnerable to enemy attack, and the earlier nuclear strategy embodied in SIOP, of targeting the other side's strategic nuclear missile bases and airfields in a first strike, became obsolete. Now, each side was attempting to build its forces up to a level of both quantity and invulnerability that they would be able to absorb a first-strike by the other side and still have enough surviving "residual force" to destroy the other side in a retaliatory response – thereby deterring both sides from attacking the other. This doctrine became known as "Mutual Assured Destruction", or MAD, and it dominated military thinking for the rest of the Cold War.

The memo concludes that both the US and the USSR had the capability to kill about 40% of the other's population in a nuclear second-strike.

STRATEGIC POLICY ISSUES

This memorandum provides a brief over-view of the strategic situation and then considers the single issue which requires immediate attention; should President Johnson's FY70 budget for strategic forces be amended now and if so, how? More fundamental issues will be addressed in the six-month review.

I. The Strategic Situation

This section provides a brief over-view of the strategic situation as background for necessary immediate decisions.

US-Soviet Force Comparisons: The present US force plan calls for the number of ICBMs to remain constant at 1,054, the number of sea based missiles to be held at 656 (41 Polaris submarines), and the number of strategic bombers to decrease to approximately 300 in the 1970's. However, US strategic offensive forces will undergo very substantial qualitative improvements over the next five years, most importantly by MIRVs. With these deployments, the number of independently targetable US strategic missile warheads will increase from the current approximately 1600 to about 5800 by the mid-1970's. Similarly, our strategic bomber force will undergo substantial improvements encompassing advanced penetration aids.

The Soviets have continued their ICBM buildup and within two years may have 1200 of these systems operationally deployed; they could have 1500 ICBMs and a few hundred mobile ICBMs by the mid-70's. The Soviets have a substantially smaller sea based force and bomber force than the US, but they have recently initiated a new submarine construction program which could give them a force comparable to our present Polaris fleet by the mid-1970s. They are estimated to be about four years away from initially deploying MIRVs on large ICBMs.

On the defensive side, the US Sentinel ABM designed against China, comprised of some 700 defensive missiles, will be initially operational in late 1972 and fully deployed by 1975. The Soviet ABM program has lagged, with completion of the small Moscow ABM (64 launchers) not to occur until the early 70s. The intelligence community estimates that the Soviets will probably deploy an ABM comparable to Sentinel by the mid-70s. There are no current signs of additional ABM deployments beyond Moscow, and the extensively deployed Tallin system is estimated to be for air defense purposes with no real ABM potential.

Relative Effectiveness. Comparing the numbers and types of US and Soviet strategic systems does not indicate how well the respective forces can perform strategic missions. Effectiveness is generally measured in terms of the ability of the forces to survive an enemy first strike and inflict large fatalities on the adversary's population.

Our currently programmed force can maintain the ability to inflict 40% Soviet fatalities (90 million) throughout the early to mid-1970s against the highest threat estimated by the intelligence community. If it is determined that a greater than expected Soviet offensive and defensive threat is emerging, a very unlikely but possible occurrence, the US has many force improvement and addition options which can be implemented soon enough to maintain the ability to deter the Soviets at at least the 25% fatality level.

With estimated probable future deployments, the Soviet Union can maintain its second strike damage potential against the US at 40% US fatality levels throughout the 1970s (80 million). Although the Soviets may have to work harder and spend relatively more money than the US in maintaining their second strike capability, we can be certain that the Soviets can and will take sufficient counteractions to retain the ability to inflict unacceptably high levels of damage against the US regardless of our force procurements.

In general, if one examines the outcome of strategic exchanges between the US and Soviet Union throughout the 1970s, both will suffer very heavy destruction regardless of who strikes first and independent of detailed differences in force level and characteristics.

Conduct of Nuclear Operations. Despite our efforts to prevent nuclear wars or major crises such events may occur. If we are to secure the most favorable possible outcome we need to be able to control forces effectively during a crisis and to employ nuclear weapons selectively. Our procurement decisions are based mainly on deterrence considerations and most of our nuclear plans assume sudden very large use of nuclear weapons. Issues requiring consideration are: (1) whether we need to pay more attention to issues of control and selective use in procuring forces and (2) whether we need more flexible plans for the use of nuclear weapons.

Political implications. The US nuclear capability is a major component of our deterrent of large conventional attacks particularly in Europe. Europeans are concerned about US strategic forces and the US-Soviet nuclear balance for this reason and because some of them desire and some fear US-Soviet strategic arms limitation agreements.

The effect on the probability and consequences of nuclear proliferation also needs to be taken into account in designing US strategic forces.

May 29, 1969

This classified memo from the National Security Council gives a discussion of the political aspects of American nuclear strategy, which underwent a change during the Nixon Administration. This was part of the diplomatic framework known as "détente", in which the United States and the Soviet Union sought out political initiatives to lessen their hostility and ease tensions, and to work together on ways to co-exist peacefully. Militarily, the US wanted to focus on the situation in Southeast Asia, and sought out ways to reduce Cold War tensions and allow for a slowdown in nuclear weapons.

As new technologies such as MIRVs drove the numbers of nuclear weapons on both sides higher and higher, there were serious diplomatic efforts to begin Strategic Arms Limitation Talks (SALT) with the goal of reducing the number of nuclear weapons through arms-control treaties. As Anti-Ballistic Missile (ABM) systems became more sophisticated and more expensive, it was realized by both sides that while such systems could never be an effective defense against a first-strike of ICBMs, they may eventually be effective at stopping a much-reduced retaliatory second-strike. By therefore potentially preventing effective retaliation, these ABM systems were having a destabilizing effect on the nuclear arms race by provoking each side to produce ever-more warheads in an attempt to overwhelm the other's defenses and maintain a lethal second-strike capability. Talks therefore began which would later lead to the ABM Treaty in which both sides agreed to avoid deploying any large-scale anti-ballistic missile defenses.

The discussion in the memo also illustrates clearly the central political problem of the entire Cold War: the US had no idea what the Soviet Union's ultimate strategic goal was or what their overarching political aims were. Were the Soviets seeking military superiority and world domination, with the short-term goal of invading Western Europe? Or were they seeking military parity with the US to defend themselves against another surprise attack such as had been launched against them by Germany in World War Two? The US had no reliable intelligence information on Soviet intentions, and therefore, throughout the Cold War, American Presidents tended to lurch from one side of the scale to the other based more on their own political ideology than on any actual data or information.

NSC REVIEW GROUP MEETING
Subject: Review of US Strategic Posture
SUMMARY OF RESULTS

The Review Group went page by page through the revised summary paper of NSSM 3 distributed May 26 and agreed to a large number of drafting changes. These were to be incorporated in the paper by the NSC staff and redistributed to Review Group members for their approval before forwarding to the NSC for its consideration. It was agreed that this NSSM 3 on strategic forces and NSSM 28 on SAT would be considered closely and consecutively in coming weeks. The NSC will devote more time to these two subjects than the usual two-hour sessions. There was general consensus that doctrinal decisions on how we should shape our strategic forces will heavily influence and guide our positions on SALT. However, strategic force decisions will not represent inflexible theology for SALT positions, particularly with regard to possible developments once arms talks are underway.

After some informal discussion at the outset of the meeting, it was agreed that on Page 7 of the summary paper there would be a notation that this study does not take into account civil defense measures which will be the subject of a separate NSSM.

Kissinger said that the Packard Committee did a massive job on this subject, as thorough a review as he had seen. He believed that this subject and SALT should be looked at together, with strategic force posture decisions being the theoretical basis for SALT preparations. He has talked to the President, who agreed the NSC would need more time to discuss these two subjects than the usual two-hour sessions. Kissinger asked the group, beginning with

Secretary Packard, what the NSC could reasonably be asked to make judgments on. This would effect the preparation of the summary report since the principals could not be expected to read all the supporting documents.

Packard said that the subject could be approached in two ways. The NSC could be asked to recommend one of the various strategic forces listed, deciding whether there should be any change in present programs and what direction to take with regard to the specific alternatives proposed. A second approach, which he favored, was to address basic questions as well as specific recommendations. These could be looked at in terms of the revised paper before the group. The President and the NSC could focus on some of the broader issues. For example, one fundamental question is how we assess Soviet strategic objectives.

Jurich noted that budgetary constraints must be considered also. Kissinger said that this aspect was covered in the basic papers, and Packard stated that the various strategic alternatives were costed out. However, the budgetary aspects could not really be addressed until general purpose forces were considered. The latter were more important in terms of the budget than strategic forces. Thus, there is some budgetary flexibility for strategic forces; one could opt for more expensive ones while lowering GPF expenses, without changing the overall budget level. Schlesinger suggested that this point be noted in the paper. Strategic forces represent the tail of the budgetary dog, a three to four billion dollar swing in expenses.

Kissinger then asked G Smith what his agency's requirements were. G Smith generally endorsed the Packard approach to the problem. He believed that we need general guidance on whether current policies are sensible or whether different emphases are needed. However, he did not want decisions on NSSM 3 to foreclose options for NSSM 28. For example, on page 9, there was a Steering Group agreement that we can and should deploy damage-limiting defenses against small or accidental attacks. He hoped that such governmental doctrine would not rule out possible SALT options under NSSM 28. Selin said that the steering Group didn't really address the question of no ballistic missile defense versus a small one; this was covered under the Safeguard decision. The Steering Group had instead concentrated on a small versus a large defensive deployment.

G Smith repeated that he did not wish NSSM 3 decisions to rule out the possibility of dropping the ABM, which the Secretary of State had intimated might be considered. Kissinger said that he understood G Smith's concern, but that we should be clear on the various components of the President's ABM decision. There were essentially three reasons for Safeguard, only one of which was directly related to Soviet positions. G Smith interjected that he hoped there would be no decision by the US now that under no circumstances would we accept a zero ABM level. Kissinger responded that neither would there be a US decision now that if the Soviets freeze their ABM deployment, we would agree to forego any deployment on their part. He thought that a US decision would tend to be in the opposite direction. G Smith wished only to keep this subject open. Kissinger repeated that we should keep in mind the different purposes of Safeguard as we consider SALT and alternative ways of dealing with the Soviets. He said that nothing decided with regard to NSSM 3 should be used as theology in developing our SALT positions. On the other hand, he did not wish to say that no decisions would be taken on our strategic force posture. The decisions on doctrinal issues taken in response to NSSM 3 should guide the decisions taken on NSSM 28, without establishing a firm, unchangeable line.

G Smith said that this point was a valid one. Nevertheless he would like to think that nothing in this paper purports to limit Presidential options when NSSM 28 is considered, that in effect a zero ABM level cannot be considered because of prior decisions on NSSM 3. Farley pointed out that discussion on Page 15, especially option 3, reflected recognition that a zero ABM level is a possible outcome that should not be foreclosed. He agreed that doctrinal decisions on NSSM 3 could seriously constrain NSSM 28 options.

Kissinger said that, for example, if the President decides, with regard to NSSM 3, not to limit MIRV testing before SALT discussions, we would not then go back on this decision when discussing NSSM 28. G Smith said that he understood that the decisions on NSSM 3 would shape some decisions on NSSSM 28 options. Packard suggested that the government try to reconcile the two subjects as it moved ahead. Kissinger declared that we could not deal with strategic force postures as if arms control were a completely different subject. The President should be aware of the interrelationship as he looks at NSSM 3. In any event G Smith would be present at discussion on both issues.

G Smith recalled BNSP papers in previous years where a single clause set theology and the government was boxed in by language ten years after it was written. Packard suggested that it was a matter of common sense, and Kissinger assured the group that the President would be aware of the longer term significance of all decisions.

G Smith again expressed his concern that the language in the paper (which he himself also had agreed to) could have a long life expectancy. Farley noted that the language confirmed that we will deploy Safeguard, while Selin repeated that the Steering Group never really addressed this question. Kissinger said that he could not reopen the ABM decision. Secretary Packard had addressed this question in great detail in March, and it could not be reopened on its merits as part of this present review. He understood that G Smith was not attempting to do this but rather was worried that the paper's language could handicap our proposing a zero ABM level in the SALT discussions. He added that he thought the President (for whom he was reluctant to speak unless he were sure) would probably not decide upon a zero ABM level, i.e., giving up the anti-Chinese aspect, on the basis of Soviet actions alone. However, he might well be inclined to drop the anti-Soviet components in response to Russian moves. Packard added that a lower level of ABM launchers would not make much difference to the Soviets. Selin agreed that the Safeguard system as approved should not concern the Soviets, whether 200 or 500 launchers, but that G Smith was worried about the principle of an anti-Chinese deployment. Packard believed that we should maintain the principle for the SALT talks that we be prepared to consider anything that would improve our position as negotiations develop. He believed that G Smith should have faith that a reasonable approach would be followed during the talks in order to get the objectives that everyone wanted. The problem here concerns our opening position, which should be consistent with NSSM 3 decisions. Kissinger noted that the paper does not specifically rule out any SALT options. Unger added that he did not believe that anything in the summary or the basic paper should constrain G Smith with regard to arms control discussions. He believed that both subjects should be considered closely at the NSC level.

G Smith said that he was satisfied if the interpretation that Packard had just outlined was accepted.

The group then went through the paper page by page and agreed on drafting changes. The NSC staff was to incorporate these and shortly get out a revised version to Review Group members for their concurrence.

Kissinger noted that the paper reflected two views concerning how conservative we should be in carrying out US strategic purposes (II A 1). We could be very conservative in our planning and decisions, leaving no doubt about out strategic posture; or we could be restrained in our actions so as not to generate Soviet over-reaction. He noted the danger of using the word "sufficiency" in a liturgical way, as if it were perfectly self-evident. Rather it should be used in contrast with other options. It would be a major accomplishment if this group could reach agreement on what constitutes "sufficiency".

Hartman suggested that it would be helpful for the Secretaries to have a summary of what our present posture looks like in terms of programs as the paper discusses maintaining our present course. Selin suggested, and Packard agreed, that certain tables now in the backup sections could be affixed to the summary paper. Packard shared Kissinger's concern about using the word sufficiency, and thought that attention should be given to its definition. Unger noted that the basic paper contained 18 force structures with their costs. The tables indicate an order of magnitude for these forces rather than laying out sufficient details for selection of one of them. In these tables one could identify current forces and the objective requirements of the JCS, i.e., what they recommend as a target 18 months from now.

Lynn pointed out that paragraph 3 on pages 8 and 9 does attempt to define "sufficiency" and wondered whether this definition was adequate to distinguish the approach from other strategies.

Kissinger said that he never understood the second point on Page 9, i.e., maintaining the capability to cause at least as many deaths and industrial damage on the USSR as they could cause on us in a nuclear war. Unger suggested that this point could be clarified by adding a fifth criterion to this section, "have the capability to insure relatively favorable outcomes if deterrence fails." In response to Kissinger's question as to what "relatively favorable" means, Unger stated that the number of deaths and industrial damage were not the only criteria to defining the outcome of a nuclear exchange. Other factors such as residual forces are also crucial, and that is why he believed a fifth point here was required.

Schlesinger did not believe that the Steering Group had agreed to this point 2 on page 9, and Kissinger wondered whether it was a meaningful statement in any event. Farley said that the Steering

Group did agree we would not want a situation where the Soviets could cause significantly more damage than we, but it had not agreed to include this point as part of a definition of "sufficiency". It was a little imprudent to enshrine sufficiency and make these conditions theological sine qua nons. Kissinger asked G Smith what effect this would have on his responsibilities, and the latter replied that he did not wish to enshrine war-fighting capability as part of sufficiency.

Lynn felt that this was a fundamental issue—are we going to make meaningful statements about structuring our strategic forces? Kissinger added that we must decide whether we want such statements and whether those under consideration were meaningful.

Packard declared that in the discussions concerning criteria for our strategic forces, the Joint Chiefs still maintained a divergent view to the effect that they wished to have more emphasis on "relatively favorable outcome" along the lines of Unger's suggested addition. The Steering Group decided, after some discussion, that rather than laying out too complex criteria, it was preferable to stick to numbers of deaths and industrial damage and that other criteria would not make much difference. Packard suggested that, if the Review Group agreed, perhaps the views of the Joint Chiefs on this point could be inserted.

When Unger suggested that this might be put on Page 1, Selin responded that the first page laid out what is desirable, while later discussion in the paper centered on what is possible. Our present analysis of nuclear exchanges indicated that sometimes we inflict more damage on the Soviet Union, sometimes the damage is about the same. He said that this analysis included weapons damage as well as fatalities. Kissinger suggested that if there were disagreement, both views should be presented fairly in the paper. Selin repeated that it was not a question of what we would like to do but whether we can assure our doing it, and Farley added: for a tolerable price.

Selin noted that point 2 on Page 9 centered upon damage limitation for smaller nuclear exchanges, not those involving 80-100 million deaths. Kissinger wondered whether we could insure relatively favorable outcomes at lower levels of exchange, and Selin responded that relatively similar light defenses could result in unbalanced outcomes. Unger said that estimating outcomes depends on how one programs the computers. Annex J of the study treats deaths only, while Annex B is preferable because it includes other factors.

Jurich said that the word "sufficiency" will always be seen in a political context. For the Soviets we will interpret it as parity, while for the American people it could mean superiority. The NSC will call sufficiency whatever it decides upon with regard to strategic forces.

Packard suggested that the group return to a discussion of purposes on page 1; sufficiency would be those forces that can accomplish these purposes. Selin interjected that the paper shows there is disagreement over which forces can do this.

Kissinger said that the President had asked to be spared agreed papers. It would be more useful to let the NSC talk about general disagreements rather than much energy being spent on reaching agreements.

Hartman suggested, and then withdrew his suggestion, that the phrase "under the weight of strategic military superiority" be dropped from the opening sentence of the paper. Under noted that the JCS had a series of recommended changes to the report. It was agreed that the substantive changes would be taken up in the course of discussion while the stylistic ones would be given to Lynn who would have the responsibility of reflecting all drafting changes in the paper. The paper would then be recirculated to the Review Group members for their concurrence before submission to agency principals.

There was some discussion of paragraph 3 on page 2 with G Smith pointing out that presumably we already practice "restraint" in making strategic force decisions, and Farley noting that references to research and development as hedging measures had been dropped.

Kissinger thought, and the group agreed, that it would be useful to add a reference to research and development as a hedge in this paragraph. Packard agreed that language could be inserted here, but commented that perhaps some would opt for restraints in our decisions even to the point of not wanting R&D.

Halperin believed that paragraphs 2 and 3 on page 2 represented two extremes, with almost everyone somewhere in the middle, and that they therefore did not give the President a real choice. Lynn mentioned Safeguard, and Halperin wondered under which optional view this decision would fall. Packard thought that these paragraphs set up a logical general range, and Kissinger added that the President could only choose a general tendency and could not make precise decisions.

Kissinger then turned to the question of assessing Soviet strategic objectives (II A 2). There were two schools identified. The first is that the Soviets look at the strategic situation and characterize our position in the same manner as we do, and are therefore looking for rough parity. The second school suggests that the Soviets are engaged in a deliberate attempt to achieve superiority. He asked whether these were the only two choices. J Smith said that these represented broad statements of Soviet objectives and established general parameters. Selin believed that our decisions should be keyed more to Soviet reactions to our moves rather than the definition of Soviet strategic objectives. In response to Kissinger's question, Selin said that if we were convinced that the Soviets were after superiority, we would have no choice but to match them. Kissinger wondered whether the Soviet positions might just be reactions to our initiatives. J Smith said this was conceivable, and that the question of defensive reactions had been left out. He nevertheless thought the paper staked out an adequate approach.

In reply to Kissinger's query, Sonnenfeldt said that we just don't know Soviet purposes. We are more geared to our evaluation of threats than they are geared to their evaluation of threats.

In continuing discussion of likely Soviet reactions to US strategic initiatives (II A 2b) on page 3, Kissinger outlined the paper's two alternatives. The Soviets would move to offset any attempts by the US to produce an unfavorable shift in the balance of power against them; or such initiatives on our part might induce the Soviets to seek détente. He did not believe that these two views were strictly inconsistent; the Soviets might do both simultaneously. Détente could happen either way, whether or not the Soviets attempted to match us. The operational question was whether it were true that the Soviets would always match what we are trying to achieve or whether they might stick to assured destruction at some point.

J Smith believed that the latter was possible. In response to Kissinger's question, he said he thought that their programs were sensitive to our own. He thought that the discussion under b on page 3 showed too much symmetry. Most people would agree that the Soviets would react to any attempt on our part to seek clearcut superiority or a first strike capability. The second point, whether the Soviets would be induced to move toward détente, is more of a tactical question. He believed that it was much less likely that they would seek détente in the face of a buildup on our part. Kissinger concluded that most agreed that the Soviets would match major efforts by us.

Sonnenfeldt wondered, in light of this discussion, what had happened to the recently held view that the Soviets want an agreement to freeze the present strategic situation so as to be in a less disadvantageous position than they foresee in the coming four to five years because of our MIRVs and other programs. He said that this was the rationale for SALT last year. Selin pointed out that this section of the paper was treating attempts at clearcut superiority, not ambiguous nuances which might not produce a Soviet response. In response to Kissinger's query whether MIRVs were ambiguous, Selin said they were. On the one hand, they could be considered a threat to the Soviet retaliatory force, while on the other hand they could be construed as our deployment against their ABM system.

Kissinger suggested that the real question was whether or not the Soviets would match us, not whether they would seek détente in the face of a US build up. J Smith noted that the Soviets were inferior strategically for a long period, but when they face gross inferiority, they act. Kissinger added that he wished to avoid presenting MIRV as an ambiguous program; this might be true, but it would not appear so to the principals. J Smith believed that the Soviets would react to compensate (though not necessarily match) unfavorable shifts, and that history supports this thesis. Kissinger suggested therefore that there was no possibility of achieving superiority, since the other side would always offset our efforts. J Smith corrected this statement to say that they always will _try_ to match us. This is a far cry from previous years when we enjoyed some superiority.

G smith wondered who supported the view in the second paragraph under b on page 3 that the Soviets would react to major US build ups by seeking détente. Halperin suggested some clarifying language to help this section of the paper. He believed that the first question, on which there was general consensus, is whether the Soviets would react to prevent our attaining a first strike capability. More difficult questions included whether they would react to offset totally improvements in our programs short of those aiming for a first strike capability. Kissinger suggested, and there was agreement, that language along these lines would be more precise.

G Smith again asked who believed that the Soviets would react to US build ups with a search for détente. Lynn replied that the evidence was not conclusive that this would not be their response if they were economically pressed. In the face of a determined effort on our part, they might decide to forego matching us temporarily and seek a relaxation in relations. Packard summarized by saying that the Soviets would react to our attempts at a first strike capability, but they might not react to US moves concerning deterrence and damage limitation.

Halperin noted that his formulation attempted to reflect this, and it was agreed that this type of presentation would be useful.

Farley believed that the first paragraph under b on page 3 referred to Soviet military reaction, while the second concerned political response. He said that State believed that in the face of major US arms initiatives, the Soviets would not only react militarily but would also generally harden their political attitudes. Kissinger said that the real disagreement centered on the political reaction rather than the hardware reaction. Ware thought that the economic situation might be one of the factors determining the Soviet political response. Kissinger said that he had seen strong arguments on both sides, i.e., that the Soviets were more conciliatory when scared or more conciliatory when not scared. Sonnenfeldt said that this was really an unknown problem and that history provided examples for each view. For example, many major Soviet weapons decisions were taken during 1955 and 1958-9, periods of relative détente.

Kissinger noted the group's agreement that in this section the Soviet military response would be rewritten while possible political reactions would be stated.

In considering Allied interests (II A 3) Unger suggested language which would indicate that our commitments impose additional requirements on US strategic forces, and Packard concurred in this suggestion.

Kissinger wondered which European countries would be scared if we increased our strategic capabilities, which was one view suggested by the paper. G Smith said that there would be a negative reaction, more distaste than fear, in the United Kingdom if the US substantially increased its strategic capabilities. Loomis pointed out the difference between more realistic governmental opinion and public opinion which is more apt to be worried by an arms build up. Kissinger received the impression from European leaders that their political publics would be amazed if they heard that we were not vastly superior to the Soviet Union. There would probably be a different reaction between letting European publics continue to think we are superior and attempting to increase our forces if they knew we were not superior. G Smith believed that public opinion was aware of the concept of sufficiency, and that in an era of negotiations new decisions to increase our forces would incur public disapproval. Kissinger thought it depended on the public's view of the strategic situation.

J Smith believed that the paper's statement on this question was a somewhat simplistic view of a highly complex problem. Europeans would be relieved if we had strategic superiority, but they prefer not to see arms build ups. Thus, they want to have both détente and superiority. Selin suggested treating this problem in concrete terms, e.g., what would be the British reaction to our building 300 new Minuteman silos. Kissinger agreed with G Smith that this might present new problems in the UK, but wondered where else in Europe this was the case. Sonnenfeldt opined that we were dealing with extremes. The Europeans would be worried either about marked US inferiority or determination by the US to go for superiority. He thought that in between these extremes there would be relatively little sensitivity to programs like MIRVs or new Minutemen. Kissinger noted that the discussion refers to strategic improvements rather than superiority. G Smith suggested Italy as another country which could have a negative reaction. Kissinger repeated that a key factor was what Europeans think of the US-USSR strategic situation. Loomis felt that the public distinguishes between defensive systems, like the ABM, and offensive ones, like 300 more Minuteman silos. This was true of public opinion throughout Europe; G Smith added Canada. Farley believed that major initiatives by us in the arms race would create European concern. Packard thought that much would depend on how our programs were presented. For example, Europeans would welcome steps needed to deter war in Europe.

Kissinger suggested that it would be useful to have a paragraph in the paper on European reactions, put in terms of their perception of strategic problems. Halperin suggested that the paper's statements were not inconsistent unless one assumed a single European opinion; there are widely different views to be reflected.

Packard said that Europeans both want détente and are worried about deterring conventional attack. Loomis believed that Europeans were always worried about increasing the chances of war, and they would be unhappy if they assumed we were taking steps which would have this effect. Selin again suggested looking at this problem in terms of specific decisions, while Hartman stressed the importance of the rationale for our actions with regard to the US public. Kissinger again noted the importance of European perceptions concerning our programs. There would be different reactions to a situation in which we were ahead and sought to increase our lead, or behind and sought to catch up, or in a situation where Europeans were not clear about the strategic relationship.

Kissinger noted a JCS suggestion concerning nuclear assurances for our allies (II A 4) and wondered about the status of such assurances. Farley thought that testimony during Senate hearings had walked us back somewhat from assurances under the NPT. Halperin said that this Administration had not made a policy of assurances along the lines of those of the previous Administration. Kissinger thought that we needed a NSSM concerning our assurances to non-nuclear countries against nuclear attacks or threats. Farley noted that our Allied commitments do not distinguish between nuclear and conventional attacks. Schlesinger believed that there was one type of general assurance given to our allies, and another type to non-allied countries. Halperin noted our reaffirmation of assurances in the United Nations, and Farley pointed out that this was through the Security Council only. Kissinger suggested to Unger that he consult with his principals; he did not believe the language recommended by the JCS was strictly accurate. Halperin agreed with General Unger that the original text of the paper on this point was not accurate either. Kissinger believed that the legal situation does not take us beyond the UN Charter except with regard to our allies.

J Smith suggested deletion of the last paragraph under 4 on page 4 which said that the issue of nuclear assurances was outside the scope of this study.

Kissinger then took up military issues in designing our strategic posture (II B), beginning with what kinds of attacks we must deter. Selin noted that the three general views on page 5 concerning this question were mistakenly set up as mutually exclusive. He suggested that the paper say that beyond assured destruction, there were other additional criteria to be used in evaluating the US strategic posture.

Kissinger said that the discussion on page 5 indicated that the Soviets would either launch a general nuclear attack or none at all. Selin replied that they are not apt to make a discriminating attack. In response, Kissinger wondered how one could rationally make a decision to kill 80 million people. To blow up the Hoover Dam might not be rational either, but it was not less rational than an all out attack. Selin and Unger noted that this doctrine of massive preemption by the Soviets reflected CIA's view.

J Smith stated that a discriminating attack was the least likely contingency—one could not believe that the Soviets would launch a few nuclear ICBMs against the US. Kissinger probed this view, suggesting the possible use of a few missiles in a Berlin crisis. Packard said that the issue is Soviet first use, and Lynn suggested the example of their hitting soft strategic targets and nothing else. Selin and Schlesinger stressed the unlikelihood of this; Lynn noted that he was the only one in the Steering Group supporting this possibility. Sonnenfeldt recalled that during the U-2 crisis Kruschev threatened the selective use of nuclear weapons. J Smith noted that we did not place much credence in this threat at the time.

Kissinger summarized the paper's view as being that if the Soviets launch a nuclear attack, it will be a general one, not a limited one. J Smith said that studies indicate that Soviet strategic doctrine allows only for all out nuclear use and not limited attack. This could change, of course, but there were no indications that the Soviets seriously considered limited attack as part of their military doctrine. Packard said that he could envisage a scenario where we would not wish to fire all our missiles in five minutes, and he suggested that this was a good reason to have effective command and control. J Smith noted that this was useful at least for accidents. Kissinger wondered whether if we make limited use of nuclear weapons, the Soviets would make an all out response. J Smith believed this was correct, for once nuclear weapons start landing, the response is likely to be irrational. Selin said that the Soviets would hope to hit our command and control and our cities, and thus avoid a suicide of 80 million lives. It would paralyze our response without hitting our weapons. Lynn suggested that the destruction of our command and control would make a spasmodic reaction more likely than if they chose to coerce us through destroying military weapons.

There was some further discussion of the language in this section. It was agreed both to delete the reference to Soviet military tradition, and to make clear that the discussion was referring to nuclear attacks only.

The group then discussed damage-limiting (II B 2). Kissinger suggested that beyond a certain level of casualties, it did not make much difference whether more destruction and death occur on one side or the other (2nd para., page 6). No one really believes that we have "won" if we lose 90 million people and they lose 110 million people.

Lynn suggested that in the 90-120 million persons range there was rough equivalence, but that one should consider wide differences, such as between 80 and 150 million people. Schlesinger said that it was the Steering Group's judgment that this was one criterion for damage-limiting capabilities. Lynn believed the President would want this problem discussed. Kissinger wondered if we would be influenced by the prospect of the Soviets inflicting more damage upon us at mutually high fatality levels, and Lynn thought that perhaps we would be influenced in this situation. Kissinger thought that a mythology of relative deaths had grown up which was no longer relevant. Lynn replied that this was true in the context of assured destruction fatalities but not at lower death levels. Kissinger said that the question was therefore whether the ratio of fatalities would make a difference below certain levels. Halperin commented that the paper (3rd para. on page 6) states that you cannot keep our damage levels down in any event. Lynn said that this view in the paper said we should care about relative damage and casualties. Kissinger said that the necessity was to get our fatalities down to their levels so that they would not believe they could inflict significantly greater damage. Lynn and Selin declared that we now have rough parity in terms of damage and casualties, unless a thick ABM system is deployed. Kissinger repeated his view that beyond a certain level the casualty ratio makes no difference. Damage-limitation might be worth the effort for 10 million lives versus five million lives, but the statement in the paper loses meaning beyond a certain point. Lynn said that we are in a poor position now to balance off fatalities and we would not wish to see the Soviets, through defensive deployment, cut into this balance even though we still maintained assured destruction. Halperin summarized that the paper's statement on this subject was meaningful only if casualty ratios above the 25-30% assured destruction level were meaningful.

Kissinger asked whether it was worth noting that we cannot get fatalities below a certain level. Selin confirmed that view. On intelligence grounds we are sure that the Soviets would respond to our initiatives, and on technical grounds it is easy for them to do this.

Unger suggested that the heading about controlling our forces in nuclear war (II B 3 on page 6) be made broader in terms of assuring a relatively advantageous outcome. Packard recommended a general observation be made in this section about the desirability of a favorable outcome which overrides other considerations in a nuclear war.

The group then discussed Section III, results of the analysis of the NSSM 3 study.

G Smith wondered whether the JCS suggestion was designed to recommend more damage-limiting capabilities even in present forces. In assessing outcomes of nuclear exchanges, they would utilize other criteria than fatalities alone, such as military targets. They were seeking how to deploy present forces with a different emphasis, but this did not necessarily mean needing more than present capabilities. Unger summarized the JCS position as wanting "present forces appropriately modified".

G Smith thought it was more a question of strategy than force structure. During 7-8 years of an assured destruction strategy, the Chiefs wanted more war-fighting and damage-limiting capabilities; this would have resulted in greater forces. They were never for a pure assured destruction strategy. He wondered whether the JCS believed that the strategy of the past few years should be changed. Unger responded that it was rather a question of assessing our posture in light of the increasing threat of the last five years and projections for future years. Selin stated that this year's JSOP objectives were closer than ever to the recommendations of the Secretary of Defense; the differences were in such areas as relative advantage and degree of conservatism in planning. The large strategic differences between the Chiefs and the Secretary have almost completely disappeared. Packard noted that there were no real OSD-JCS problems with strategic forces. The principal issues concerned general purpose forces.

Kissinger raised the question of protecting our allies against attack, and Sonnenfeldt/Lynn said that this would be covered in the remaining portion of the Packard study. Selin and Unger noted that it was decided not to attempt to discuss defense of our allies in strategic terms alone because of the close relationship with our conventional forces in Europe. Lynn noted on page 9 reference to the need for additional study on strategic forces required to support theater forces, while Selin added that decisions on general purpose forces affect our strategic forces.

Kissinger recalled that in NATO debates our allies expressed their belief that theater forces support strategic forces rather than vice versa. Packard believed that the issue of tactical nuclear weapons policy in Europe was a very important one, and would be extremely significant both in his overall report and for SALT discussions. Kissinger suggested a cover note to this study saying that we have not included allied considerations.

Under believed that the conventional situation in Europe impacts on the strategic relationship. G Smith underlined the importance of our commitments in Western Europe to cover targets crucial to our allies. Under questioned if our conventional strength were below that of our adversaries in Europe, how we would deter them if our strategic forces are on a par with or below theirs. Kissinger said that this important issue could be covered in a note that he and Packard could agree upon. Kissinger questioned the degree of deterrence we now have against ground attack in Europe, given the changing strategic relationship of the past years. G Smith did not believe the issue was so clearcut.

With our 7th Army, tactical nuclear weapons, and strategic forces, the Europeans should not sense that our umbrella is eroding. He believed that the uncertainty factor for the Soviet was crucial and just as high as it was ten years ago. Packard thought that we did have some problems. Our tactical nuclear weapons cannot reach the USSR. Given the prospect of 80-90 million fatalities, would we intervene with nuclear weapons if the Soviets moved into Berlin? Packard disagreed with G Smith's assertion that the situation was not different than it was ten years ago. G Smith repeated his view that the Soviets have no greater appetite than they did to invade West Germany, and that tactical nuclear weapons were a factor in this situation. Selin declared that it would take a very large Soviet conventional attack to raise the question of whether we should go to nuclear weapons.

Kissinger believed that if our nuclear weapons deter the USSR, our different strategic relationship today must be reflected in the degree of deterrence. G Smith said he was disturbed to hear the implication that Europe is in greater danger today with regard to the US nuclear umbrella. In response to Packard's belief that the President would be hard pressed to use nuclear weapons in Europe, G Smith said that this has always been the case and that Europe is not in a different state of security today. J Smith opined that he just did not know what constitutes deterrence. Kissinger continued to question how one could write a long disquisition on the changed strategic relationship that all agreed has taken place during the past few years, without acknowledging its impact on the ability of American strategic forces to provide local defense. He was not saying that local defense was not possible. He thought those questions should be flagged for the decision-makers' attention without prejudging them.

Farley referred to the four conditions on pages 8-9 which appeared to define strategic sufficiency. He asked whether we would have insufficiency if we could not fulfill one of those four conditions. Packard reviewed each of the conditions and thought there was agreement that the first two (maintaining our second-strike capability and insuring that the Soviets would have no first strike incentives) were ones that all could agree were necessary for sufficiency. There were questions about the meaningful casualty levels of the third condition (relative outcomes in a nuclear war) and arguments over the fourth condition (damage-limitation against small or accidental attacks).

Unger suggested his fifth condition of relatively advantageous outcomes, which Packard suggested be added. Farley said that the Steering Group had not agreed to this condition. Selin did not believe this element should be added; it could mean that one was always confronted with the choice of either insufficiency or an arms race. Packard suggested, and it was agreed, that the JCS suggestions would be inserted as their position, accompanied by a statement on OSD objections.

The group then reviewed Section IV, Strategic Options.

G Smith emphasized the importance of our public posture. The way in which we describe our strategic forces is crucial to world opinion, and ACDA should have a look at any public statements. Kissinger promised that ACDA would have a crack at any Presidential statements arising from NSSM 3.

In discussing the question of uncertainties in the future US-USSR strategic relationship, J Smith pointed out that the role of intelligence was to give the President a tool for dealing with such unknowns. Intelligence can serve to mitigate uncertainties, given the lead times of 18-24 months required for most major weapons systems.

There followed a discussion of several of the pros and cons under the options in this section, and several drafting changes and additions were agreed to.

Under the discussion on estimating the threat (IV A 1) Selin pointed out that option A referred to the greater-than-expected threat and that therefore the first con should read to the effect; forces probably greater than needed.

It was agreed to drop the phrase "offsetting the least part of our advantage" under the third con for option A. Selin pointed out that our current policy is option B, not option A. Kissinger suggested that a pro for option B could be that it provides the greatest incentive to the Soviets to enter arms limitation talks. Lynn believed that option A could also provide incentive for SALT talks. It was agreed that pros along these lines would be inserted under both options A and B.

Farley thought that the first con under option C was overstated, and it was agreed to tone this down. The group also concurred in a JCS suggestion to change the first pro under option C to read; "forces needed against the estimated likely threat".

Kissinger wondered whether the second paragraph on page 12 was accurate, i.e., that option C would reduce our confidence in crises. He wondered whether 20% more missiles, for example, would give us more confidence in a crisis. Selin noted that we had confidence in past crises when we enjoyed a superior relationship. Lynn said that the thinner you slice your relative strategic posture the riskier it becomes to be firm during a crisis.

In response to Kissinger's query about our sensitivity to minor changes in the Soviet threat, Selin said that it was a question of which threat one was discussing and how much redundancy was needed beyond the assured destruction level of 25-30% fatalities. The discussion then centered on the question of redundancy (IV A 2). Halperin pointed out, and Selin agreed, that redundancy is related to deterrence, not damage-limitation.

Packard said that, speaking frankly, one had to admit that the issue of redundancy was being treated strictly in the context of the current components in our strategic forces, rather than taking a hard look at redundancy that might be caused by competition among the military services. Thus, this issue was being treated only in terms of the present facts of life, and there was no vigorous examination of possible new forces. Lynn suggested a background paragraph to this effect, and Kissinger agreed. There followed a brief discussion of the question of the mix of our forces which Unger noted was relevant to all the conditions listed for sufficiency. Packard said this had been studied. G Smith wondered, in this regard, why we placed our missiles near cities; he agreed with the Navy's emphasis on getting them out into the seas. Lynn noted the command and control problems of sea-based forces.

There was some discussion of how the options in this section would complicate Soviet planning. It was agreed that in addition to option A, option B would also serve this purpose to some extent.

Farley noted the seeming paradox between the two cons for option A (with regard to the adequacy of the force). Unger pointed out that the first one referred to assured destruction, while the second one covered other factors such as damage limitation, contingencies, etc.

(Kissinger had to leave the meeting at this point, and Packard became Chairman.)

Discussion continued about the pros and cons. Unger noted the second pro under option C, a sea-based force only would reduce Soviet incentives to attack the continental United States. Lynn again recalled the command and control problems related to submarines.

There was considerable discussion about the thrust of section B, beginning on page 13, and it was agreed to highlight the political and public aspects in the title for this section. Halperin noted that we will call whatever option we choose sufficiency. Selin suggested deleting a reference to emphasizing this concept under option 1, and this was agreed upon.

J Smith wondered whether the first option, which included proceeding with MIRVs and Safeguard, could be characterized as emphasizing moderation. After some discussion it was agreed to reverse options 1 and 3, and to say that the new option 3 emphasized moderation in comparison to the new option 1. Selin did not perceive the difference between options 1 and 2 in terms of our strategic force decisions. He did not see how under the new option 2 we might be passing up opportunities to improve our relative strategic capabilities. Packard and Unger felt this was a fair statement. Packard said that the discussion was merely treating the broad options of increasing, decreasing or maintaining present strategic forces. This was an overlook at the general effect before dealing with specific programs; therefore under this broad option we might be passing up some opportunities to improve our capabilities. Farley said that if the con for the new option 1 of perhaps inducing the Soviets to seek détente was to be retained, there should also be a con to the effect that this option might harden Soviet attitudes, given our uncertainty about Soviet reactions.

After some further discussion on this section (IV B) Selin suggested, and it was agreed, to pick up language contained in the Steering Group report.

With regard to the final section on unresolved issues (V), Halperin suggested adding the problem of requirements generated by our NATO commitments. It could be noted that this issue, unlike the other three unresolved questions listed in this section, was being addressed in the remaining portion of the Packard study. This was agreed to.

There being no further questions, the meeting was then adjourned.

November 8, 1969

Another classified memo giving some details about the SIOP-4 as it stood in 1969. The SIOP consisted of three different categories of targets ranked in order of priority, which were designed to eliminate Soviet military centers and to destroy at least 70% of Soviet urban industrial capacity.

The SIOP had five different options for execution, ranging from a preemptive American "counter-force" first strike against only Soviet military targets located outside of the urban areas (the lowest-casualty option) to a full-out retaliatory attack on all targets. The counter-force first-strike option would use 1750 nuclear warheads (about 58% of the total nuclear force). The intent in all of the attack options was to prioritize the destruction of Soviet strategic nuclear capabilities, following that up if necessary with attacks on urban-industrial targets. Within each plan were options to attack one category of targets only, two categories, or all three: there were also a number of "withhold" options to spare particular types of targets or particular nations.

MEMORANDUM FOR DR KISSINGER
SUBJECT: The SIOP
To follow through on our discussions of the SIOP, I have summarized below the salient features of the current SIOP to include:

--The current National Strtaegic targeting Policy, drawing from Mel Laird's paper (attached at Tab A);

--The JCS rationale for this Policy and some argumentation pro and con;

--Specific issues that should be pursued in refining or revising the SIOP.

I believe the next step is for you to meet with General Wheeler and raise a number of issues, answers to which will enable you to furnish the President with a clear picture of the SIOP, present sub-SIOP options and rationale, and possibilities for SIOP revisions. Accordingly, I have also identified specific questions you might want to pursue (talking points at Tab B).

The Current SIOP

The present SIOP is designed primarily for a general nuclear war with the USSR. For lesser conflicts, reliance would be placed on theater contingency plans, such as those SACEUR has developed. For substantial efforts against the CPR, some strategic forces would be needed (primarily from SAC); but, we do not know how the planning and targeting would be done.

The present SIOP target list has been subdivided into three tasks:

--<u>ALPHA</u>: To destroy Sino-Soviet strategic nuclear delivery capabilities located outside urban areas. As part of this task, the highest Soviet and Chinese political and military control centers would be attacked — the Moscow-Peking Missile Packages (MPMP).

--<u>BRAVO</u>: To destroy other elements of the Sino-Soviet military forces and military resources not included in ALPHA which are located outside the major urban centers.

--<u>CHARLIE</u>: To destroy Sino-Soviet military forces and military resources which were excluded from ALPHA and BRAVO because of their location within urban centers and at least 70% of the urban industrial bases of the USSR and Communist China.

These tasks have been further combined into five attack options. The smallest attack, a pre-emptive strike on the ALPHA targets, would involve 58% of our SIOP committed forces. Roughly 1750 weapons would be expected to arrive on or near their targets in the USSR. More forces would be needed for this option if the Soviets had been forewarned of the attack.

The basic attack options are:

SIOP ATTACK OPTIONS

	Attack Options	Tasks Normally Included	Tasks Withholdable
Pre-emptive	1	A	(MPMP)
	2	A, B	—
	2X	All	—
Retaliatory	3	A, B, C	B & C, or C
	4	All	—

Two points might be underscored:

--Under present plans we always attack the Soviet nuclear threat, in its entirety, before engaging "value" targets. This is what makes even the smallest strike so large.

--We initially can withhold an element of a task (MPMP in ALPHA), a task of an attack option (CHARLIE in option 2), or both.

I understand that there are other "withhold elements", as well as the MPMP, which would permit as many as 90 sub-variations on these attack options. How these work—and what degree of real alternatives they afford—we do not know.

--I think we should ask General Wheeler for information about the withhold packages.

--I strongly recommend also asking him about the possibility of designing additional withhold packages as a way of obtaining sub-SIOP attack options. This could be your way of obtaining other attack options in ways that would involve the least friction with the strategic planners.

Discussion Points: Task ALPHA Rationale

I believe you should focus discussion about the substance of the SIOP strictly to the ALPHA task. That task is always included in the SIOP options and it requires the largest part of our forces.

I also believe it would be useful to consider only pre-emptive strikes, at least initially. The issue of retaliation involves debatable assumptions about the enemy attack which must be agreed to before a discussion can be manageable.

You could proceed by asking General Wheeler for the JCS rationale on the ALPHA task. I expect he will give the reasons indicated below. (I have also indicated some counterpoints you may wish to raise.)

The JCS believe there are strong arguments for beginning a nuclear exchange on Russia with something like the complete ALPHA list. They give five different reasons:

1. "Soviet knowledge that the US would contemplate a small-scale nuclear attack could downgrade the deterrent value of our strategic posture."

One could equally assert, of course, that willingness to cross the nuclear "firebreak" with a small-scale attack will clearly indicate that the US might "go all the way", thus increasing our deterrent.

2. "That such an attack might warn the Soviets of US intentions (real or imaginary) and induce them into a state of readiness less advantageous to us in the event larger attacks are necessary later."

This argument actually applies only to the special case where the Soviets are completely surprised. This is unlikely during a period of tension. It does not apply to US attacks against the soft Soviet targets, where one US weapon would destroy a number of Soviet non-alert or soft but mobile weapons. Our attack could be designed to destroy those forces that could be moved to a higher state of readiness.

In fact, I think this counter-argument is sufficient without further evidence, but it could be supported by analysis if the following information were available:

--a list of the soft force targets in the USSR;

--US weapon effectiveness against these targets (using various systems and warheads).

Some of the work has been done for NSSM 64. That analysis shows a great pay-off for the initial strikes on soft force targets by either side in strategic counterforce attacks.

One could object to this reasoning. Perhaps the soft targets are co-located with highly populated urban/industrial complexes. If they were attacked, the USSR might consider itself compelled to respond, perhaps against a similar or somewhat smaller US city. Could a President take that risk?

3. "A small attack might trigger an immediate large-scale Soviet response, particularly of their soft nuclear forces."

This argument is clearly a corollary of the dilemma referred to in the previous paragraphs. If the initial US attack is too small to get all soft Soviet forces, the argument is valid. The Soviets might attack with their remaining soft systems rather than see them destroyed in a subsequent US attack. Perhaps the Soviets cannot distinguish a small from a large attack and would feel compelled to retaliate (this is another issue).

Much of the argument turns on an analysis of soft target vulnerability and collateral effects. This issue can be resolved by analysis, provided we know;

--surrounding urban/industrial complexes near soft USSR nuclear systems targets.

4. "Rapid execution of a small strike could leave a large portion of our own strategic and theater forces at a relatively low level of force generation, making them particularly vulnerable to Soviet retaliations."

This argument is valid in the following case: an attack during which we left non-alert bombers and submarines in tender in a state of non-readiness, and we used only day-to-day ready forces in our initial strikes, perhaps to obtain maximum surprise. Thus, US reliable and accurate systems would be used up, leaving the average or net reliability of the remaining forces somewhat less than it is now.

This condition could be eliminated if our forces were readied in secret or simultaneously with the strike, if advance plans and orders were given so that communications systems were not overloaded after the strike, and if reconnaissance requirements were kept to a minimum. Moreover, the JCS supposedly instituted a faster procedure for selective options last July (1969).

An important issue not directly related to the JCS point is what happens in the USSR and what its likely response to the crisis situation might be. Once the attack hits, Soviet crisis management capabilities will be severely strained. All sorts of rumors will abound initially. With respect to Soviet forces, if part of the force targeted survives, what will it do if communications with headquarters has been lost? Would the Soviet operators respond against their general war targets?

5. "Any strike against the USSR should include consideration of suppressing or penetrating Soviet air and or missile defenses; several hundred weapons are included for this purpose in every SIOP option as an integral and mutually supporting element."

This conclusion is not obvious. Like SAM suppression over NVN, the desirability of expending sorties on air defenses can be evaluated in terms of the reduced effectiveness of attack sorties when the defenses are left intact. The measures are higher attrition, higher abort rates, and less accurate delivery.

With respect to strategic attacks, attacking radar sites or air defense launchers with a small number of missiles could be more than repaid by the "wide open door" provided for the follow-on attack forces.

However, these attacks could also be destabilizing if they rendered the defended Soviet systems vulnerable.

In attack planning we could minimize this destabilizing risk and the "overhead" cost of removing defenses. For example, we could design attacks so that the defense systems were not attacked, or were attacked only enough to penetrate through to the soft targets they covered. To do the analysis, we would need:

--Attack corridors into Soviet soft nuclear systems including defenses only for the soft target and defenses for other targets as well.

--US system effectiveness in attacks on these Soviet defenses.

6. The last JCS argument is "that there are existing theater forces under CINCPAC and SACEUR command and contingency plans for less than all-out attack."

One might say that this is the JCS "hedge" on the logic of JCS posture on the ALPHA list, including ALPHA targets in all the attack options.

Practical Problems in Changing the SIOP

There are certain practical problems involved in working with the SIOP.

--annually, there is a review of the SIOP during which targeting of systems is changed. At present, adjusting the SIOP after these reviews takes about six months.

--The retargeting time can be improved. When SAC obtains the integrated command and control system for Minuteman, costing up to $700 million, retargeting time could be reduced from 90 to 180 days to 17 days. Now, however, it is about six months.

--Another restraint on retargeting Minuteman is the time and technical resources needed to change the guidance and control instructions in the missile itself. A specialized team is needed (there are about 100 of these) and the task can require up to eight hours per missile. This latter constraint will keep SIOP retargeting time above 14 days.

--Changes in submarine targets can be accomplished more quickly. However, during a period of alert there is no way of ascertaining whether the submarine has received the new instructions because the submarine cannot communicate to the NCA without giving its position away.

--Present weapon laydown criteria optimize target destruction for the full ALPHA list. To do this and protect against failures in launch, penetration, or weapon delivery, extensive cross targeting is done: this means a system with multiple warheads will engage several targets. In order to optimize destruction of a few specific targets, some changes to targeting would be necessary.

I believe that by focusing on withhold options you can obtain an "expanded SIOP" giving the President attack options which would be part of the SIOP, they could be promptly executed on Presidential order, without:

--Elaborate readjustments of the weapons and delivery systems which would take from several days for a few weapons to a very minimum of three weeks for the entire force (using computer reprogram capabilities not yet available).

--Degrading the general deterrent by expending crucial parts of it.

Proposed ALPHA Withhold Options

In think it would be useful, in order to start moving ahead on expanding the SIOP, for you to propose one of two ALPHA withhold options. This could be done by asking General Wheeler to have the Joint Targeting people design two options, along the following lines;

ALPHA SUB-OPTIONS
(Withhold all ALPHA but these targets)

Option	U.S. Force Requirements
Attack soft undefended Soviet nuclear systems in remote areas (not near urban/industrial complexes).	In each case, U.S. forces expended should be less than Soviet forces destroyed. This means the USSR targets must be co-located or that re-loadable U.S. systems would be used, e.g. bombers or SSBNs.
Attack soft USSR nuclear systems (in remote areas) where only the defenses for the system attacked are eliminated.	

RECOMMENDATION:

I recommend that you meet with General Wheeler to discuss the SIOP. At the meeting, you would raise some of the issues mentioned above (taking points are attached at Tab B).

In addition, I recommend that you ask General Wheeler to have the Joint Staff targeting analysts examine ALPHA withhold options involving only a few attacks on some soft Soviet targets. I have also prepared a description a description of the two options discussed above (see Tab C).

January 29, 1971

This classified memo discusses a policy of "launch on warning".

By this time, newer ICBMs and MIRV warheads were becoming more accurate, raising the possibility that one side could soon be able to launch a pre-emptive first strike that could knock out the enemy's ICBMs in their silos, preventing an effective retaliatory strike. Under these circumstances, some military planners felt, the only way to maintain a retaliatory ability was to launch the missiles as soon as warning is received of an enemy launch, allowing the ICBMs to be on their way and out of their silos before the enemy warheads could arrive to destroy them.

Throughout the 70's and 80's, as the number of warheads continued to climb, and as ever more accurate missiles like the Minuteman III and the MX Peacekeeper appeared, the debates over a "launch on warning" policy would be repeated again and again.

MEMORANDUM
SUBJECT: Your Memorandum on "Launch-on-Warning"

I want to thank you for your memorandum of December 28 on launch-on-warning. It is a thoughtful memorandum. It will probably come as no surprise to you, however, that it leaves me less than satisfied.

My dissatisfaction stems in part from the semantics used. The term "launch-on-warning", perhaps because of the earlier debates on the policy issues involved, seems to generate strong reactions and, in the process, obscures the central points I previously made to you and Sey.

To refresh your memory, in our previous discussion I was questioning the degree of our vulnerability to Soviet nuclear attack, and thus the need for our resorting to measures, such as hard-point defense, which most informed observers feel would blow up the possibility of a SALT agreement. I was also raising in this context the feasibility of an ABM-only agreement consistent with adequate protection of our security interests.

Stripped to its essentials, my reasoning was, and still is, as follows:

1. Our fundamental protection against nuclear attack—and nuclear blackmail—lies in our capability to inflict such intolerable damage on the enemy as to deter him from possible attack.

2. We would appear to have that capability in part in our capacity to get our Minutemen off the ground before any Soviet ICBMs could knock them out should the Russians attempt a nuclear first strike. That is, there would be time between the launching of Soviet missiles and their hitting US targets to get our own missiles on the way.

3. The Soviets would know that we had this capability.

4. Knowing this, they should be deterred from the possibility of undertaking a first strike. Even if the Soviets might calculate that there is a substantial chance we would not employ this capability, they would still have to allow for the possibility that we would; and even if the possibility were small, it should be sufficient to deter them because of the intolerable destruction they would suffer if the possibility became a reality. In other words, because of the intolerable level of destruction with which they might be visited, they would have to assume "the worst case" in judging what they themselves might do.

5. Thus, I concluded that despite the SS-9s and possible future qualitative improvements by the Soviets we still have a significant deterrent so long as our own Minutemen could get off the ground in time.

6. In addition, and more important, of course, we still have our sea-based missiles and heavy bombers, and the political factor would provide a further heavy constraint on the Soviets as well as ourselves

on any first resort to nuclear weapons, though for the sake of analysis we left these considerations aside to focus on the deterrent capability of a land ICBM force.

In these terms your memorandum still leaves me unpersuaded:

1. If I understand your argument correctly, it is in large part that the deterrent is not credible. It implies that we might "launch everything in a spasm" even when the Soviets might launch only a few missiles, and that the Soviets would calculate that we would not engage in mass destruction when they are hitting us with just a few. You suggest, accordingly, that the Soviets would have a strong temptation "to probe below the threshold" of the number of missiles they could launch before we could react.

I don't find this a very plausible argument. Nuclear weapons are of such tremendous destructive capability that I find it difficult to conceive of the Russians "probing" even with only a few of them. Were they to probe in the sense of actually sending some over, they would have to calculate that we would respond at least to the extent of the amount they may have thrown at us; and they would have at least to allow that the initial exchange would escalate into a more massive one, and thus they should be deterred from starting things in the first place. If they should reason this way—as I would expect them to if they are rational—then I doubt they would even threaten "to probe below the threshold", as you suggest, since they would appreciate that the threat is not credible. In general, I find this whole concept of probing below some threshold highly unrealistic politically.

2. You appear to question the technical feasibility of developing a system which would be sufficiently fast, discriminating and unambiguous in providing the warning required to make such a deterrent credible. I am no expert in these matters but I am advised by Frank Perez and others who are more knowledgeable that this is quite feasible.

3. You also suggest that such a warning system would be very costly, perhaps as costly as increased Minutemen survivability. I am advised that the cost is not as great as you suggest. Even if it were, however, I would prefer to see the money going into such an effort than to plunge into hard-point defense with the adverse impact it would have on the possibility of reaching a SALT agreement.

4. I fully endorse your point that "the essence of a strategy of deterrence is to exploit the existence of weapons without actually

using them". That is precisely what I am talking about. It seems to me that if in fact we have the capability to strike the Russians a devastating blow if they should attempt a first strike, the Russians cannot afford—as we couldn't either—to assume anything else but that the capability will be used. And in making that assumption, neither they nor we would resort in the first instance either to small ("probing" in your terms) or massive employment of nuclear weapons.

5. Finally, so that our perspective is not lost, let me emphasize that in arguing as I have (a) against ABM action by ourselves which would prejudice the chance of getting a SALT agreement, and (b) for an ANM-only agreement if a more comprehensive agreement covering offensive weapons is not negotiable, I have raised the question of the deterrent capability of our land ICBM force as a subordinate aspect of our total deterrent capability. I expect our principle deterrence to lie in our sea-based force. I have raised the launch-on-warning capability only to illustrate further the immense power at our disposal and to suggest that the concerns about the survivability of our nuclear force and the threat to our security have, in my view, been greatly exaggerated.

Enclosed is a memorandum by Frank Perez which discusses in greater detail some of the technical aspects of the issues raised in your memorandum.

FROM: Frank H Perez
SUBJECT: Thoughts on Launch-on-Warning

During the past decade major advances have occurred in the technology relating to ballistic missile early warning, detection, tracking and discrimination. Utilization of these advanced techniques provides high confidence that a flock of geese or an accidental or unauthorized missile launch would not serve to trigger a spasm response with all of its catastrophic results. In fact, technology has progressed to a stage where the unpopular and distasteful subject of "launch-on-warning" should be re-examined in a more rational and less emotional manner, particularly in view of the growing impact of Soviet technology on the survivability of our strategic forces. At this stage, however, it would be more appropriate to talk about a <u>capability to launch on unambiguous warning</u>.

In order to provide such a capability, it would be necessary to construct—in addition to systems already in operation or nearing operational status—perimeter acquisition radars (PAR type) along ICBM approach corridors. The resulting combination of systems would provide unambiguous information on the numbers of attacking objects, where they were launched from, and where they would impact.

The rationale for considering this approach is as follows: if the Soviets were to develop a credible counterforce capability against Minuteman, the possibility of their using it first in a crisis situation would exist. The current DPRC study on strategic force survivability shows that technical advancements, particularly in the form of highly accurate MIRVs, indicate that the Soviets could attain a counter-force capability against the US Minuteman force in the 1975-80 time period.

A significant deterrent to any temptation on the part of the Soviets to use their counterforce capability in a first strike in order to gain an advantage would be the threat to launch Minuteman before it came under direct attack. If the Soviets were uncertain as to the US response, it is doubtful that they would consider a counterforce first strike against Minuteman to be a viable option. The possibility of trading Soviet cities for empty US silos would weigh heavy on the Soviet political leadership in reaching such an awesome decision.

In order to convince the Soviets that the US might respond to an all-out Soviet surprise attack against Minuteman by launching some part or all of the force would require the US to have in being a highly reliable ballistic missile early warning and tracking capability. Such a system would provide warning of a massive missile launch at the time it occurred and would be capable of accurately and reliably determining the nature of the attack in sufficient time for the Minuteman force to be launched on the basis of an informed judgment by the President.

The key to a credible capability would be highly sophisticated and reliable systems to detect mass launches from the Soviet Union as soon as they occurred and then to quickly define the attack in terms of its size and the intended target areas. It would also require rapid procedures to communicate with the President and the National Command Authority.

We already have systems in operation which are designed to provide immediate and continuous warning of mass missile launches from the Soviet Union. These are the 440-L OTH system and the 647 early warning satellite. 440-L is now operational and functioning satisfactorily. The first 647 satellite was launched recently but failed to achieve the desired stationary orbit over the Soviet Union. Instead, it went into a highly elliptical orbit. Nevertheless, we have received sufficient data from the satellite to indicate that its design objective probably will be achieved.

Determining that a mass launch had occurred, while a very important part of a launch-on-warning capability, would not be enough. We would have to have absolute assurance as to the size of the attack and would need to know specifically where the attack originated and to where it was directed. With the deployment along ICBM approach corridors of advanced phased array radars of the type we are putting into Safeguard (Perimeter Acquisition Radars—PARs) we would be able to accurately and reliably determine such factors as the number of attacking objects, where they were launched from and where they were intended to impact. Thus, we would know of a large-scale attack directed against Minuteman in time to be able to launch the Minuteman force or a given portion of it before it comes under direct attack.

In terms of cost, such a warning and tracking capability would not appear to be excessive. The 440-L OTH system is already in being and the program for the 647 early warning satellite system already has been approved and is in the initial phase. We are also in the process of constructing PAR radars at Malmstrom and Grand Forks which will perform the acquisition function for all of our Safeguard deployment at defended Minuteman complexes. Additional PAR type radars required to assure a highly reliable and redundant assessment of the threat would not be significantly less expensive than other solutions being considered for the Minuteman survivability problem—ABM defense of Minuteman, rebasing Minuteman in a mobile mode or the phase-out or phase-down of Minuteman with greater emphasis on SLBMs and bombers.

The argument could be made that the Soviets might first attack ballistic missile detection and tracking radars (PAR type) so as to blind the US, and then follow with an all-out counterforce attack against Minuteman. This, however, would be a dangerous tactic on the part of the Soviets. Such a radar attack would alert the US and could permit the US to launch its missiles after a mass missile launch against the US was detected by 440-L and 647. To mitigate the remote possibility of such a radar attack the US could elect to protect a key segment of its ballistic missile warning and tracking network with ABMs. In the SALT context we could propose our NCA defense be not around Washington, but rather at Malmstrom which is one of two Safeguard sites currently being constructed. From Malmstrom alone we probably would still be able to track and identify with sufficient precision and reliability a major ICBM attack directed at our Minuteman complexes.

Once the attack had started, the Soviets would know that around 30 minutes would be available in which to alert the US President and the National Command Authority and to make a decision to launch Minuteman. However, about 15-20 minutes probably would pass before the nature of the attack would be sufficiently defined so as to determine whether it was in fact a major attack directed against Minuteman. Thus, in any system designed to permit launching of Minuteman on unambiguous warning would require highly sophisticated and reliable procedures for alerting the President and the National Command Authority so that they would be fully informed on a continuing basis of developments as they occurred. However, <u>it is most unlikely that a Soviet first strike would occur except in a period of extreme tension</u>, and in such a situation the President and the National Command Authority would be especially alert to react to Soviet initiation of an attack.

A Soviet counterforce attack against Minuteman might be conducted without concurrent attacks against US population and industrial centers. Launching the Minuteman force against SIOP targets, which include Soviet population and industrial targets, probably would cause the Soviets to retaliate in kind. Therefore, it might be prudent to earmark a certain portion of the Minuteman force, say 200 or 300 missiles, which could be launched against high value military targets away from population and industrial centers while the remainder of the Minuteman force rode out the attack. In such an attack, high value targets could include heavy bomber bases, submarine bases, nuclear storage sites, military depots, R&D centers, etc. Thus, if the Soviets did destroy the bulk of the remaining Minutemen, they will have suffered relatively greater losses and will have expended a large number of their missiles.

On balance, even if we were to provide ABM defense of Minuteman as a deterrent to a first strike, there would still be considerable merit in having a highly reliable integrated ballistic missile early warning and tracking system which would give the President the option to respond to a Soviet attack based on his assessment of the situation. This would seem preferable to no option other than to ride out the attack and then respond with what residual remained. As noted in the draft DPRC study on strategic force survivability, uncertainties surround even a dedicated hard-site defense of Minuteman because "there is considerable uncertainty about future Soviet penetration aids and re-entry vehicle technology."

In summary, unambiguous launch-on-warning capability could serve to deter the Soviets from seeking to develop a counterforce capability against Minuteman. More importantly, it could serve to significantly reduce any incentive to use such a force in a pre-emptive strike in the hopes of gaining some strategic advantage. This latter consideration is particularly important, since the primary objective of US strategic forces is to deter nuclear attack on the US. To obtain the deterrent effect inherent in the capability to launch-on-unambiguous-warning would not require the US to announce a launch-on-warning policy. The mere fact that we had developed and deployed the sophisticated components required for such a capability would serve as a signal to the Soviets that the US was prepared to exercise this option.

It is recognized that this memorandum has only scratched the surface of this very complex and emotional issue. It is emphasized that this memorandum is not advocating the adoption of a launch-on-warning policy; rather it is raising issues and arguments which need more careful examination and study in light of changing conditions, both in terms of the military threat and technological opportunities.

January 3, 1972

This classified memo gives a detailed look at the SIOP-4 and the nuclear arms race as it existed at this time. By 1972, both the Soviet and American arsenals were expanding rapidly, as newer more accurate ICBMs like Minuteman III and the Poseidon submarine-launched missile began to come into play. In conventional forces in Europe, however, where it was assumed any aggressive actions by the Soviets would come, the USSR had always had a huge numerical advantage, and the announced policy of NATO and the US throughout the Cold War was that the west would use tactical nuclear weapons in response to any large-scale Soviet invasion. The US in 1972 had roughly 3600 tactical nuclear weapons within the country's borders (as anti-air and anti-submarine weapons) and 12,900 across the world, including 7400 in Western Europe. (About 4000 of these were defensive, either anti-air, anti-ship/submarine, or anti-missile.)

The SIOP by this time had approximately 4200 strategic nuclear weapons available. There were five major options for the SIOP, with three of these involving a pre-emptive attack by the United States (presumably in response to a Soviet invasion of Western Europe) and two involving a retaliatory attack by the US after a Soviet first strike. However, the memo notes, while the US could knock out many of the Soviet bomber bases and intermediate-range missile launchers in a first strike, it did not have the capability to knock out a significant portion of the Soviet ICBM forces in their hardened silos, and was unable to prevent a devastating Soviet retaliatory response. And the opposite was also true – the Soviets could not knock out the American Minuteman missiles, and even just 100 surviving US ICBMs from a Soviet first strike would be able to wipe out 15% of the population of the USSR in retaliation.

Within each option were three different target priorities, known as "tasks": ALFA representing Soviet strategic weapons and delivery systems, BRAVO representing secondary Soviet command centers and targets like airfields, and CHARLIE representing soft military targets and urban/industrial areas.

The plan was designed with the intent to "moderately damage" at least 70% of the industrial capacity of the USSR and to kill at least 30% of its population. About 3200 nuclear weapons were aimed at Soviet ICBM forces and their command centers (counterforce), and about 700 were aimed at Soviet cities. The public policy of both sides was that they were not deliberately targeting civilian populations or cities, but that was a polite diplomatic fiction: everyone knew what "MAD" meant, and both sides knew full well that military targets were located in or near cities, and that attacks on "urban industrial targets" would mean the destruction of the city around them. Any large-scale attack by either side on any category of target could be expected to kill at least 100 million people.

But the SIOP also contained contingency plans for the use of very small attacks during a crisis, even just a single missile or bomber strike. Such an attack could be on its way within 15 minutes of the decision.

The memo also contains a section describing the strategic situation between the US and China. Although China was not considered as much a threat as the Soviet Union, the SIOP targeted almost 600 nuclear weapons at Chinese nuclear delivery systems and cities. Nearly all of these were submarine-launched missiles or bombers – the US did not want to launch ICBMs over the north pole towards China because they would cross Russia on their way, and the Soviets would assume the missiles were targeted at them and launch a counter-attack.

Because China at this time was still a largely rural nation, it was expected that an American nuclear strike against Chinese targets would eliminate most of its industrial capability (the goal was 70% destruction), but only 7% of China's population – which still amounted to 60 million people.

US STRATEGIC OBJECTIVES AND FORCE POSTURE
Executive Summary
C. Nuclear Weapons Employment Plans

Employment plans for nuclear weapons include the Single Integrated Operational Plan (SIOP) and various contingency plans of SACEUR and other theater commanders. These are discussed below, as is our current capability for ad hoc planning of nuclear strikes.

1. SIOP

The National Strategic Targeting and Attack Policy (NSTAP), prepared by the Joint Chiefs of Staff, provides guidance for preparing employment plans of US nuclear offensive forces against the Soviet Union and other communist nations. The SIOP integrates US strategic forces and designated theater nuclear forces for preplanned attacks on targets for the purpose of accomplishing the NSTAP objectives, of which there are three:

--Destruction of nuclear offensive threats to the United States and its allies, in order to limit damage.

--Destruction of a comprehensive military target system, in order to assist in destroying overall Soviet and other Warsaw Pact military capability.

--Destruction of war-supporting urban and industrial resources. {The NSTAP goals are to inflict moderate damage in 70% of the war-supporting industry and to destroy 30% of the people.) (Note: The JCS representative notes that destroying people is not a specific NSTAP objective.)

To meet the above objectives, there are three SIOP tasks, designated ALFA, BRAVO and CHARLIE.

--Task ALFA includes strikes on ICBM and IR/MRBM sites, bomber bases, ballistic missile submarine bases, local military command and control sites, nuclear weapon storage sites, and defense suppression targets.

--Task BRAVO includes strikes on tactical airfields and other military targets critical to the overall conduct and direction of military operations.

--Task CHARLIE includes strikes on urban/industrial targets and military targets collocated with cities.

Table III-2 shows the number of targets and the number of weapons assigned to each task:

Table III-2
Summary of SIOP Targeting
(SIOP) Revision H; Numbers Rounded)

Task	Total Installations Targeted	Preemptive U.S. Attack		Retaliatory U.S. Attacks	
		Installations Targeted	Warheads Programmed	Installations Targeted	Warheads Programmed
ALPHA	2800	1700	3200	1600	2900
BRAVO	1800	500	300	500	300
CHARLIE	-6400a/	4300a/	700	4300a/	800

a/ An installation is a particular target within a city. The 4300 installations targeted are located in cities.

There are five attack options which can be selected by the NCA in executing SIOP strikes. Three of these options (designated Attack Options 1, 2, and 2-extended) provide for executing the SIOP tasks in a preemptive attack. Table III-3 shows the relation between attack options and the SIOP tasks:

Table III-3
Summary of SIOP Options
(X=executive; other tasks are reserved for possible later use)

Task	U.S. Preemption			U.S. Retaliation	
	1	2	2 Extended	3	4
ALFA (nuclear threat targets)	X	X	X	X	X
BRAVO (other military targets)		X	X	X	X
CHARLIE (urban/industrial targets)			X		X

Under each attack option, the SIOP provides for selective withholding, by task and by country, of attacks against China and the Far Eastern and East European communist nations. In all options, however, the Soviet Union would be attacked. Moreover, attacks on the government centers in Moscow and Peking may be withheld in all attack options. On the other hand, SIOP strikes against China and North Korea can be expected without ordering SIOP attacks against the Soviet Union or other communist nations.

The following points are of importance:

--Task ALFA (nuclear threat targets) is included in all attack options.

--The smallest preemptive SIOP attack which the NCA can order against the Soviet Union, with the option of withholding against the Soviet NCA) includes Task ALFA which involves about 2500 weapons.

--The smallest SIOP retaliatory strike against the Soviet Union (again with the option to withhold) includes tasks ALFA and BRAVO which involves about 2600 weapons.

Given these employment plans, US strategic forces as currently targeted have the following capabilities for achieving the NSTAP objectives:

--They cannot destroy a significant part of the Soviet nuclear delivery capability.

--They can destroy about half of a comprehensive Soviet military target system.

--They can inflict damage on 70% of the war-supporting economic targets in the USSR and China.

--They can support our allies by destroying a significant number of Soviet bomber bases and soft, fixed IR/MRBM launchers.

--They cannot significantly limit damage to the United States and its allies.

--They cannot insure termination of hostilities under conditions advantageous to the United States as measured in terms of residual military resources and limitation of damage to the US urban/industrial base.

Unless there are changes to current strategic programs or to current SIOP planning objectives, these capabilities will remain unchanged through the 1970s, except our ability to support NATO operations will decline if the Soviets harden more of their IR/MRBM sites.

(An annex with more detailed information and a separate analysis of the SIOP by the JCS are being distributed on a selective basis.)

2. Contingency Plans

The contingency plans of SACEUR and SACLANT for employment of NATO theater nuclear weapons are coordinated with the SIOP, and many of the NATO theater nuclear strike forces have common target assignments under both the SIOP and the NATO plans.

There are also contingency plans for the use of nuclear weapons (primarily tactical air forces), limited use of B-52s, and very limited use of SLBMs by US unified commanders for tasks not incorporated in the SIOP. These plans are coordinated with the SIOP and with one another.

3. Capabilities for Selective Release and Ad Hoc Planning

In addition to the SIOP attack options and the above contingency plans, the President can currently use selective release procedures or ad hoc planning if he wants to execute a limited strike with nuclear weapons. Although CINC selective release procedures for tactical nuclear weapons are periodically exercised, those for strategic nuclear weapons are not and, therefore, their responsiveness in a crisis is uncertain.

--The emergency action message procedures contain provisions for selective release of individual bomber or missile sorties which are programmed in the SIOP. This procedure could be extended to incorporate pre-planned or ad hoc limited strike options.

--Small attacks tailored to a specific crisis would be planned on an ad hoc basis, using current forces, staff organizations, and command and control systems.

Selective Release

Once the President has selected specific SIOP sorties for release, these sorties can be executed within 15-20 minutes after his decision. The time required for Presidential review and selection of these sorties is, however, uncertain; it could be several hours or over a day, depending on the number of political-military factors which must be taken into account. There are routine drills involving the communications systems, but we do not have systematic provisions for interface between the President and the planning staffs for the purpose of reviewing SIOP sorties for selective release.

Moreover, several factors, bear on the choice of pre-programmed sorties from the SIOP for execution in a crisis:

--The most obvious factor is that the pre-programmed sorties may not provide the attacks most suitable to the crisis.

--SIOP attacks are planned with a high degree of mutual support among individual sorties for penetration of Soviet defenses. Thus, individual bomber sorties into areas with extensive air defenses or missile strikes into areas defended by the Moscow ABM system may not have much chance of success if the attack size is to be kept low.

--A pre-programmed sortie with the MIRVed Minuteman III or Poseidon would generally be targeted against several targets, some of which the President might not want to attack.

--Execution on a selective basis of many SIOP sorties would start to raise concerns about erosion of the effectiveness of the SIOP attack options, because of the high degree of mutual support among individual sorties. This threshold is uncertain and would depend on the sorties which were selectively released.

--If SAC headquarters had been destroyed, the President could still review SIOP sorties for selective release, using airborne command posts, but capabilities to estimate prospective strike results, particularly collateral deaths, would be very limited.

Ad Hoc Planning

Ad hoc strike planning could permit a small strategic nuclear strike to be tailored to fit any crisis situation. The time required for this planning is uncertain and would depend on the attack size. It might be possible to plan and execute a small attack (10-20 weapons) in 24 hours or less. However, as with selective release, we do not exercise our capabilities for ad hoc strike planning. Nor do we have provisions for interface between the President and planning staffs for the purposes of providing ad hoc responses. In fact, there are no staffs dedicated and trained for planning such strikes. (Note: The JCS representative notes that while the statement is true in respect to a dedicated staff, it is misleading since it is not clear that a "dedicated" staff would be necessary for these operations. In respect to training, selected individuals probably possess adequate training.

IV. SPECIAL ISSUES

Several outstanding issues should be discussed in some detail before considering the basic choices regarding US strategic policies. These include:
  --Support of allies;
  --Strategic stability;
  --Strategic flexible response;
  --Improved missile counterforce capabilities.

A. Support of Allies

(Note: The State Department believes the section on Support to Allies inadequately treats the subject. In particular, the political and psychological aspects of maintaining a credible deterrent are not fully considered, and all relevant alternatives (e.g. greater allied control over US nuclear forces, a European nuclear force) are not considered. Moreover, the ability of each of the general strategic (offense) alternatives to meet the objective of support to Allies is asserted rather than demonstrated.)

The US has stated on many occasions that it could and might use its strategic nuclear forces to support its Allies in the event of threats or attacks. (Note: The JCS representative notes that in the Final Decision on MC 14/3 the United States is committed, as a member of the NATO Alliance, to act jointly and maintain a credible capability to conduct a general nuclear response as the ultimate deterrent. MC 14/3 further specifies that should aggression occur, the Alliance should initiate the appropriate major response if the aggression were a major attack.) The implications of these statements can best be analyzed by asking:

--What are the nature and levels of the US strategic commitment?

--What contributions can strategic forces actually make?

--Under the current balance, how credible are our commitments to the Soviets and Allies?

This section will focus on support of our NATO Allies. A subsequent section on China will discuss our commitment to Allies vis-à-vis China.

1. The Nature and Level of the US Commitment

This study did not attempt to reassess US commitments. It did conclude that existing commitments vary widely in their specificity and in the degree of US vital interests involved.

2. The Contribution Which Strategic Forces Can Make

Strategic forces are part of a continuum of forces for ensuring the security of our Allies; our theater nuclear forces and conventional forces couple and extend our strategic nuclear commitment down to any level of aggression, coupling the loss at one level to the risk of escalation to another.

With regard to this continuum of US forces supporting the Allies:

--NSDM 95 established US conventional force policy in Europe and directed further study of tactical nuclear issues in Europe:

--NSSM 69 is studying the US conventional and tactical nuclear policy in Asia, as well as the strategic policy.

However, even when trying to focus only on strategic nuclear policy, we must note that the planning distinction between "strategic" and "theater" weapons is often overlooked in practice. On one hand, strategic forces might be employed for theater operations. For example, the President has recently approved commitment of Poseidon warheads for supporting the SACEUR strike plan thus continuing the support which had been provided by Polaris for several years. SACEUR's strike plan covers a wide area extending out to about 55 degrees east longitude. On the other hand, theater forces contribute to strategic planning. For example, US tactical nuclear forces in Asia directly support the SIOP against China; 32% of SIOP weapons planned against targets in China are by theater forces.

Table IV-1 summarizes our tactical nuclear stockpile and deployments by major weapon class. There are, in addition to those shown in the table, about 2500 tactical nuclear warheads and 1100 ASW/AAW nuclear warheads stockpiled in the United States. Table IV-2 shows the number of tactical offensive weapons which are available for delivery on the Soviet Union and China, given their current deployment.

Table IV-1

Tactical and ASW/AAW Nuclear Weapons Deployment Authorization
(End FY-72)

Type	Number Deployed in Theaters				
	Atlantic	Western Europe	Pacific	Afloat	Total
Tactical Offensive a/	0	6000	1600	1300	8900
Tactical Defensive b/	0	1200	200	0	1400
Fleet ASW and AAW	50	200	150	2200	2600
Total	50	7400	1950	3500	12,900

a/ Includes tactical bombs, surface-to-surface missiles, and artillery
b/ Includes atomic demolition munitions, air-to-air missiles, and surface-to-air missiles.

Table IV-2

Number of Offensive Tactical Nuclear Warheads Which
Could be Employed Outside of Battlefield Area
(End FY-72)

Type	Number Capable of Striking a/		
	Warsaw Pact Nations	USSR	China
Surface-to-Surface Missiles	600	0	0
Tactical Bombs	2600 b/	2600 b/	1700

a/ From current deployments.
b/ There are 2600 tactical nuclear bombs in Western Europe and afloat which could be delivered against either Warsaw Pact nations or the Soviet Union.

As for the contributions which strategic forces can make in strategic support of allies, there is sharp debate. Strategic forces in the SIOP are planned against targets threatening our allies. However, our present employment planning would use these strategic forces in the context of a large strike; we have very limited capabilities for a small strategic attack. (Note: The JCS representative believes that our capabilities for support of Allies should not be incredible and that a counterforce capability to support our commitments reinforces credibility.)

--Many question how helpful these capabilities are given the current balance. Presumably we would hesitate to launch a large strategic strike unless the Soviets had launched such a strike or were apparently on the verge of launching such a strike. Our capability to launch a limited strike is small at present and there is great uncertainty over the Soviet response to be expected. Those who question the present contribution of our strategic forces often argue for improvements in the capabilities of these forces. These improvements could include: increased flexibility, improvement in counterforce capabilities, and/or the ability to insure favorable relative outcomes. Such improvements and their implications are discussed in subsequent sections.

--Others say that the existence of sufficient strategic forces, such as we have now, deters Soviet use of strategic weapons. The Soviets would fear a large US response to any large attack by them and would be uncertain how the US would react to a more limited strategic attack against the Allies. Improvements in capabilities such as those suggested above and discussed in detail later, would not substantially increase the contributions of strategic forces, since they would not reduce the uncertainty of the Soviet responses. Moreover, such improvements might lower the threshold of strategic warfare.

--Others argue that it is not clear that procuring new or additional systems including defenses will in itself alleviate allied concern about the US nuclear guarantee which, in turn, is related to the broader issue of their concern about future US commitments to their security. While allies' questioning the commitment might in part be due to the changed strategic balance, it is also due to unilateral US political and economic moves as well as the growth of bilateral US and Soviet negotiations. Therefore, whether any General Strategic Alternatives will improve allied confidence in the US commitment and the credibility of the deterrent is unclear. There are also political and psychological factors which may not be addressed by force improvements or new deployments. Some believe it might require other, more far-reaching measures. For example, greater allied participation in planning, targeting or control of US nuclear forces might be considered, or we might encourage an independent allied nuclear force. Obviously, such measures would involve far-reaching changes in US policy and involve a series of considerations beyond the scope of this study. The key element is not the US telling our allies we can do this or that, but their "seeing" it can be done and participating in the process. Others believe that such measures would not be in the US interest.

3. The Credibility of Our Commitments

It is difficult to assess how credible our commitments are to ourselves, the Soviets, our Allies, and other countries. Confidence is often elusive, not directly tied to actual capabilities.

--Some feel that the recent Soviet buildup and the US reactions have whittled away at the confidence which many have in our commitment.

--Others feel that there is no evidence of any dangerous erosion of this confidence.

Even if the US were to plan and maintain fully sufficient capabilities supporting all functions judged necessary to meet our objectives, the Soviets could end up with a strategic posture which seemed to have "more" than the US. For instance, they could have more strategic delivery vehicles. Such a disparity in "visible" postures might affect perceptions of credibility.

If there is a serious problem of confidence in US commitments now or if one does develop, there are several alternatives for dealing with it;

--We could make the effort to educate and convince our Allies of our evaluation of sufficiency, and of the complexity of defining balance with numerous indices.

--We could choose a more ambitious policy on sufficiency based on building real military capabilities for a relative advantage.

--Between these two alternatives, if we observe a significant erosion of confidence, we might take military measures such as changes in deployment policies, operating procedures, or new procurement in order to restore an apparent imbalance in weapon inventories with the Soviets. We would do so at minimum cost to restore the strategic balance in terms of a political rather than a military requirement. Also arms control offers another alternative for maintaining political, visible balance of forces.

B. Strategic Stability

Strategic stability has two aspects: (1) Crisis stability and (2) the long-term balance of strategic arms between the United States and the USSR.

1. Crisis Stability

The term "crisis stability" refers to the degree to which both the United States and the Soviet Union would tend to avoid the use of nuclear weapons if facing one another in a deep political or military crisis.

The incentive which either side might have for use of nuclear weapons in a crisis is dependent on many factors, including how much they felt their vital interests threatened, their perceptions of the other side's capabilities, intent and resolve, assessments of risk and gain, the political and psychological factors prevailing during the crisis, the personality of the leaders involved, and their own military force characteristics.

This section focuses on the characteristics of US nuclear postures. Concerns can arise in many ways about how the US strategic posture decreases of increases Soviet incentive to strike first in a crisis. But a major crisis stability question which must be faced now—because of pending SALT and budget issues—relates to the possible future vulnerability of fixed land-based missiles. (Note: The JCS representative, however, believes that the Soviet Civil Defense Shelter Program is also a factor in crisis stability.)

There is general agreement that a principle contributor to stability in a crisis is a well-hedged retaliatory capability against urban/industrial targets. If each side has such a capability, there probably will be no assured advantage (in terms of absolute levels of U/I damage) to either side in preemption, since neither side could hope to greatly reduce its opponent's U/I retaliatory capability.

Analysis shows that, with current capabilities, neither the United States nor the Soviet Union can, by striking first, reduce by more than a few million the deaths or by a few percent the industrial damage they might expect in a general nuclear war. Both sides currently have sufficiently survivable and diverse strategic offensive forces that they can, either in a first strike or a second strike, almost totally destroy the urban population and industry of the other.

Also related to crisis stability is the relative balance of U/I damage after a general nuclear war. This question is treated in Annex C.

There is also general agreement that other factors besides a well-hedged U/I retaliatory capability have a bearing on stability in a crisis. There is not, however, a consensus regarding how and to what extent to change our current strategic force posture, if at all, in order to reduce (or avoid increasing) Soviet incentive to strike first in a crisis. Some changes which have been considered, however, include the following:

--Changes in the command and control system to improve some or all of the following: (1) Presidential survivability in a crisis; (2) continued and positive NCA control of US forces; (3) NCA knowledge of the status of US forces; and (4) NCA knowledge of the damage caused by US conventional and nuclear military actions during a crisis or the early phases of a slowly escalating nuclear exchange.
--Greater flexibility in the employment of nuclear forces.
--Greater attention being given to the positive or negative contribution of US tactical nuclear weapons (especially their survivability and forward deployment) to stability in a crisis.
--Provision for rapid communications between the governments of the United States and Soviet Union during a crisis. We and the Soviets have recently signed agreements which lay out procedures in the event of nuclear accidents and which will result in improvements to the US-USSR direct communications link.

Many of these factors and their relation to crisis stability are discussed below in connection with general strategic alternatives. An issue which is, however, relatively independent of the general strategic alternatives is that of a vulnerable force component. <u>There is wide disagreement about the value of insuring that no US strategic offensive force components becomes very vulnerable to a Soviet first strike.</u>

Some argue that a substantial decrease in survivability of a force component could be destabilizing in a crisis by making it easier for Soviet leaders to perceive—rightly or wrongly—an advantage to striking first in a crisis if they believed war was imminent. Attack on a vulnerable Minuteman force is the most common example, although SSBNs, bombers, or strategic C3 and surveillance targets have also been suggested. The Minuteman example is of particular importance because, if large threats to Minuteman develop, the currently envisaged means of maintaining Minuteman survivability (i.e., active defense or a land-mobile ICBM program) could be precluded by SALT agreement, by fiscal restraints, or by Congressional refusal to fund such programs.

On the question of whether an excessively vulnerable Minuteman force would unacceptably degrade crisis stability, there are two views:

One view is that this question must be answered affirmatively and we must keep Minuteman survivable or phase it out (or at least reduce it to a lower level, say less than 100-200). Proponents of this view argue as follows:

--If the United States allowed Minuteman to become vulnerable to a Soviet strike which could destroy perhaps 900 or more Minuteman launchers, the Soviets would probably be convinced that we intended Minuteman primarily for first-strike counterforce attacks, particularly in view of the public emphasis we have placed on survivable forces.

--During an intense crisis, our primary leverage on the Soviet Union is the implied threat of military action to preserve our vital interests. Resolute US actions in a crisis would of necessity cause the Soviets to consider nuclear war to be more likely and could lead them to believe we were about to launch Minuteman. In such a situation, the Soviets might decide that their only alternative short of general nuclear war would be to launch an attack on Minuteman, seek to forestall retaliation by threatening to attack US cities, and negotiate with the United States.

--The feasibility of a strike on Minuteman and the credibility of their threat to US cities would be considerably increased if they could do so with only part of their ICBM force (possible in the mid-to-late 1970s) or if they could quickly reload their ICBM launchers. (Note: Regarding the present Soviet reload capability, the intelligence community estimates that each of the soft SS-7 and SS-8 launchers has a capability to launch a refire missile 2 to 4 hours after the initial launch. Silo launchers currently deployed do not have a refire capability.)

In summary, proponents of this view assert that an excessively vulnerable Minuteman force could be destabilizing in a crisis, even if we had strong bomber and SLBM forces, because the threat to our cities might deter us from using these forces after an attack on Minuteman. At the very least, they argue, the President's options for diplomatic and military actions in a crisis would be more constrained if Minuteman were vulnerable, in order to avoid any suggestion that we intended to launch Minuteman in a first strike.

Another view of crisis stability is that a vulnerable Minuteman force is not destabilizing so long as we can insure that the Soviets would not perceive substantial gains in lives, industry or military targets saved by striking first, rather than second. Proponents of this view argue as follows:

--The President's options in a crisis would not be limited by the existence of a vulnerable Minuteman force. In a crisis both sides would take action to avoid false interpretations of first strike intent, whether or not ICBMs were vulnerable. The overall evaluation shows that any constraint on Presidential options is only a small element in the many factors that condition crisis stability.

--The above concern about the destabilizing effects of a vulnerable Minuteman force rests on the premise that Soviet objectives in a crisis would warrant their risking over 100 million lives and almost all their industrial capability. Save for totally reckless actions by the United States in making direct threats to the Soviet homeland, proponents of the second view do not believe the Soviets would have such objectives.

--The Soviets realize that the survivable Minuteman force was designed for a second-strike capability. Reduction in Minuteman survivability because of Soviet force improvements would not necessarily convince the Soviets that this would cause the US to shift from a second-strike to a first-strike policy.

--Arguing the plausibility of a Soviet attack on Minuteman assumes that the nuclear war follows a "start-stop" scenario, which depends on the Soviet ability to deter US nuclear attacks after the initial Soviet strike. But, the Soviets would assess the risk of a US bomber and SLBM counter-strike after a nuclear attack on Minuteman as extremely high.

--A Soviet planner preparing for a first-strike on Minuteman would have to consider the possibility of a US launch on warning.

Because of the extreme consequences of such a counter-strike on the USSR, the Soviets would have to seriously weigh their possible gains and losses if the nuclear war continued after their initial strike. (Note: The JCS representative notes that this presupposes that the Soviets calculate the results of simulated nuclear exchanges using US-type analytical models in the same manner as US analysts. This assumption may not be correct.) Recent analyses for SALT show that Soviet fatalities could be reduced by at most 30 million from a fatality level of 140 million, and save at most 30% of their soft military targets if they destroyed 900 Minuteman. Hence, it is argued, Soviet attacks on Minuteman in a crisis are unlikely, provided we maintain high survivability in alert bombers and SLBMs.

--In assessing the risk of attacks on Minuteman, the Soviets would have to take into account the expected number of US deaths from fallout. Depending on the time of year, the prevailing weather, and the size of the Soviet attacks, fallout deaths could vary from as low as 2 million to as high as 40 million over a six-week period. Moreover, the Soviets would have to take into account the operational uncertainties of attacking Minuteman (greater-than-expected collateral deaths, less-than-expected damage to Minuteman, and launch-on-warning), and the retaliatory capability of even a hundred surviving Minuteman missiles which could destroy up to 15% of the Soviet population with zero or NCA ABM.

--If Minuteman is phased out or reduced to low levels, crisis stability could be reduced because the Soviet problem of simultaneously attacking US bombers and land-based ICBMs would be eliminated. Thus, it is argued, the Soviet incentive to strike the bombers would be increased.

--The Soviets could gain little military advantage in a strike on Minuteman. At best, they would be trading part or all of their ICBMs for ours. With the capabilities inherent in our bomber and SLBM forces (especially as these forces would be fully generated in a crisis) for attacking U/I and soft military targets, attacking Minuteman would reduce our capability to attack their ICBMs.

Judgment is required to determine which view to emphasize as a guide for strategic force planning and for resolving SALT issues. In particular, judgment must be exercised on the following points (Note: the JCS representative believes that an immediate issue is how much to invest for protection of sunk costs in our present systems over the next 8-10 years):

--The degree to which the danger of Soviet miscalculation of US intentions and strategic force capabilities might be increased if we had a large force of vulnerable Minuteman launchers;

--The extent to which the President's options in a crisis might be constrained if we had a large force of vulnerable Minuteman launchers.

--The plausibility that any objective other than protection of their homeland could cause the Soviets to make a large attack on even a vulnerable Minuteman force and to accept the risks that general nuclear war might result.

2. Long-Term Strategic Stability

Other sections will consider in detail the possible impact of specific policies and programs on the long-term strategic stability between US and the Soviet Union. There is, however, an underlying uncertainty about Soviet goals which affects evaluation of this impact. A major difficulty in assessing Soviet goals involves, of course, fundamental differences in strategic views. Moreover, our perceptions are inevitably distorted since the application of a US analogue (our basic approach) is only partially appropriate at best.

Our perceptions of Soviet goals are especially uncertain at this time. The Soviets demonstrate an apparently serious interest in achieving a SALT agreement and other forms of improved relations with the United States and its allies. On the other hand, there is clear evidence of a continued Soviet arms buildup—e.g., new ICBM development, the deployment of new silos and Y-class SSBNs (there are currently 25 Y-class SSBNs operational and 16 under construction), the development of a new strategic bomber, and a very active ABM R&D program. Such ambiguity leads to a variety of views about Soviet goals and perceptions of the strategic balance. A range of views is presented below (Note: It should be noted that these views are overly simplistic. In fact, motivations are probably more complex and interrelated than suggested):

--The Soviets are driving hard for strategic superiority and will be influenced only by a US show of strength. In this view, the United States should not be concerned about stimulating Soviet weapon deployments. Rather, these deployments will continue independently of US programs and US efforts at moderation will only be viewed by the Soviets as signs of weakness and further encourage them to continue to deploy strategic arms.

--The Soviets are striving to achieve nuclear parity with the United States. They are seeking a stable strategic balance and want to avoid needless expenditures on strategic arms, but their perceptions as to what constitutes a stable balance are different than ours. In this view, negotiations and dialogue with the Soviets are particularly important in order to bring the views of both sides closer together. US sensitivity to the effect of our strategic programs on Soviet weapon developments and deployments, as well as on the diplomatic positions of the Soviet government, should be a major factor in our planning.

--The Soviet government is split into at least two major factions, those advocating strategic superiority and those seeking long-term stability in the strategic balance. In this view, the anomalies we see in the Soviet strategic arms policies are caused by conflict and compromise between these two factions. This would imply that US strategic programs and discussions in SALT should be structured so as to reinforce those in the Soviet government who are seeking strategic stability, but also so as to hedge against the advocates of superiority achieving the upper hand.

C. Strategic Flexible Response Options

The earlier review of current US nuclear weapon employment plans found that:

--These plans consist primarily of preplanned nuclear strike options which provide for large attacks against various Soviet and Chinese military targets, as well as options for large urban/industrial strikes. A notable example is that the smallest preplanned SIOP option which can be ordered against the territory of the Soviet Union involves about 2500 weapons.

--We currently have some capability for rapid selective release of SIOP weapons and for planning small ad hoc strikes within a day or so, but these capabilities are not systematically directed or exercised toward providing limited and flexible strategic nuclear strike options.

--These plans do not provide options appropriate to all situations that the President might want to be prepared to deal with.

Greater flexibility in the employment of strategic nuclear weapons would entail planning and organizational changes to provide options for smaller strikes than currently in the SIOP and for selection of weapon-target combinations suitable for both the political and the military situations in which they might be used. Improvements in command and control or in counterforce capability might also be entailed, but increased strategic flexibility could be attained without necessarily increasing the number of US strategic forces.

1. Purposes of Strategic Flexible Response

There are at least three circumstances in which limited nuclear strikes might be an effective US action:

First, the Soviets do not understand what constitutes vital US interests and take hostile actions in the belief that we will not resort to the use of nuclear weapons.

Second, they do correctly understand what constitutes vital US interests, but (possibly misreading our resolve) seek to coerce us by posing unacceptable choices designed to drive the United States to acceptance of Soviet demands.

Third, through Soviet design, Soviet miscalculations, or failures in US diplomacy, the credibility of the US deterrent is called into serious question.

Any of these circumstances might or might not include the first and limited use of nuclear weapons by the Soviet Union.

There are three major purposes for US strategic flexible response options; deterrence, early war termination, and demonstration of resolve to our allies.

--<u>Deterrence</u>. One purpose for a known capability for limited and flexible strategic nuclear option would be to reinforce US deterrent by providing suitable responses to a Soviet threat or attack on a limited set of US targets. It could also help deter Soviet nuclear or conventional attacks on US allies by increasing Soviet uncertainty about US responses. These aspects of a flexible response capability suggest primarily US second use of strategic nuclear weapons, although the implied threat of US first use in response to tactical nuclear or conventional attacks on our allies is an element of deterrence.

--<u>Early War Termination</u>. In our analysis, we found it difficult to identify credible scenarios for deliberate Soviet nuclear attacks, although this does not completely rule out such threats. We did identify circumstances of miscalculation which could lead to such attacks. In such cases, a combination of limited US strategic nuclear strikes (showing at the same time restraint and resolve) and diplomatic initiatives might bring an early termination to a nuclear conflict without sacrificing vital US interests. The threatened or actual use of limited strategic strikes could also assist in halting tactical nuclear or large conventional attacks on US allied forces, although this could involve US first use of nuclear weapons.

--<u>Demonstration of Resolve to Allies</u>. The NATO Allies, in particular, favor a strong coupling between their forces and the US strategic force. They reason that if even a small-scale conflict could be rapidly escalated to a general nuclear war, then the Soviets would be deterred from initiating even smaller-scale aggression. A US flexible response option might demonstrate to our Allies our resolve not to permit the Soviets to decouple US strategic forces from allied forces.

To be consistent with these purposes, a strategic flexible response capability could have some or all of the following elements to varying degrees, depending on the improvements in command and control deemed appropriate:

--Provisions for a high degree of interaction between the President and military commanders in selecting specific attack options and in attack timing.

--The ability to control Soviet deaths to within desired margins.

--Avoidance of attacks which would reduce or destroy the control of Soviet political leaders over their strategic forces.

--Continued positive Presidential control over US nuclear forces throughout a series of limited nuclear exchanges, including the provision of appropriate information to the President concerning the status of US forces and the results of US and Soviet strikes.

<u>a. Weakening of the US Deterrent</u>

--Some argue there is a risk that a US flexible response posture could weaken the deterrence of conventional and nuclear attacks on NATO and other US allies and of limited strategic attacks against the US. The risk, in effect, is that the Soviets would interpret a US flexible response posture as an "admission" that we would not respond to Soviet attacks on our allies with large nuclear strikes on either urban or military targets and thus broaden the range of hostile actions the Soviets believed they could get by with.

--Supporters of flexible response options argue to the contrary, stating that our extended deterrent is less credible unless we have the capability for any level of response in a spectrum varying from conventional defense to general nuclear war. They point out that strategic flexible responses would fill a gap which currently exists in this spectrum. Moreover, these options in no way decrease the US U/I retaliatory capability and, hence would not reduce the risks the Soviets would face in an escalating crisis with the United States.

<u>b. Increased Pressure for Use of Nuclear Weapons</u>

--Some assert that the existence of a systematically planned and institutionalized capability for limited strategic nuclear strikes would make it more "tempting" to exercise that capability in a crisis which might otherwise be satisfactorily resolved without resort to nuclear weapons. Staffs and other personnel involved in planning for the limited use of nuclear weapons could constitute a persuasive group of advocates for their use during a crisis. Moreover, the existence of a group of people psychologically conditioned to the limited use of nuclear weapons in a deep crisis will always exist and that systematic provisions for development and review of limited nuclear strike options in such a crisis will enhance the President's capability to evaluate the utility of employing nuclear weapons. Moreover, they assert that careful attention to the details of institutionalizing a flexible response capability and to the selection of staff personnel can mitigate the risk of creating an independent pressure group.

2. Issues

The following major policy issues were identified in this study and are evaluated below:

--Should we have greater flexibility for employment of strategic nuclear weapons in unlimited numbers?

--Should there be command and control improvements to support flexible nuclear strike options?

--Should there be improvements in US missile counterforce capability to support flexible nuclear strike options? This question will be discussed in conjunction with other counterforce issues.

3. Should We have Greater Flexibility for Employment of Strategic Nuclear Weapons?

Although one can visualize circumstances in which limited US strategic strikes could help halt an escalating conflict with the USSR, it is difficult to devise credible scenarios leading to these circumstances. On the other hand, many major crises and conflicts have occurred under conditions which were not foreseen in advance (e.g., the Pearl Harbor attack and the Cuban missile crisis).

Some assert that we should have more flexibility for employment of strategic nuclear weapons than provided by current plans, even though the precise circumstances for use of flexible response cannot be predicted in advance. They emphasize the potentially severe consequences of being faced with a choice between general nuclear war and backing down in a deep crisis with the Soviet Union, because our war plans could not provide appropriate strike options in a timely manner. They also emphasize the escalatory risks inherent in selective release or ad hoc strike planning if the use of limited nuclear strikes has not been carefully planned in advance.

Others point to the low likelihood of ever having to use flexible response options and emphasize the risks associated with a strategic flexible response posture. There are three types of risk:

c. <u>Unwanted Escalation</u>. Probably the most serious risk associated with the limited use of nuclear weapons during a crisis is that it could trigger uncontrolled escalation to general nuclear war. Although this relates to the use of flexible response options, it is also relevant to the issue of <u>whether to have such options</u>, since it bears on their utility in a crisis.

Soviet doctrine regarding the use of nuclear weapons is one critical factor in assessing this risk. The evidence is limited and ambiguous.

The Soviets have long maintained that a US-USSR military conflict would rapidly escalate to general nuclear war, even if it began conventionally. Soviet military theorists appear to be nearly unanimous in their belief that a limited conflict is both unlikely and inherently unstable. Moreover, there is no reliable evidence whether the Soviets plan for limited nuclear strikes (although they have the capabilities for such attacks.)

On the other hand, the Soviet political leaders are not bound to follow the doctrine of military theorists. At SALT, the Soviets have indicated that they place a high premium on being able to communicate with US leaders during crises (e.g., accidental launches or provocative attack by a third country), with the putative aim of precluding general nuclear war. Moreover, some argue that achievement of strategic equality may cause the Soviets to rethink their attitudes toward limited nuclear exchanges. But there is no evidence of a recent shift in Soviet views regarding the instability of limited nuclear war.

Thus, if the United States were the first to use nuclear weapons in limited strikes, there is no sound way, based on currently available intelligence, to predict the Soviet response, which could be to negotiate, to launch limited nuclear strikes, or to escalate to large nuclear attacks.

If US limited nuclear strikes were made in response to Soviet limited nuclear strikes, we would still only know that the Soviets were willing to launch an initial nuclear strike; their next step would still be uncertain. However, the risks to the US of initiating a limited first-strike as compared to responding to a Soviet first strike seem substantially different. If we observe a limited Soviet strike, there is a strong presumption that they are willing to play the flexible response game, i.e., to keep the conflict limited. For a US first strike, we have no idea whether the Soviets would even try to keep their response limited in nature.

This analysis carries two implications regarding the utility of increased strategic nuclear flexibility:

--The United States should consider execution of flexible response options (particularly the first use of such options) only if faced with a challenge to vital national interests and only if the consequences of other alternatives make acceptable the risk of escalation to general nuclear war.

--If the United States executed a limited strategic strike, every precaution should be taken to reduce the likelihood of unwanted escalation, including appropriate use of diplomatic channels and public announcements, direct communications with Soviet leaders via the hot-line and strict avoidance of attacks which would lessen the control of Soviet leaders over their nuclear forces.

4. Command and Control

Some argue that improvements in command and control would be needed in order to effectively provide greater flexibility in the employment of US strategic forces. Some or all of the following improvements might be necessary.

--Provision of a survivable command post from which the President could direct flexible nuclear operations during a crisis. Options include ABM defense of NCA, and Advanced Airborne Command Post (AABNCP) with capabilities for directing and monitoring flexible strategic responses, air defense of the NCA against air-supported threats including cruise-missile and low-altitude bomber attacks, and the construction of a Deep Underground Command Center (DUCC) to withstand several large-yield nuclear bursts.

--Plans could be made for placing a designated successor in a survivable command post during a crisis.

--Improvements in the survivability and resolution of the early warning satellite system to assure prompt accurate assessment of attacks on the United States throughout a series of limited nuclear exchanges and to improve our capability for assessing the results of US strikes. Survivability improvements could include redundant satellite coverage, spare satellites, decoy satellites, and satellite relay of downlink data and survivable readout antennas. The current system requires readout antennas which are too large to allow airborne readout.

--Improvements in the survivability of communications links, e.g., through deployment of military communications satellites, possibly including silent spares and decoys.

--Provision of a rapid retargeting capability for Minuteman to improve ad hoc strike planning capacity. Minuteman II can now be preprogrammed with up to eight targets and the Minuteman III MIRVs can now be preprogrammed with up to three sets of targets. Currently, however, under current policy about half of these preprogrammed target slots are reserved for implementing new SIOP revisions and would not be available for retargeting during a crisis or after an attack. Additional retargeting requires 24-35 hours. New retargeting hardware (Command Data Buffer) could reduce this to about one hour for each additional missile in a flight of ten, assuming the target data was available at the Launch Control Center. (Note: The JCS representative notes that new retargeting improvements (Command Data Buffer) would reduce this time to about five minutes for the new improved computer unit and one hour for the D-37 computer unit. Concurrent retargeting allows a full wing (150 missiles) to be retargeted in two hours with the improved computer and fifteen hours with the D-37 computer.) Command Data Buffer does not now contain provisions for retargeting Minuteman from airborne control centers (this would cost about $100 million). Polaris and Poseidon SLBMs can now be retargeted within 15 minutes after receipt of orders to do so, although there is a question whether the orders can be communicated quickly and reliably in all circumstances to submarines, using current systems. However, Sanguine could order specific pre-planned options already stored on board the SSBNs. Additionally, it could complement a survivable satellite system by selectively calling specific SSBNs to the near surface for brief real time communications via satellite for such options as battle management or ad hoc retargeting. There is a question as to whether we would want direct, 2-way communications with SSBNs and require acknowledgement of instructions in view of the possible increased vulnerability.

Detailed trade-off studies have not been performed which would permit selection of specific command and control improvements to support flexible responses. The considerations set forth here show a range of improvements (and their costs) and are intended only to support decisions on broad planning guidance.

Table IV-3 summarizes current estimates of costs and lead times of possible command and control improvements for flexible response: this table also shows the current status of these programs. Depending on the extent of the command and control improvements, there would result an increased TOA of as much as $3-4 billion in FY 73-77 over the current program. Our current command and control program has a TOA of about $3 billion in FY 73-77, which includes about $1 billion for some of the improvements in table IV-3. In addition, the current FYDP provides funds for the 12-site Safeguard program which includes defense of the NCA.

There are three broad approaches we could take with regard to survivability of command and control systems for flexible responses, no improvements, modest improvements, and a concerted survivability program. The basic judgment which must be made is whether we should rely on Soviet and third country restraint from attacking our command and control.

--<u>No improvements</u> beyond those needed for a well-hedged U/I retaliatory posture. Such a posture might require some of the improvements described in detail above. This issue is also being studied in the NSSM-126 study. This would be the least-cost approach and its effectiveness would depend on Soviet restraint from attacking command and control targets during a crisis. On the other hand, even granting Soviet restraint, our flexible response capability could be reduced or lost through accidental or unauthorized Soviet attacks or through third country attacks.

--<u>Modest survivability improvements</u>. Critical fixed command posts, surveillance systems, and communications systems could be made sufficiently survivable that several weapons would be needed to destroy each target. These measures would reduce the likelihood of destruction of vital command and control systems by accidental, unauthorized, or provocative attacks. Survivability of these systems against deliberate Soviet and Chinese attacks could not be assured.

--<u>Concerted survivability program</u>. A vigorous and concerted R&D program to explore all feasible technical approaches to improving command and control survivability could provide assurance of survivability against all Chinese attacks and against a range of Soviet attacks short of general nuclear war. This program would, however, entail substantial and currently ill-defined costs and would have high technical risk of not achieving all of its objectives.

As for post-strike damage assessment, current and programmed surveillance and intelligence systems can provide rough, indirect indicators of success or failure of limited nuclear strikes within minutes of the planned strike times. But direct and more accurate assessment of damage can only be provided within one to two days of the strike and even then some areas of the Soviet Union could not be covered. Programmed systems which are planned to be operational by the mid-1970s could reduce this time to less than a day under favorable conditions. Further reduction in damage assessment time could not be provided until late in the 1970s and would entail a development program costing several hundred million dollars.

Our current and programmed intelligence systems, including data readout and processing facilities, are designed for peacetime operations and are not survivable. Measures to provide high survivability to these systems have not been carefully studied with respect to flexible response requirements, but would probably involve very costly programs with large technical risk. Relatively low cost measures to increase the effort required to neutralize these systems probably could be developed.

--Some argue that Soviet uncertainty about the function of various systems and their role in US command and control would reduce the likelihood of their being attacked in limited exchanges. They further assert that precise, rapid, and direct assessment of the results of US limited strikes is not essential for the conduct of limited nuclear war and that the large number of diverse US intelligence systems (current and programmed) can provide adequate information to support the President in such a crisis.

Table IV-3

Costs, Leadtimes and Status of Possible C3 Improvements for Flexible Responses

			Cost ($ Millions)		
	IOC a/	FOC a/	FY 73-77	FY 73-82 Cost	Program Status
C3 Survivability Improvements					
Advanced Airborne Command Post (AABNCP)	1975	1976	540	700	AABNCP development funded in the FY 73 Budget.
Deep Underground Command Center (DUCC)	1975	1975	400	500	No program
ABM Defense of NCA	1979	? b/	2700	3600	Current Safeguard program would need redirection.
Survivability improvements to the early warning satellite system	Mid 1970s		330	600	No program.
FL. .COM (Navy Communications llite)	1975	1975	300	400	Production decision Pending. 6 additional A/C required but not currently approved
TACAMO IV (AVLF)	1972	1975	96	96	
Survivable Communications Satellite	1978	1978	200	350	Exploratory development
Sanguine ELF Com. System	1971	1982	190	470	Eng. Dev. decision pending. Add. 10 M required in FY 73.
Minuteman Retargeting					
Command Data Buffer (MCIII)	1973	1975	250	300	In Engineering development. Production funds included in FY 73 Budget
Post-Strike Damage Assessment					
Greater Survivability for Existing Systems	Mid 1970s		300	800	No program.
Development of New System with Greater Survivability and Responsiveness	Late 1970s		1200	1800	No program.

a/ Assumes FY 73 deployment decision.
b/ The inability to relate to an FOC is caused by the fact that the configuration for the NCA is unknown.

238 *Massive Retaliation*

--Others argue that the concept of a series of limited nuclear exchanges punctuated by negotiations and dialogue, requires that the President be fully apprised of the results of previous US strikes and of any information which might indicate Soviet intentions for subsequent actions. Intelligence systems for post-strike damage assessment could be prime targets for Soviet limited strikes, because destruction of these systems would not create the escalatory pressures that attacks on US early warning sensors would cause. At the minimum, R&D programs to improve the survivability of systems for post-strike damage assessments should be pursued.

D. Improved Missile Counterforce Capabilities

US ballistic missiles currently have a <u>limited</u> capability to destroy hardened targets, as is shown in Table IV-4. Existing Poseidon has virtually no counterforce capability, MMII and Minuteman III only a limited hard target counterforce capability. However, currently planned improvements for Minuteman III will provide a marginal hard target counterforce capability which could be made a significant capability either by the addition of a new RV or a new guidance system or both. Current improvements planned for Poseidon will not provide it with any credible counterforce capability but a new warhead plus SIG would provide a very credible capability. Note that, by using more than one warhead per target, the US does have some counterforce capability. For example, four Minuteman II warheads have an 80% chance of destroying an SS-9 silo. Phrased another way, 500 Minuteman III missiles (with 3 RVs each) could destroy 250 out of the 288 SS-9 silos with probability 0.8 .

Minuteman I or Polaris, not included in the table, have essentially no hard-target counterforce capability.

We can expect some improvement in missile accuracy without new programs, simply through quality improvements in such guidance components as gyroscopes and accelerometers. These are reflected in the table. For example, Minuteman II might improve sufficiently so that only two warheads are needed for an 80% chance of destroying an SS-9 silo.

It should be noted that current Soviet estimates of Minuteman III as reported in the open press are 0.20 MT yield and 400 meter CEP (0.22 nm). A Soviet view of Minuteman III for the late 1970's would probably estimate 0.4-0.5 MT yield, three RVs per missile, and a 200 meter CEP (0.11 nm).

TABLE IV-4 [1]

Number of Inventory U.S. RV's Required for a Minimum .8 Damage Expectancy [2]

		AVE Whds Carr	CEP [3]	(MT) Yield	WSR [3]	TARGET HARDNESS (psi) 300	600	900
A.	Current U.S. Weapons							
	MINUTEMAN II	1.0	.43	1.20	.85	3	5	6
	MINUTEMAN III	2.5	.25	.17	.71	5	7	9
	POSEIDON	10.0	.28	.04	.80	4/	4/	4/
B.	Currently Planned Component Improvement Programs							
	MINUTEMAN III	2.5	.13	.17	.71	2	3	3
	POSEIDON	10.0	.25	.04	.80	9	4/	4/
	New Guidance Improvements Not Presently Programmed and New RV's							
	MINUTEMAN III							
	Only new Guidance	2.5	.10	.17	.71	2	2	3
	Only new RV	2.2	.13	.50	.71	2	2	2
	New Guidance & RV	2.2	.10	.50	.71	2	2	2
	POSEIDON							
	Only New Guidance	10	.12	.04	.80	3	4	5
	New Guidance & RV	10	.12	.06	.80	3	4	4

[1] Second revision to DDR&E data.
[2] Computations were produced using the DIA Blast Damage Computer (PBC-8).
[3] Based on SIOP planning factors.
[4] Greater than 10 RV's required.

Also shown in the table are the improvements in counterforce capability which would result from the following new development programs, none of which are currently being funded:

--Improved Minuteman III accuracy through development and deployment of an inertial measurement unit system and other guidance improvements, at a ten-year cost of $400 million and with an IOC in FY 77.

--Development and deployment of a new, large-yield warhead for Minuteman III (0.35-0.5 MT), at ten-year cost of $750 million and with an IOC in FY 77.

--Improved Poseidon accuracy through development and deployment of stellar inertial guidance, at a ten-year cost of $310 million and with an IOC in FY 76.

--Development and deployment of a new warhead for Poseidon, i.e., either 10 RVs at 70 to 100 KT or 3 RVs at .5 MT, each with ten year costs of $600 million and an IOC in FY 77.

There are strategic counterforce roles for other US forces: bombers and ASW forces.

Bombers, provided they penetrate to their targets, have high accuracy and can carry large yield gravity bombs, giving them an excellent capability to destroy hardened targets. There is, however, disagreement about their utility against time-urgent targets such as missile launchers, because of their long time of flight to such targets after penetrating early warning.

--Some believe the combination of a missile and bomber attack on hard silos would be effective. The missile attack would arrive first to disable the silo for long enough to permit bombers to arrive and destroy the silo.

--Others believe that a combined missile-bomber attack on silos makes little sense and that bombers have little utility against time-urgent targets. They argue that if missile attack cannot destroy the silo, then it will provide only low confidence of keeping the silo disabled until the bombers arrive. If the missile attack has high probability of destroying the silo, then it would be more efficient to use the bombers on other targets.

--Still others believe that bombers could be used in limited strategic strikes on missile silos, arguing that the Soviets probably would not launch their missiles if the attack were small, because of the threat of US retaliation with a large U/I strike.

With current technology, ASW forces have little prospect of limiting damage to US cities from SLBM attacks and attempts to do so would be very costly (perhaps $1-2 billion per year over the next five years). Some believe, however, that R&D should be funded to seek technological improvements in strategic ASW, rather than assuming the task is impractical.

There is, however, a counterforce role for current ASW forces in disrupting and degrading the Soviet potential for SLBM attacks on our bomber force. By harassing and attacking Soviet SSBNs near our shores during a crisis (nuclear weapons need not be used in such attacks), ASW forces could provide extra time for escape of alert bombers on warning of an SLBM launch. By knowing the approximate position of enemy SSBN, SAC forces could significantly reduce their vulnerability by increasing alert posture or temporarily dispersing alert aircraft.

1. Issues

The fundamental policy issue to be decided is whether programs should be undertaken to make major improvements in the accuracy or yield of US ballistic missiles.

There are three purposes for which an improved counterforce capability could be sought:

--To provide disarming strike options against the PRC throughout the 1970s;

--To provide options for limited missile strikes on hard military targets;

--To help insure a favorable US advantage in war outcome. Evaluation of the feasibility and utility of a disarming strike option against China in the 1970s depends on many factors, including the possibility of concealment of Chinese missile sites, Chinese development of a launch-on-warning capability, and Chinese deployment of ballistic missile submarines. These factors are discussed in Section V-D which deals with the US strategic posture vis-à-vis the PRC.

2. Improved Missile Counterforce Capabilities for Strategic Flexible Responses

The key judgment regarding improved missile counterforce capability for strategic flexible response options is whether the benefits of such options outweigh the possible adverse effects this capability might have on the long-term stability of the strategic balance.

Arguments supporting missile counterforce improvements for flexible response include the following:

--Unless we have such options as part of our flexible responses, we may not be able to effectively deal with all of the crisis situations which we could face. Our present and expected hard-target kill capabilities are not adequate for efficient responses in kind to Soviet attacks on US ICBM launchers. Supporters of improved missile counterforce capability argue that an essential leverage in limited war is military leverage; the most significant military leverage in strategic war is counterforce, even limited counterforce.

--Improved US counterforce would enhance allied confidence in our nuclear shield.

--As for crisis situations, we could limit the extent of our deployments of counterforce improvements in an effort to allay Soviet concerns about an effective damage-limiting strike. Alternatively, we would have such a retaliatory capability that the Soviets would recognize that a first-strike by them would have little benefit.

--US counterforce improvements within the limits of some SALT agreements would not be destabilizing. A SALT agreement could effectively constrain Soviet arms levels even if they felt a need to react to US counterforce improvements.

--An ability to respond "in kind" to any attack is an essential element of deterrence and war termination.

Arguments against an improved counterforce capability for flexible response include the following:

--The analysis for this study has been unable to identify scenarios in which a flexible response capability to strike hardened military targets would have clear utility for deterrence or for early war termination.

--We already have and, through expected quality improvements, will increase a limited counterforce capability. Thus, there is no need for an additional counterforce improvement program.

--Heightened Soviet perceptions of a strong US counterforce capability could be destabilizing in a crisis, particularly a crisis in which limited nuclear exchanges had already occurred and could lead to unwanted Soviet escalation. It is unlikely that we could convince the Soviets that our missile improvements were for use only in limited strikes.

--Our Allies have long known that a counterforce strike would have little damage limiting benefit for them. They are more concerned with establishing the coupling of US strategic forces to their defense. This can be demonstrated with other options.

--We do not need a capability to respond exactly in kind to deter or counter Soviet attacks on our ICBMs. Appropriate responses, such as attacks on their bomber bases, submarine ports, and/or roll-up of their defenses may offset any Soviet perception of altering the strategic balance by such an attack.

--Programs to improve US counterforce capabilities could convey to the Soviets the signal that we are seeking a disarming strike capability against them. This, in turn, could work counter to our diplomatic efforts with the Soviets, including SALT. Moreover, it could strengthen the hand of those in the Soviet government advocating increased strategic armaments and could stimulate further Soviet deployment of strategic weapons.

3. Improved Counterforce Capabilities for Relative Advantage in War Outcome

Some maintain that improved counterforce capability is an essential element of the US deterrent and warfighting posture. They argue as follows:

--The relative post-war military position is a critical factor which affects the decisions of a government contemplating aggression or the threat of aggression. This implies that our deterrent must include a sufficient counterforce capability to secure relative advantage in surviving military forces after a nuclear war, or, at the minimum, to deny the Soviets the certainty of a favorable balance.

--Our current posture, even though it now provides extensive targeting of soft military installations, may not do so in the future as the Soviet and Chinese threats to our forces grow. Moreover, it will not necessarily provide forces optimized for efficient use against soft military targets, particularly the command and control needed for such attacks.

--The current emphasis on a well-hedged U/I capability has precluded imaginative R&D programs on counterforce options such as strategic ASW, order-of-magnitude accuracy improvements, and battle management systems which could render Soviet countermeasures ineffective. Without accomplishing such programs, we cannot conclude that efforts to improve our counterforce capability will be fruitless.

--The threat of a US damage-limiting strike on Soviet forces should have little destabilizing effect during a crisis since the Soviets would recognize that a preemptive nuclear attack on the US would still leave them in an unfavorable military position.

--In the long run this posture will achieve the most stable strategic balance. The Soviets cannot hope to match the US because of US economic and technological superiority. The US can therefore maintain a strategic force which will guarantee relative favorable outcomes if it announces such a policy and consistently takes action to maintain it.

Others assert that increased counterforce capability will add little to the US deterrent or to an effective nuclear warfighting capability, but will have an adverse effect on the stability of the long-term strategic balance. They make the following arguments:

--At the level of destruction which would result from general nuclear war, achieving a favorable relative advantage in surviving military capability is a meaningless goal. Such considerations of advantage are unlikely to affect a political decision to start a war, once levels of destruction are incommensurate with any possible objectives.

--A well-hedged U/I retaliatory capability provides (and will almost certainly continue to provide) an extensive capability to destroy soft military targets, some capability to destroy time-urgent hardened targets, and extensive capability, with bombers, to destroy hardened non-time-urgent targets. This will support our allies by providing for effective attacks on all Soviet installations except hardened missile launchers.

--Efforts to achieve an increased counterforce capability against hardened Soviet missile launchers will not be effective if the Soviets take offsetting measures which are readily available to them. These include further hardening, proliferation of SLBMs, deployment of land-mobile ICBMs, dispersal and increased alert for bombers, and possibly, launch-on-warning of attack.

Increased US counterforce capability would create uncertainty in the minds of the Soviet leaders about the ability of their forces to ride out a US attack and would increase their incentive to adopt less stable launch-on-warning tactics or to strike first in a crisis.

--This would very likely stimulate offsetting Soviet force deployments, leading to needless increases in weaponry on both sides and possibly to heightened US-Soviet tensions.

4. Command and Control

A comprehensive analysis has not been made of the command and control necessary to support improved counterforce capabilities in an effort to insure a favorable balance after a nuclear war with the Soviet Union. A preliminary examination suggests that adequate command and control for such a posture could cost $3-4 billion more in FY 73-77 than the current program. Our current command and control program will cost about $3 billion in FY 73-77. Command and control improvements which could be associated with improved counterforce capabilities include the following:

--A survivable and near real-time satellite system to determine which Soviet missile launchers have been fired, in order to allow surviving US missiles to be concentrated on Soviet launchers which still contain missiles.

--An Advanced Airborne Command Post (AABNCPs) for US commanders to manage strategic forces during a large nuclear war.

--Survivable missile retargeting capabilities.

--Survivable and reliable communications for force management during a large nuclear war, to include:

-Airborne VLF TACAMO force sufficient to provide VLF communications worldwide.

-ELF Sanguine to provide survivable communications to SSBNs on station at significant operating depths throughout the world.

C. China

Regarding US strategic objectives and force posture vis-à-vis the People's Republic of China (PRC) this section discusses the question of whether we should take measures to provide for a disarming counterforce strike capability against the PRC nuclear capability throughout the 1970s.

A complete analysis of possible requirements for a disarming strike capability against the PRC nuclear threat must also consider issues involving US conventional and tactical nuclear force posture in Asia. These are discussed in considerable detail in the NSSM 69 study (US Strategy and Forces for Asia). Decisions on our strategic posture vis-à-vis the PRC should be made in the context of both the NSSM 69 study and overall US strategic objectives.

The Chinese Nuclear Threat

Our knowledge of Chinese nuclear delivery systems is limited because of serious deficiencies in the quantity, quality, and nature of the evidence. Consequently, intelligence projections and judgments are characterized by a high degree of uncertainty. (Note: The views of the intelligence community on current and future Chinese strategic nuclear capabilities are contained in NIE 13-8-71 Communist China's Strategic Weapons program.)

Two broad alternatives are available to the Chinese under this estimate: (1) emphasis on peripheral delivery systems and (2) emphasis on intercontinental delivery systems. Available evidence indicates that the Chinese have opted for the former course of action. They are currently emphasizing the continued development, production, and deployment of a regional force of jet medium bombers and peripheral strategic missiles. This may, however, reflect short-term capabilities rather than long-term intent.

Annex D contains a more detailed description of the PRC nuclear threat and shows postulated force projections for each of the above alternatives.

Chinese Nuclear Doctrine

PRC nuclear doctrine in the 1970s is expected to emphasize defense of the homeland and nuclear deterrence. The possibility of the Chinese resorting to "nuclear blackmail" in the absence of direct threats to their national interests is believed remote because:

--With larger conventional forces than any neighboring Asian country, direct use of nuclear weapons would seem an unnecessary and risky course of action.

--The Chinese appreciate their substantial nuclear firepower disadvantages vis-à-vis the United States or the Soviet Union and they would undoubtedly be reluctant to become involved in a nuclear encounter. The Chinese are surely aware that to become involved with one of the two superpowers would leave it exposed to threats by the other.

While direct nuclear blackmail is considered remote, the Chinese may attempt to intimidate their neighbors in Asia through indirect means short of overt blackmail. That is, the Chinese might exert more subtle means of pressure which could possibly be effective. They can be expected to exploit politically whatever leverage their nuclear capability gives them, consistent with not jeopardizing their national security.

Prestige will also be a principle objective of Chinese nuclear policies. The possession of nuclear weapons—and the implications of these weapons regarding scientific, technological, and military capabilities—will give China an elevated status not only among Asian nations, but throughout the world.

For these reasons, the possession of nuclear weapons can be expected to work to the advantage of the PRC, although it might be offset by the presence of US nuclear forces in Asia or by a US disarming strike capability against China.

Elements of a US Strategic Policy Towards China

With even a limited nuclear capability, the Chinese are in a position to threaten the security interests of the United States and its Asian allies; this capability will increase during the 1970s. Yet, China poses some issues different than those of the Soviet Union, because:

--The nuclear capabilities of the PRC will be for the foreseeable future far less than those of the United States or the Soviet Union.

--Our operational capabilities against China are different than those against the Soviet Union. In particular, destroying large percentages of the population is much more difficult, destroying industry is much easier, and limiting damage is substantially easier than is the case against the Soviets.

--Tactical delivery systems can cover a higher percentage of strategic targets than in the case of the Soviet Union.

Beyond these general observations, the study group delineated the agreements and disagreements regarding key elements of US strategic policy vis-à-vis China.

--There is general agreement that the Chinese policy makers are no less rational than those in the US and USSR and should be treated accordingly.

--An essential element of US deterrence policy is a capability to destroy PRC cities. But there is disagreement about the circumstances under which this threat will deter Chinese nuclear or conventional attacks on our allies or, in the late 1970s, nuclear attacks on the United States. Although Chinese population is dispersed (see Table V-3), PRC leaders realize that Chinese cities, including most PRC industry, could easily be destroyed in a nuclear attack. The top 1,000 cities contain only 11% of China's total population (but 80% of her industry), making it impractical to strive for the same capability—on a percentage basis—to inflict deaths that we have against the Soviet Union. The table below illustrates the relative vulnerability of China's industry and the effects of her dispersed population.

Table V-3
Damage from 100 Arriving Warheads (1 MT)

	U.S.	USSR	China
% Population	21	17	6
% Industry	19	32	42
Population (millions)	49	43	51
% Urban population	35	34	70

--There should continue to be strategic strike options against China which do not involve overflight of the Soviet Union. But the Chinese cannot ignore the total US spectrum of nuclear weapons and all US strategic weapons (including Minuteman) should be considered as contributing to deterrence of Chinese nuclear attack on the United States.

--There is no agreement concerning the degree to which a disarming strike capability is feasible, desirable, or necessary in order to enhance deterrence, to prevent coercion of allies, or to support our alliances. The desirability of a disarming strike capability is related to our conventional and tactical nuclear force posture in Asia. If we reduce conventional forces in Asia and depend primarily on tactical nuclear weapons for defense of our allies from attacks by PRC conventional forces, a disarming strike capability might be desired if we wanted to be able to prevent China from escalating the conflict by making nuclear attacks on US bases, on our allies, or even on CONUS. The feasibility of a disarming strike is analyzed below.

Strategic Alternatives

In the overall context of the General Strategic Alternatives, we developed two options vis-à-vis China which differ basically in regard to a disarming strike capability.

Option A. U/I Retaliatory Capability Plus Limited Counterforce capability

1. Purpose and capability. This option would provide those capabilities against China which result from a posture designed primarily for a well-hedged U/I retaliatory capability against the USSR. There would be no improvements in missile counterforce or ASW capabilities for the purposes of limiting or denying damage from PRC attacks.

Forces procured on this basis would maintain the following capabilities against China:

--The capability to destroy about 70% of Chinese industry and 70% of the urban population (about 60 million people or 7% of the total population).

--The capability to destroy most soft military targets (conventional and nuclear) and hardened, non-time-urgent targets.

--A limited capability to destroy some time-urgent targets of some degree of hardness (e.g., missile silos), although this would require overflight of the USSR with Minuteman or deployment of Poseidon in the Pacific (not currently planned).

We currently have the first two capabilities against China, using about 600 warheads targeted in the SIOP (no overflight of the Soviet Union would occur); the third capability is not currently at issue because China has no hardened missile launchers.

Moreover, we currently have a disarming strike capability against known Chinese nuclear threats. But China may already have deployed some MRBMs which have not been detected (see Annex D). (Note: Under the most likely assumptions, the Chinese could deploy

IRBMs in silos of unknown hardness by 1974/75 and their first nuclear-powered ballistic missile submarine as early as 1976; initial deployment of ICBMs will probably be in silos of unknown hardness and could occur as early as 1974, but more likely in 75. There is no evidence of construction of deployed silos, and it has been possible to estimate what the hardness of deployed silos would be from analysis of the ones involved in R&D.) Under Option A, our disarming strike capability will be seriously eroded if the Chinese increase the number and survivability of their nuclear force or if they develop a launch-on-warning capability. (Note: A crude warning system, sufficient for launch-on-warning against missile attacks, could be deployed late in the 1970s. The Chinese probably now have the capability to respond to a bomber attack by launching their bombers on receipt of warning. As they deploy land-based missiles, they will probably be able to launch them on warning of a bomber attack.)

2. <u>Forces and costs</u>. This option would not require additional forces or costs over those appropriate to any of the General Strategic Alternatives. Nor would it require an area ABM defense.

3. <u>Key issues</u>. The key issue under this option is whether the threatened destruction of PRC cities and soft military targets, in conjunction with US tactical nuclear forces and US and allied conventional forces, would be sufficient to deter PRC attacks on the United States, its bases overseas, and its allies. (Evaluation of this issue depends on part on tactical and conventional force posture in Asia, discussed in NSSM-69.) While this option would provide some damage-limiting capability, we could not deny damage from Chinese nuclear attacks throughout the 1970s. This implies the following:

--For deterrence of PRC <u>conventional attacks</u> on our allies, we would depend primarily on either (a) a combination of US and allied conventional forces, or (b) battlefield use of tactical nuclear weapons, with the risk that the Chinese would respond with nuclear attacks.

--For deterrence of PRC nuclear attacks on our allies, we would depend on US theater nuclear weapons in conjunction with the threat of strategic nuclear weapons.

4. <u>Relation to General Strategic Alternatives</u>. China Option A is most consistent with Alternatives 1, 2 and 3A, which do not provide improved counterforce capabilities. It could be consistent with Alternatives 3B and 3C if counterforce improvements in these alternatives were directed primarily toward the USSR (i.e., improvements in Minuteman or improvements in Poseidon, but

without deploying Poseidon in the Pacific) would be more consistent with the damage denial objective of China Option B.

Option B. U/I Retaliatory Capability Plus Enhanced Counterforce Capability Designed for Damage Denial

1. Purpose and capability. This option would add to Option A an improved missile counterforce capability against hardened time-urgent targets and a strategic ASW capability against Chinese submarines in order to extend the time during which we could threaten China with a disarming strike.

There are two possible uses for a US disarming strike capability:

--First, to contribute (in concert with tactical nuclear weapons) to deterrence of Chinese conventional attack on our allies and to reduce the credibility of Chinese nuclear threats to our allies.

--Second, a disarming strike could be executed in an attempt to prevent Chinese nuclear responses if the United States is required to make battlefield use of nuclear weapons to support allied or US troops engaged in battle against PRC forces.

2. Forces and costs. In order to have high confidence of destroying Chinese missiles in silos (Note: A few IRBMs could be deployed in silos by 1974/75; ICBMs will probably be initially deployed in silos. Until more evidence is available and deployed silos are constructed and analyzed, there is no way of estimating what their hardness may be) without overflying the USSR, the counterforce capability of US SLBMs would have to be improved. If we relied on bombers for such attacks, success would be critically dependent upon the Chinese not launching their missiles on warning of the attack.

We could develop and deploy a Polaris missile with improved counterforce capability (no current program) or deploy Poseidon in the Pacific (not currently planned, but under study by the JCS) and improve the Poseidon accuracy (means for improving accuracy are under development, but a higher yield warhead is not; however, it would take about 4 years to IOC for an improved Poseidon guidance package, i.e., early 1976). If Poseidon is deployed in the Pacific, we would face a choice of covering Chinese hard targets at the expense of uncovering some Soviet targets or of buying additional SSBNs.

Bombers and tactical nuclear delivery systems could be used for many targets, such as urban/industrial and soft military targets.

To support a disarming strike capability, once the Chinese deploy their first nuclear-powered ballistic missile submarine (perhaps as early as 1976), dedicated strategic ASW forces would be necessary.

Moreover, an area ABM defense (Defense Level B or C), would be necessary if we were to limit or deny damage to the United States from PRC missiles surviving a US attack, forces not located for targeting, or missiles launched on warning of the US strike. Alternatively, we could threaten the destruction of PRC cities in order to deter PRC attacks on the United States with their surviving weapons.

3. <u>Key issues</u>. Differing assessments of risks under this option produce the following issues:

(a) Would missile counterforce improvements significantly affect the US-Soviet relationship?

The Soviet Union could interpret improvements in US missile counterforce capabilities as a step toward a first-strike capability against the USSR.

--Some believe this would lead to further proliferation of Soviet strategic offensive and defensive forces and to complications in SALT or other US-Soviet diplomatic efforts.

--Others believe deployment of an improved Poseidon in the Pacific would not be interpreted as a threat by the Soviets.

<u>(b) Is a US disarming strike feasible?</u>

Even before a Chinese SSBN becomes operational (1976 at the earliest) or 6000 n.m. ICBMs in silos could be deployed in significant numbers (1978/79), executing a disarming strike would, for the following reasons, involve significant risk of damage to US allies and overseas bases from attack by surviving PRC nuclear forces.

--Possible failure to locate with accuracy all deployed Chinese missile launchers. For example, since 1969 we have observed Chinese troop training with MRBMs and they have deployed a few. We have yet to locate a deployed missile site, however, which may mean MRBMs are deployed in a concealed mode. New intelligence collection capabilities will improve this situation, but there is still considerable uncertainty associated with locating all Chinese missiles.

--If the Chinese develop and deploy the necessary warning systems, they could adopt a launch-on-warning doctrine which could seriously detract from the effectiveness of a US disarming strike. A crude warning system, sufficient for launch-on-warning of missile attacks, could be deployed late in the 1970s. They probably now have a capability to respond to a bomber attack by launching their own bombers on receipt of warning. While we might jam Chinese radars to deny them precise information about an incoming attack, the jamming itself during a crisis might cause them to launch their bombers and possibly even their missiles.

--When the Chinese perceive that the United States is developing a disarming strike capability, they might be induced to accelerate the development and deployment of missiles in a survivable mode (concealed missiles, SLBMs, or land-mobile missiles). On the other hand, perception of an improved US disarming capability might cause them to slow down their deployment of nuclear weapons.

--Only a few residual weapons launched by the PRC could inflict massive casualties and damage on allied population centers and US overseas bases should the Chinese choose to target them.

Faced with the above risks our allies may not place much confidence in a US posture which depends upon the effectiveness of a disarming strike to deter attacks on them.

After the Chinese deploy SSBNs or 6000 n.m. ICBMs in silos, the risks of damage to the United States from residual PRC weapons would increase, particularly if we could not deploy an area ABM defense because of a SALT agreement with the USSR or because Congress continued to refuse funding for such a defense. For example, without an ABM system which protected major populated areas, three surviving Chinese ICBMs or SLBMs with thermonuclear warheads could kill 5-8 million US people, if targeted to maximize fatalities. Twenty surviving missiles could kill 16-20 million US people. We could, however, threaten destruction of PRC cities in an attempt to deter retaliatory strikes on the United States or its allies. (Collateral fatalities and damage connected with a disarming strike would be only _____, thus, this threat would have strong deterrent value.)

US ASW forces would probably be effective against the small number of relatively noisy and unsophisticated SSBNs the Chinese could be expected to deploy in the last half of the 1970s. Nonetheless, the outcomes of ASW engagements are strongly dependent on tactics and environmental factors and we could not predict with certainty the destruction of Chinese SSBNs before they launched their missiles.

Faced with these risks, the United States might be willing to execute a disarming strike against China in defense of an Asian ally. A crisis which would confront us with such a decision is most likely to arise because of a Chinese conventional attack on one of our Asian allies. It is likely that the Chinese would take military and diplomatic actions designed to encourage opposition by the US public to US first use of nuclear weapons (on the battlefield or for a disarming strike) in such a crisis. If the Chinese believed that this opposition would inhibit us from using nuclear weapons in defense of an Asian ally, then the effect of a disarming strike posture in helping deter conventional attacks would be significantly eroded.

In spite of these limitations, some argue that a disarming strike capability can be politically useful, especially as Chinese planners would conservatively make more pessimistic assessments than we, and our allies might lack the sophistication to tell the difference. Others point out that survival of a few residual weapons are easy for all to imagine, that this would be enough to erode the political leverage we might gain from an imperfect disarming capability.

4. <u>Relationship to General Strategic Alternatives</u>. China Option B is most consistent with Alternative 4, which would provide major counterforce improvements, and with Defense Level B. Defense Levels D or E would not be inconsistent inasmuch as they also involve at least a light area defense. As noted above, it could also be consistent with Alternatives 3B and 3C.

April 3, 1974

A comprehensive and detailed classified look at US nuclear weapons policies as they stood in 1974. The political aims sought by the US in its nuclear policies were to first prevent a war through deterrence, second to attempt to limit any military conflict as much as possible, and third to guarantee that the US emerges as a more powerful force than its enemy in the post-war world, both by protecting American economic and political resources and by destroying those of the enemy. Rather than simply mutual destruction, the reasoning now went, maybe a nuclear war could be "won".

Thus, although détente was still the diplomatic preference, the Nixon Administration simultaneously developed policies for successful nuclear war-fighting, spelling out a series of military options which carried the Kennedy-Johnson idea of "flexibility" to much higher levels. Nuclear attack plans were expanded to include not only an American first strike and a retaliatory strike after a Soviet attack, but also a series of "limited war" options intended to utilize nuclear weapons without setting off a full-scale war, and also a series of actions intended to ride out a full-scale nuclear exchange and still leave the option for further nuclear actions (termed a "trans-attack" strategy) to end the war on terms favorable to the US. Each of these broad plans was divided into a large number of target categories, with numerous options and withholds, which allowed some or all of them to be hit with the first attacks, not hit at all, or reserved to be hit later if escalation became necessary. These options included soft military targets like airfields, urban/industrial areas, and the civilian leadership of the opposing nation.

Under these options, nuclear war was expected to be a series of steadily-escalating small steps, each one intended to dissuade the opponent from going any further. "High value targets" such as major cities or the civilian government leaders themselves, could be spared in the initial strikes and held in reserve as virtual hostages, to be destroyed later if escalation is not halted.

The strategic options spelled out by these new political policies were incorporated into a new nuclear war plan, SIOP-5, which was adopted in January 1976.

POLICY GUIDANCE FOR THE EMPLOYMENT OF NUCLEAR WEAPONS

1. Purpose and Scope

This document sets forth US national policy for the employment of nuclear weapons. It includes planning assumptions, objectives and guidelines which take into account current and near-term military capabilities and foreign policy objectives of the United States.

The purpose is to provide guidance to the Joint Chiefs of Staff for the preparation of capabilities plans for the employment of strategic and nuclear-capable theater forces in nuclear attacks against the territory or forces of the Soviet Union, the People's Republic of China, and their allies. Air defense, anti-ballistic missile, and anti-submarine warfare forces are not covered by this guidance. This policy will be reflected in the Single Integrated Operational Plan and other nuclear weapons employment plans. This guidance does not cover the policy for development, acquisition, and deployment of US forces. These are set forth in the Defense Policy and Planning Guide.

2. Objectives

a. Deterrence

The principle objective of US strategy is the deterrence of nuclear and conventional attacks or attempts at coercion under a threat of nuclear and conventional attacks against the United States, its allies, and any nation whose security is vital to the US interests.

b. Escalation Control

To the extent that deterrence fails, the major objectives are to assure a US position of power and influence and to limit the conflict and its consequences to the United States and its allies. These objectives are to be accomplished through control of escalation, that is: (i) by conducting selected military operations to protect vital US interests and to foreclose enemy opportunities for further aggression; (ii) by attempting to limit the level and scope of violence; and (iii) by holding some vital enemy targets hostage and threatening their subsequent destruction in order to coerce the enemy into negotiating a war termination.

c. General War

To the extent that escalation cannot be controlled, the US objective is to maximize the resultant political, economic and military power of the United States relative to the enemy in the post-war period in order to preclude enemy domination. This is to be accomplished: (i) by destruction of those political, economic and military resources critical to the enemy's post-war power and influence and national and military recovery; (ii) by limitation of damage to the United States and its allies through counterforce operations; and (iii) by maintaining a strategic force in reserve for protection and coercion during and after the war.

3. Strategic concepts

a. Control of Escalation

In efforts to control escalation, initial US military operations should focus on actions to protect those interests immediately threatened and actions to foreclose opportunities for further enemy aggression. Such actions, if effective, would serve to diminish enemy expectations of successful aggression. Control of escalation requires both sides to show restraint. Such restraint could stem from a combination of self-interest and coercion. In an effort to deter the enemy from escalation and to coerce him into negotiating a termination of the war acceptable to the United States, the US should maintain the capability to effectively withhold attacks from additional targets highly valued by the enemy leadership.

The following concepts should be embodied in US attack options to permit operations intended to control escalation:

(1) <u>Escalation Boundaries</u>. US nuclear weapon employment plans should provide the National Command Authorities with the ability to conduct nuclear war at various levels of intensity within clearly defined boundaries. These boundaries are intended to signal to the enemy our desire to keep the war limited. To complement escalation boundaries, attack options should be developed which, when selectively withheld by the United States and perceived by the enemy, will serve to deter enemy escalation by holding high value targets hostage.

(2) <u>Trans-Attack Stability</u>. US nuclear attack options most likely to be withheld for the purpose of deterring further enemy escalation

should be planned to provide trans-attack stability. That is, there should be high confidence that these options can be withheld over an extended period of conflict and then executed in a timely, effective manner.

(3) Avoidance of the Enemy's National Command and Control. Options should be developed to withhold attacks on: (i) the enemy's highest command structure including soft and hard command centers serving high civil or military authority, and (ii) sensors and communications systems needed by the enemy leaders to discern the nature of US attacks. The survival of these elements would facilitate control of enemy forces and negotiations to limit and end the war.

b. Relative Post-Attack Power and Influence

Targeting concepts fundamental to securing the relative power and influence of the United States and its allies include: (i) destruction of the national political controls of the enemy; (ii) destruction of those urban, industrial, economic and other resources most necessary for the enemy's national and military recovery from nuclear war; (iii) destruction or neutralization of those enemy military forces which otherwise could exercise internal control over the post-attack recovery, secure external resources for the enemy's post-attack recovery, and continue to threaten the United States and its allies.

4. Planning Concepts

a. Pre-Planning and Review

It is desirable to pre-plan nuclear employment options to the extent practical for several reasons: (i) to enhance the efficiency and effectiveness of the forces used; (ii) to provide for rapid and effective communication of orders for execution from the National Command Authorities, and (iii) to provide a solid basis for estimating the consequences of execution. Periodic reviews of the risks, limitations and effectiveness of nuclear employment plans by the National Command Authorities is critical to obtaining timely and appropriate decisions under crisis and combat conditions.

b. Flexibility

Since the full range of politico-military conditions cannot be anticipated, nuclear employment plans should be designed to allow flexible adaptation as events unfold prior to execution. Some sacrifice in overall force effectiveness may be necessary in order to provide optional withholds and adaptation of pre-planned options. Where only general plans may be laid in advance, appropriate organizations and procedures should be established and exercised for the rapid development, assessment and execution of specific options.

c. Responsiveness to Political and Military Objectives

Planning for the employment of nuclear weapons should also take into account the overall objectives, particularly of the United States; the interests of friendly and allied states, those on whose territory any such operation might be undertaken; existing arrangements for coordination with allied forces and commands in appropriate geographical areas; as well as the immediate and overall military situation.

d. Crisis and Conflict Management

To control escalation will require timely coordination between, and control of, political and diplomatic actions and military actions in the face of rapidly, often obscurely, unfolding events. Accordingly, crisis management procedures and nuclear employment planning procedures should be developed to provide for substantial interaction, during crisis and conflict, between the National Command Authorities, their political and intelligence advisors, the Joint Chiefs of Staff and Unified and Specified Commanders with nuclear forces. Such procedures should be periodically exercised and evaluated.

It should be assumed that military actions undertaken during limited nuclear conflict will be conducted with a high degree of control and direction by the National Command Authorities.

e. Attack Option Structure

Employment plans will be structured according to four categories of attack options as follows: (i) Major Attack Options, (ii) Selected Attack Options, (iii) Limited Nuclear Options, and (iv) Regional Nuclear Options.

5. Major and Selected Attack Options

Planning for Major and Selected Attack Options will be directed toward the following objectives and governed by the priorities set forth below.

a. Objectives

(1) Destroy, under all conditions of war initiation, selected economic, and military resources of the enemy critical to post-war recovery. The level of such destruction should be sufficient to achieve a decisive reduction in the enemy's economic power and influence and to prolong markedly the duration of the enemy's post-war recovery.

(2) Destroy the political leadership of the enemy, its control of resources, and its military command structure to the extent necessary or practicable in order to neutralize its ability to engage in effective warfare and to exercise internal political control.

(3) Destroy or neutralize, to the extent practicable with available, allocated nuclear forces, the nuclear offensive capabilities of the enemy that threaten the United States and its allies in order to assist in limiting damage and to reduce the enemy's forces for nuclear coercion.

(4) Destroy or neutralize, to the extent practicable with available, allocated nuclear forces, the enemy conventional forces, in order to assist in the neutralization of the enemy's overall military capability and to assist in denying the enemy access to external resources.

It is not the intent of this policy guidance to target civilian population per se. Accordingly, planning directed toward the above objectives will not include residential structures as objective targets. Substantial damage to residential structures and population may nevertheless result from targeting that meets the above objectives.

The Joint Chiefs of Staff should commit such forces to plans for Major and Selected Attack Options as necessary and appropriate. This commitment is for planning purposes and should not interfere with appropriate planning and use of such forces in Limited and Regional Nuclear Options. Forces intended for maintenance of a strategic reserve with high trans-attack stability may be included. However, such forces must be withheld unless explicitly authorized for execution and their use must not be essential to meeting the above objectives.

Major and Selected Attack Options should be encompassed in one integrated plan of which individual options cover sub-sets of targets. This integrated plan should provide for selective and sequential execution of individual options. Annex A provides additional guidance for Major and Selected Attack Options.

b. Priorities for Weapon Allocation

The relative emphasis to be used in allocating committed weapons among the objectives listed above is outlined below. The relative emphasis is different for the two sets of planning assumptions listed, namely:

Set I—Alert forces with damage—Day-to-day readiness posture, tactical warning received, maximum effort enemy attack on US nuclear forces.

In this case allocate sufficient weapons to meet objective a(1), then allocate in order of decreasing emphasis to objective a(2), objective a(4) and objective a(3).

Set II—Generated forces without damage—Advanced readiness posture, no pre-launch damage to US nuclear forces.

In this case allocate sufficient weapons to meet objective a(1); then allocate in order of decreasing emphasis to objective a(3), objective a(2) and objective a(4).

6. Limited and Regional Nuclear Options

a. Limited Nuclear Options

Options may be desired which are intended to observe different or more limited escalation boundaries or seek different or more limited objectives in order to persuade an enemy to terminate hostilities without resorting to larger nuclear exchanges. Options of these characteristics and that attack fixed targets are termed Limited Nuclear Options. They will be generally of lower intensity than attacks specified in the Selected Attack Options. Limited Nuclear Options may be developed during the normal planning process in anticipation of crisis situations, during the course of crises and during hostilities. The procedures for developing Limited Nuclear Options may also be useful in developing specific modifications of Major or Selected Attack Options that are requested by the National Command Authorities.

Limited Nuclear Options should serve three principle objectives:

(1) To indicate to the Soviet Union or the People's Republic of China that issues attendant to local conflicts are part of the vital interests of the United States.

(2) To provide options for establishing or increasing the military superiority of US and allied forces in a local conflict and to inhibit further enemy military operations.

(3) To provide responses to limited nuclear attacks by the Soviet Union or the People's Republic of China on the United States, its allies, or its forces.

b. Regional Nuclear Options

The use of nuclear-capable theater forces in preplanned or preplannable attacks on fixed targets is covered by the guidance for Major, Selected, and Limited Nuclear Options. However, circumstances might arise in which the interests of the United States can best be served by responding directly against attacking enemy forces with forces and resources immediately available within a theater of operations and clearly committed to the tactical defense of that area.

Such options are designated Regional Nuclear Options. The objective is to counter deployed enemy military forces engaged in aggressive actions and to create a state of affairs permitting the continuation or resumption of political arrangements to terminate the conflict. Plans developed for the defense of a specific geographic region or area should, as appropriate, include Regional Nuclear Options to provide selective, coordinated nuclear strikes on deployed enemy combat and service units, reserves, reinforcements, tactical nuclear delivery systems, local controls and field logistics facilities.

Every reasonable effort will be made to limit attacks in the vicinity of densely populated areas. Further, damage to non-military targets and friendly military forces will be minimized through selection of the lowest weapon yields necessary, delivery vehicles with suitable accuracies, and alternative targets to accomplish the desired objective.

7. Responsibilities and Review

Joint Chiefs of Staff

The Joint Chiefs of Staff will be responsible for:

(1) Transmitting this policy guidance together with necessary implementing guidance to appropriate Unified and Specified Commands.

(2) Directing and monitoring nuclear employment planning and evaluating the resultant operational plans and their impact on related and ancillary activities, especially crisis management activities.

(3) Advising the President and the Secretary of Defense, as required, of actions taken and their overall evaluation of the effectiveness, utility, limitations and risks of the resultant operational plans.

ANNEX A.

Planning guidance

A-1 Objectives and Guidelines for major Attack Options

A-2 Objectives and Guidelines for Selected Attack Options

A-3 Guidelines for Targeting and Damage Criteria

A-4 Guidelines for Prohibited Target Categories and Optional Withholds

A-1 Objectives and Guidelines for Major Attack Options

Note: Overall guidance for Major Attack Options is given in the basic document. The degree to which each set of objectives given below can be accomplished will be constrained by conformance to the guidelines for weapon allocation given in Section 5b. Representative Target Categories are intended to amplify the stated objective. The Prohibited Target Categories serve to prohibit certain targets from being included in attack options. The Optional Withholds provide for a choice, at the time of execution, with respect to certain targets or types of overflight. Definitions of the target categories listed as Prohibited Target Categories and Optional Withholds are given in Section A-4 below.

M-1 <u>Objective</u>: As specified in the basic document, Sections 5a(3) and 5a(4) with respect to the Soviet Union and its Eastern European allies.

<u>Representative Target Categories</u>: A comprehensive military target system in the Soviet Union and its Eastern European allies to include a) nuclear and conventional threats to the United States and its allies world-wide, and b) the national and intermediate military controls over these forces.

<u>Prohibited Target Categories</u>: None

<u>Optional Withholds</u>: Urban, Country, National Government, and National Military Control.

M-2 <u>Objectives</u>: As specified in the basic document, Sections 5a(1), 5a(2), 5a(3) and 5a(4) with respect to the Soviet Union and its Eastern European allies.

<u>Representative Target Categories</u>: All target categories in M1 above, plus the urban, industrial, political, economic and military resources in the Soviet Union necessary to post-war recovery as defined in Section A-3, below.

<u>Prohibited Target Categories</u>: None

<u>Optional Withholds</u>: Country

M3 <u>Objectives</u>: As specified in the basic document, Sections 5a(3) and 5a(4) with respect to the People's Republic of China and its Asian allies.

<u>Representative Target Categories</u>: A comprehensive military target system in the People's Republic of China and its Asian allies to include a) nuclear and conventional threats to the United States and its allies world-wide and b) the national and intermediate military controls over these forces.

<u>Prohibited Target Categories</u>: None

<u>Optional Withholds</u>: Country, Urban, National Government, National Military Control, and Soviet Union overflight.

M4 <u>Objectives</u>: As specified in the basic document, Sections 5a(1), 5a(2), 5a(3) and 5a(4) with respect to the People's Republic of China and its Asian allies.

<u>Representative Target Categories</u>: All target categories in M3 above plus the urban, industrial, political, economic and military resources in the People's Republic of China necessary to post-war recovery as defined in Section A-3 below.

<u>Prohibited Target Categories</u>: None

<u>Optional Withholds</u>: Country and Soviet Union overflight.

<u>A-2 Objectives and Guidelines for Selected Attack Options</u>

Note: Overall guidance for Selected Attack Options is given in the basic document. The degree to which each set of objectives given below can be accomplished will be constrained by conformance to the guidelines for weapon allocation to target categories given in Section 5b. Representative Target categories are intended to amplify the stated objective. The Prohibited Target Categories serve to prohibit certain targets from being included in attack options. The Optional Withholds provide for a choice, at the time of execution, with respect to certain targets or types of overflight. Definitions of the target categories listed as Prohibited Target Categories and Optional Withholds are given in Section A-4 below.

S1. <u>Objective</u>: Neutralize the Soviet nuclear threat to the United States.

Representative Target Categories: a) ICBM sites, b) homeport locations, submarine bases, and shipyard facilities for missile-launching submarines, c) active bomber home bases, related dispersal bases, and arctic staging bases, d) national and regional nuclear storage facilities, e) sensors and associated communications that would allow the Soviet leaders to execute a timely launch of their strategic nuclear forces, f) Soviet national civilian and military controls including alternate command centers, regional military headquarters and control over nuclear delivery forces, but which are not collocated with these forces.

<u>Prohibited Target Categories</u>: Urban

Optional Withholds: Country, National Government, National Military control, Attack Assessment.

S2. <u>Objective</u>: Neutralize the Soviet nuclear threat to major urban areas of members of the North Atlantic Treaty Organization (NATO) other than the United States and Canada.

Representative Target Categories: a) IRBM and MRBM sites, b) SS-11 sites located in IR/MRBM fields, c) SLBM homeports, d) bomber home, dispersal and logistics bases, e) supporting national and regional nuclear storage facilities, f) Soviet command centers, regional military headquarters and control over nuclear delivery forces, but which are not collocated with those forces, and g) sensors and associated communications that would allow the Soviet leaders to execute a timely launch of their strategic nuclear forces.

Prohibited Target Categories: Urban

Optional Withholds: Country, National Government, national Military Control, Attack Assessment.

S3. Objectives: Neutralize the nuclear and conventional aircraft threat to NATO other than the United States and Canada.

Representative Target Categories: Aircraft home, dispersal, and logistics bases together with associated support facilities and nuclear storage sites.

Prohibited Target Categories: Urban, National Government, National Military Controls, Attack Assessment.

Optional Withholds: Country (particularly the Soviet Union)

S4. Objective: Neutralize the ground-based military threats to NATO.

Representative Target Categories: a) military controls and major military headquarters, b) transportation and other logistics facilities, c) major fixed ground force installations, d) and other military targets critical to the overall conduct and direction of conventional military operations.

Prohibited Target Categories: Urban, National Government, National Military Control, Attack Assessment.

Optional Withholds: country (particularly the Soviet Union)

S5. Objective: Neutralize the threat to NATO posed by the naval forces of the Soviet Union and its Eastern European allies.

Representative Target Categories: Home ports, bases, shipyards, and support facilities for missile launching submarines and other naval forces.

Prohibited Target Categories: National Government, National Military Control, Attack Assessment.

Optional Withholds: Urban, Country (particularly the Soviet Union)

S6. <u>Objective</u>: Provide a nuclear defense of NATO, except the United States and Canada, without the use of CONUS-launched forces.

<u>Representative Target Categories</u>: A comprehensive military target system threatening NATO including nuclear missiles and associated storage sites, and target categories listed under S3, S4 and S5.

<u>Prohibited Target Categories</u>: National Government, National Military Control, Attack Assessment.

<u>Optional Withholds</u>: Urban, Country.

S7. <u>Objective</u>: Neutralize the Soviet nuclear threat to US forces and US allies in Asia.

Representative Target Categories: a) SLBM related facilities, b) SS-11s, c) SS-12s, d) MRBM/IRBMs, e) appropriate airfields, f) tactical nuclear missiles, and g) associated support facilities and nuclear storage sites. (This threat is generally based east of 55 degrees east longitude.)

<u>Prohibited Target Categories</u>: Urban, National Government, National Military Control, Attack Assessment.

<u>Optional Withholds</u>: None

S8. <u>Objective</u>: Neutralize the Soviet conventional threat to US forces and allies in Asia.

<u>Representative Target Categories</u>: a) appropriate airfields, b) major ground force installations, and c) naval facilities. (This threat is generally located east of 55 degrees east longitude.)

<u>Prohibited Target Categories</u>: Urban, National Government, National Military Control, Attack Assessment.

<u>Optional Withholds</u>: None.

S9. Objective: Neutralize the operational nuclear threat of the People's Republic of China to the United States, US forces and allies in Asia and the means necessary for rebuilding this threat, separately or combined.

<u>Representative Target Categories</u>: a) submarine related facilities; b) bomber bases, c) land-based ballistic missiles; d) nuclear production and storage facilities and e) research, development and testing facilities for aircraft, missiles, nuclear weapons, and chemical, biological, and radiological warfare.

<u>Prohibited Target Categories</u>: National Government, National Military Control, Attack Assessment.

<u>Optional Withholds</u>: Urban, Soviet Union overflight.

S10. Objective: Neutralize the national, civilian, and military controls of the People's Republic of China.

Representative Target Categories: a) national command centers, alternates thereto, regional military headquarters, and control centers, and communications facilities related to control over nuclear delivery forces, but which are not collocated with these forces, and b) sensors and associated communication that allow the People's Republic of China leaders to discern the nature of nuclear attacks on the People's Republic of China and its allies.

Prohibited Target Categories: None

Optional Withholds: Urban, Attack Assessment, Soviet Union overflight.

S11. Objective: Neutralize the conventional threat from the People's Republic of China and its allies to US forces and allies in Asia.

Representative Target Categories: a) port facilities, b) major ground force installations, and c) airfields.

Prohibited Target Categories: National Government, National Military Control, Attack Assessment.

Optional Withholds: Urban, Soviet Union Overflight.

A-3 Targeting and Damage Criteria

The following general guidance applies when programming forces:

a. Relative Target Importance

Available forces will be programmed to permit attainment of damage expectancies consistent with target importance in achieving the attack objectives of this policy guidance. (Damage expectancy DE as used above is defined as the average damage that would be achieved if the attack were repeated many times.) When programming weapons which contribute only a small, relative, incremental increase in damage expectancy, the application should be examined from the standpoint of possible alternative application to other targets with a view toward achieving more compensatory returns for the programmed effort.

b. Measures to Increase Confidence

Measures should be employed to increase confidence in our estimates of attack results, e.g., cross targeting; however, in cases where such measures might conflict with other considerations, e.g., trans-attack stability, measures chosen shall minimize such conflicts.

c. Overall Damage Expectancy

The overall damage expectancy to any Designated Ground Zero (DGZ) in an allied attack option resulting from weapons programmed for delivery by US and allied forces, where appropriate, should not normally exceed 90 percent. The determination of damage expectancy on each DGZ will include collateral damage effects from weapons programmed on proximate DGZs within the same attack option. In addition, fatalities due to fallout will be included where appropriate, e.g., Limited Nuclear Options. The programming of theater forces against DGZs programmed for attack by other US forces will not be precluded by the 90 percent restriction, if such additional effort is required to reduce time of attack or cover targets critical to theater commanders. The cumulative damage expectancy to a DGZ resulting from forces programmed in a Limited Nuclear Option, or to a DGZ in a defense suppression attack, may exceed 90 percent.

d. Nuclear Threat Target Coverage

In a US attack planned with fully generated undamaged forces on the Soviet nuclear threat to the United States and its allies, not less than one warhead should be applied to each ICBM site, each IRBM and MRBM site, each base for heavy, medium, and light bombers, and each base for missile-launching submarines, even if a high damage expectancy cannot be achieved or only short-term damage can be realized.

e. Urban, Industrial, Political and Economic Base

A very important purpose of attacks on urban, industrial, political and economic base of the Soviet Union and the People's Republic of China, as described in the basic document, is to minimize the strategic power and influence of these countries in the post-war era and to prolong their post-war recovery. To this end targeting will meet at least the following four criteria: (1) inflict moderate damage on facilities comprising approximately 70% of each nation's war-supporting economic base, (2) program at least one weapon on an industrial facility in the top 250 urban areas in the Soviet Union and in the top 125 urban areas in the People's Republic of China (ranked by economic worth), (3) program at least one weapon on major centers of government, and (4) neutralize other targets, including military targets, critical to post-attack recovery not covered above.

It is not the intent of this guidance to target civilian population per se. Accordingly, targeting to meet the above criteria will not include residential structures as objective targets. It is recognized, however, that substantial damage to residential structures and population may result from targeting that meets the above criteria.

A-4. Prohibited Target Categories and Optional Withholds

The objectives and guidelines for the development of attack options contain references to Prohibited Target Categories and Optional Withholds. The names and definitions of the Prohibited Target Categories and Optional Withholds used in Major and Selected Attack Options are given below. The objectives and guidelines for Limited Nuclear Options and Regional Nuclear Options may contain additional Prohibited Target Categories and Optional Withholds.

(1) <u>Urban</u>. To prohibit or withhold attacks on targets that are in or collocated with major urban areas of 100,000 or more population. A target is defined to be collocated with a major urban area if attacking the target alone or in combination with other targets would result in moderate damage to 10 percent or more of the residential floor space, Deviations from this guideline may be made in exceptional cases if necessary to avoid major degradation in accomplishing the political/military objectives.

(2) <u>Country</u>. To prohibit or withhold attack on targets in any country.

(3) <u>National Government</u>. To prohibit or withhold attack on the centers of government within the urban areas of Moscow or Peking.

(4) <u>National Military Control</u>. To prohibit or withhold attack on targets composing the national level military controls of the Soviet Union and/or the People's Republic of China including communications facilities.

(5) <u>Attack Assessment</u>. To prohibit or withhold attack on sensors and associated communications used by the Soviet or People's Republic of China national leadership to assess the nature of nuclear attacks against their own countries or forces.

(6) <u>Soviet Union overflight</u>. To withhold those sorties that overfly the Soviet Union in attacks on the People's Republic of China and its allies.

July 25, 1980

The Nixon Administration's policy of flexible nuclear options that would allow the US to fight a nuclear war and attempt to maintain dominance in the post-war world was continued by the Carter Administration, even as the US sought diplomatic détente and continued negotiations with the Russians towards limiting nuclear weapons. The Soviets, meanwhile, made large and rapid investments in their nuclear forces, particularly ICBMs and intermediate-range IRBMs, through the 1970's, and by 1980 had reached rough parity with the US in terms of strategic quantity, quality, and accuracy. In 1979 the US and USSR signed the SALT II treaty placing limits on the number and types of strategic weapons that each side could deploy, but later that year the Soviet Union invaded Afghanistan, international tensions rose, and the period of détente ended.

This classified memo, Presidential Directive NSC-59, spells out the Carter White House's understanding of the "nuclear war-fighting" doctrine. Carter's directive added methods for changing nuclear plans and options during a nuclear conflict in response to circumstances, and also added options to integrate the use of a limited strike with nuclear weapons alongside conventional forces. By 1980, SIOP-5 had almost 40,000 potential targets for nuclear weapons, ranging from Soviet nuclear forces to command centers to urban industrial sites. The doctrine was called "tailored counterforce" — it envisaged a series of carefully targeted selective attacks, each one escalating in severity, along with deliberate withholding of particular targets as "bargaining chips" to encourage the Soviets to negotiate and end the conflict.

To carry out this policy, the President Carter ordered the expansion of the US nuclear force capabilities, and began research programs that eventually led to many new strategic weapons systems, including the B-1 bomber, the "MX" ICBM missile, the nuclear cruise missile, the neutron bomb, and the highly-secret Stealth bomber, and also began programs to improve the survivability of US command and control to allow for changes in planning even while nuclear weapons were falling on the US.

These policies were highly controversial. Some military officials doubted the whole idea of attempting to wage a "limited" nuclear war in clearly defined stages – they argued that any initial use of nuclear weapons would quickly and unavoidably lead to a an all-out exchange. In particular, there was heavy criticism of the added "launch-on-warning" option. Other military experts concluded that it was unlikely that the command and control system needed to manage a limited-escalation strategy would survive the initial attacks, making the idea of a "protected war" impossible. Public opinion, fueled by leaked versions of the directive appearing in the New York Times *and* Washington Post, *saw the strategy as an attempt by the US to develop the ability to fight and win a nuclear war – a dangerous and provocative move that, aside from being impossible, could make the use of nuclear weapons more likely.*

Presidential Directive/NSC-59
SUBJECT: Nuclear Weapons

In PD-18, I directed a follow-on study of our targeting policy for nuclear forces. I have reviewed the results and considered their implications for maintaining deterrence in the present decade, particularly in the light of the growing Soviet strategic weapons arsenal and its capabilities.

The most fundamental objective of our strategic policy remains nuclear deterrence. I reaffirm the directive of PD-18 to that effect. The purpose of this directive is to outline policies and actions in the nuclear force employment field to secure that continuing objective.

Our strategic nuclear forces must be able to deter nuclear attacks not only on our own country but also on our forces overseas, as well as on our friends and allies, and to contribute to deterrence of non-nuclear attacks. To continue to deter in an era of strategic nuclear equivalence, it is necessary to have nuclear (as well as conventional) forces such that in considering aggression against our interests any adversary would recognize that no plausible outcome would represent a victory on any plausible definition of victory. To this end and so as to preserve the possibility of bargaining effectively to terminate the war on acceptable terms that are as favorable as practical, if deterrence fails initially, we must be capable of fighting successfully so that the adversary would not achieve his war aims and would suffer costs that are unacceptable, or in any event greater than his gains, from having initiated an attack.

The employment of nuclear forces must be effectively related to operations of our general purpose forces. Our doctrine for the use of forces in nuclear conflict must insure that we can pursue specific policy objectives selected by the National Command Authorities at that time, from general guidelines established in advance.

These requirements form the broad outline of our evolving countervailing strategy. To meet these requirements, improvements should be made to our forces, their supporting C3 and intelligence, and their employment plans and planning apparatus, to achieve a high degree of flexibility, enduring survivability, and adequate performance in the face of enemy actions. The following principles and goals should guide your efforts in making these improvements.

Pre-planned options. The Single Integrated Operational Plan will provide pre-planned targeting for strikes against the Soviet Union, its allies and its forces. It should provide for retaliatory strikes that will be effective, even if the Soviets attack first, without warning, and in a manner designed to reduce our capability as much as possible. It will be developed with flexible sub-options that will permit, to the extent that survival of C3 allows, sequential selection of attacks from among a full range of military targets, industrial targets providing immediate military support, and political control targets, while retaining a survival and enduring capability that is sufficient to attack a broader set of urban and industrial targets. [*In addition, to the maximum extent possible, pre-planned contingencies (including attacks on Cuba, SRV and North Korea as appropriate*) [censored]

While it will remain our policy not to rely on launching nuclear weapons on warning that an attack has begun, appropriate pre-planning, especially for ICBMs that are vulnerable to a preemptive attack, will be undertaken to provide the President the option of so launching.

Flexibility. In addition to pre-planned options we need an ability to design nuclear employment plans on short notice in response to the latest and changing circumstances. This capability must be comprehensive enough to allow rapid construction of plans that integrate strategic force employment with theater nuclear force employment and general purpose force employment for achieving theater campaign objectives and other national objectives when pre-planned response options are not judged suitable in the circumstances.

To assure that we can design such plans, our goal should be to have the following capabilities on a continuing basis in peacetime, during crises, and during protracted conflict:

--Staff capabilities, within all unified and specified commands which have nuclear forces, to develop operational plans on short notice and based on the latest intelligence.

--Staff capabilities at the seat of Government to support the NCA for coordinating and integrating the nuclear force employment for all commands.

--Intelligence and target development capabilities which permit damage assessment and acquisition of a broad range of targets, fixed and mobile, on a timely basis for military operations.

Reserve Forces. Pre-planned options should be capable of execution while leaving a substantial force in secure reserve and capable of being withheld for possible subsequent use. The forces designated for the reserve should be the most survivable and enduring strategic force capable of being effectively employed against a wide target spectrum and withheld if necessary for a prolonged period. The secure reserve force will be increased over the next two years to support a more flexible execution of our countervailing strategy. This will be done according to the Secretary of Defense's guidance.

Targeting categories. Overall targeting planning appropriate to implement a countervailing strategy will result in a capability to choose targets. Military targets must be selected for the purpose of destroying enemy forces or their ability to carry out military operations. Strategic and theater nuclear forces should to the extent feasible be used in combination with, and in support of, general purpose forces to achieve that objective.

More specifically, the following categories of military targets, with appropriate sub-options for different theaters, should be covered in planning:

--strategic and theater nuclear forces, including nuclear weapons storage;

--military command, control, communications, and intelligence capabilities;

--all other military forces, stationary and mobile;

--industrial facilities which provide immediate support to military operations during wartime.

In addition, pre-planned options, capable of relatively prolonged withhold or of prompt execution, should be provided for attacks on the political control system and on general industrial capacity.

There must be extensive and effective coverage in the pre-planned options of all categories. Methods of attack on particular targets should be chosen to limit collateral damage to urban areas, general industry and population targets outside these categories, consistent with effectively covering the objective target, and, where appropriate, overall plans should include the option of withholds to limit such collateral damage.

Command, Control, and Communications, and Intelligence. Flexibility in contingency planning and in operations will be highly dependent on our C3I capabilities, including their ability to acquire targets, assess damage, and survive attack. Strategic stability in an era of essential equivalence depends as much on survivability, endurance and reconstitutability of C3I capabilities as it does on the size and character of strategic arsenals.

PD/NSC-53 directs that our C3I programs and our guidance to telecommunications common carriers support the development and maintenance of such capabilities. In addition, PD/NSC-41 directs that we seek greater continuity of government should deterrence fail. Implementation of PD/NSC-53 and PD/NSC-41 must be pursued in parallel with that of this employment directive.

The relationship of acquisition policy to employment policy. Our acquisition programs must be evaluated in terms of their support for the employment policy ordered by this directive. The required flexibility, survivability, endurance, and target destruction capability must be taken into account in developing programs for acquiring nuclear weapons systems, and their supporting C3I systems, needed to support our countervailing strategy.

Implementation. As new targeting capabilities are developed, and as our operational staffing support change to meet the foregoing directives, they must be reviewed and tested to validate their feasibility and soundness. For that purpose:

--At least two exercises involving the National Command Authorities should be conducted each year to evaluate our capabilities and our employment doctrines.

--Continued study and analysis of means to improve and refine our countervailing strategy of general conflict should be conducted by the Department of Defense.

--The results of these exercises, studies and analysis will provide the bases for modification and any further development of employment and acquisition policy.

--A report will be rendered to the President at least annually on our employment plans, including, but not limited to, on the size and capability of the reserve forces, the degree of flexibility available, limiting factors in achieving flexibility, and the status of programs to provide improvements.

--Any change or new pre-planned options will be submitted to the President for his review and approval, in accordance with current procedures.

NSDM-242 is superseded by this directive.

November 3, 1986

The Reagan Administration accepted and embraced the "war-fighting" strategy followed by the Nixon and Carter Administrations, but modified it further by increasing the emphasis on counterforce targets. By the mid-1980's the United States either had or would have soon a number of new operational strategic delivery systems, such as the B-1 and B-2 bomber, Air-Launched Cruise Missile (ALCM) and Submarine-Launched Cruise Missile (SLCM), and the MX Peacekeeper ICBM, in large enough numbers and with high enough accuracy, to begin to think seriously about the possibility of a successful American first strike. The Peacekeeper ICBM, moreover, was originally designed to be a mobile system, in which a number of missiles would be randomly shuffled by rail cars between a large number of hardened shelters, to increase their survivability against Soviet missile strikes. (Because of budgetary limits, however, this plan was dropped and the Peacekeeper was deployed in the existing Minuteman silos.)

One important development at this time was advanced research work into Earth-Penetrating Warheads, which would allow a nuclear missile warhead or a bomber-dropped gravity bomb to burrow a distance underground before exploding, producing a much greater shock effect that would be capable of destroying even hardened targets like Soviet underground command bunkers and ICBM silos. For the first time in the Cold War, one side now had the realistic prospect of gaining the capability to launch a preemptive attack that would eliminate a significant portion of the opponent's retaliatory capability.

The Soviets, whose ICBMs were not accurate enough for their own first-strike counterforce capability against the US, greatly feared this impending imbalance. Their fears increased further in 1983 when the US announced it would leave the ABM Treaty which had banned anti-missile defenses, and would attempt to develop a Strategic Defense Initiative, known popularly as "Star Wars", to use satellite-based laser weapons to destroy enemy missiles on their way to the target. This, the Russians concluded with alarm, would end MAD and give the Americans overwhelming superiority — US earth-penetrating weapons would be able to destroy Soviet ICBMs in their silos, and the SDI system would be able to stop any retaliatory response by SLBMs or surviving ICBMs.

Then in 1985, Mikhail Gorbachev took over as leader of the Soviet Union. Along with sweeping economic and political reforms, Gorbachev wanted to end the military arms race that hobbling the Soviet economy, and began new diplomatic efforts with the United States.

This classified memo is NSDD-250, spelling out the American positions in regards to negotiations with the Soviets, including the summit meeting between Reagan and Gorbachev in Reykjavik, over the SDI, the ABM Treaty, and agreements to limit Intermediate Nuclear Forces in Europe (INF) and Strategic Arms Reduction Talks (START).

In 1989, the Soviet Union collapsed, the Cold War was over, and the 40-year nuclear arms race came to an abrupt end.

NATIONAL SECURITY DECISION DIRECTIVE NUMBER 250
POST-REYKJAVIK FOLLOW-UP

At my meeting with General Secretary Gorbachev in Reykjavik, Iceland, on October 11-12, 1986, we were able to reach a series of understandings that will serve as the foundation for future progress in a number of areas. With respect to nuclear arms control matters, the common ground that exists between positions of the two sides was substantially expanded in both the START and INF areas. A path toward progress was also uncovered in the area of nuclear testing. However, as we neared the end of the time allotted for our second day of discussions, the General Secretary placed great emphasis on the Soviet need for the United States to agree not to exercise its existing right to withdraw from the ABM Treaty for a period of time in excess of 10 years. At the same time, he asked me to accept additional restrictions on some aspects of our SDI program that go well beyond the existing treaty restrictions. He ultimately tied making further progress at that meeting, even on those areas of understanding which we had already reached, to US willingness to make such a commitment with respect to a "strengthened" ABM Treaty.

I did not intend to leave Reykjavik with any potential path to progress left unexplored. Therefore, I told the General Secretary that, for the US part, we would be willing to consider any approach as long as it did not demand of us that we compromise our fundamental principles, our security and that of our allies, or our hopes for a more stable future through a transition to an increased reliance on defenses that threaten no one.

Further, I made it clear that I believed that we should make progress in each substantive arms control area based on the individual merits of the understandings reached in that area. We should not hold the potential increased mutual benefits to security and stability achievable by such processes hostage to either side's desires in other areas of discussion.

With respect to the specific Soviet demand for a US commitment not to exercise our existing right to withdraw from the ABM Treaty, I explained that a blanket commitment to waive all rights of withdrawal would not be acceptable, and that any US attempt to meet Soviet concerns in this regard should not be interpreted by the Soviet Union as US readiness to forfeit its existing right to withdraw from the ABM Treaty due to supreme national interest or in the face of material breach of the treaty by a party.

Therefore, as an attempt to see if I could find a way to respond to the General Secretary's concern in a manner that met the criteria outlined above, I reviewed the various elements of the previous US proposals to see if they could be reformulated in a novel way so as to meet both US and Soviet concerns. As a result of this effort, I offered the following initial proposal which laid out the conditions under which I was prepared to consider meeting the basic thrust of the Soviet request.

"Both sides would agree to confine themselves to research, development and testing, which is permitted by the ABM Treaty, for a period of 5 years, through 1991, during which time a 50% reduction of strategic nuclear arsenals would be achieved. This being done, both sides will continue the pace of reductions with respect to all remaining offensive ballistic missiles by the end of the second five-year period. As long as these reductions continue at the appropriate pace, the same restrictions will continue to apply. At the end of the ten-year period, with all offensive ballistic missiles eliminated, either side would be free to deploy defenses."

The General Secretary responded to this with the following Soviet proposal.

"The USSR and the United States undertake for ten years not to exercise their existing right of withdrawal from the ABM Treaty, which is of unlimited duration, and during that period strictly to observe all its provisions. The testing in space of all space components of missile defense is prohibited, except research and testing conducted in laboratories. Within the first five years of the ten-year period (and thus through 1991), the strategic offensive arms of the two sides shall be reduced by 50 percent. During the following five years of that period, the remaining 50 percent of the two sides strategic offensive arms shall be reduced. Thus by the end of 1996, the strategic offensive arms of the USSR and the United States will have been totally eliminated."

This Soviet proposal was clearly unacceptable in a number of respects. It sought to have the US accept restrictions on research on advanced defenses well beyond those specified in the existing ABM Treaty. It redefined the conditions for the subsequent five-year period to involve the elimination of *all* strategic forces of the US and the Soviet Union. And, it did not include a positive commitment that, following the ten-year period, either side could then begin the transition to increased reliance on advanced defenses.

Having evaluated the Soviet offer, I again attempted to find an appropriate bridge between the US and Soviet positions. In this effort, I tried to use as much as possible of the Soviet proposal. The result was the following second US offer which was designed to correct the key problems associated with the Soviet proposal while making it clear that in this context the US was prepared to meet what was perceived to be the central Soviet concern by an appropriately limited US commitment not to exercise its existing right to withdraw from the ABM Treaty through 1996 for the purpose of deploying advanced defenses. It was this US offer which was the US offer of record when the discussion ended without further agreement.

"The USSR and the United States undertake for ten years not to exercise their existing right of withdrawal from the ABM Treaty, which is of unlimited duration, and during that period strictly to observe all its provisions while continuing research, development and testing, which are permitted by the ABM Treaty. Within the first five years of the ten-year period (and thus through 1991), the strategic offensive arms of the two sides shall be reduced by 50 percent. During the following five years of that period, the remaining offensive ballistic missiles of the two sides shall be reduced. Thus by the end of 1996, all offensive ballistic missiles of the USSR and the United States will have been totally eliminated. At the end of the ten year period, either side could deploy defenses if it so chose unless the parties agree otherwise."

Eliminating All Offensive Ballistic Missiles. At the heart of the last US proposal made at Reykjavik is the expressed US commitment to join a bilateral agreement to delay any deployment of US and Soviet advanced defenses against ballistic missiles until after the elimination of all US and Soviet offensive ballistic missiles, with this US commitment made in return for a corresponding Soviet commitment to join a parallel bilateral agreement to complete this elimination within a specific period of time. The ten-year period of the US proposal was associated with the period through 1996 because I will not permit the possibility of the US moving to a more stable deterrent, unilaterally if need be, to slip further into the future. This specific ten-year period was chosen to balance the Soviet desire to have the US commitment not to deploy defenses for as long as possible against the US desire to find an appropriate means of eliminating the threat currently posed by offensive ballistic missiles as quickly as possible.

The elimination of all offensive ballistic missiles is not a new objective for the US. In 1983, when I announced the establishment of the SDI program I did so with the specific objective of making offensive ballistic missiles obsolete. It was examined as a part of our review and response to the proposals made by General Secretary Gorbachev in January, 1986, which went beyond this to call for the total elimination of all nuclear weapons within the next 14 years. In short, it is an objective that we have studied and discussed both within the US government and with our allies, most recently in the deliberations that led to my July 25, 1986, letter to General Secretary Gorbachev.

In the preparations for that letter, I initially focused on my desire to make a concrete proposal which would formalize my offer to share the benefits of advanced defenses with the Soviet Union should our research into such defenses meet the objectives that we have set. However, when considering this idea, the Secretary of Defense correctly pointed out that it made little sense to commit to share the benefits of advanced defenses with the Soviet Union if the Soviet Union insisted on continuing to retain large numbers of offensive ballistic missiles which would, in turn, attempt to defeat our defenses. After discussion and study by my principle advisors, it was agreed that the new US proposal should contain a specific call for a plan for the elimination of all offensive ballistic missiles. Therefore, my July 25 letter to the General Secretary was framed to incorporate this objective as a key element of the new US proposal presented in that letter. After full consultation with our allies on this and the other elements of the proposal to be contained in the correspondence, I finalized and sent the letter.

Additionally, the objective of the elimination of all offensive ballistic missiles is consistent with what we have been trying to do for some time both in START and in INF, and also with the fundamental goal that I specifically set for the SDI program.

With respect to the START negotiations, our position has long been that while each side may need nuclear forces for some time to deter conflict and underwrite its security, neither side needs fast-flying, non-recallable offensive ballistic missiles for this purpose. From the very first, in START, we have been trying to draw a clear distinction between fast-flying ballistic systems, which are uniquely suited for an attempted first-strike by an aggressor, and slow-flying systems which are better suited for deterrence through the prospect of retaliation. As a result, we have been attempting to focus on reductions in ballistic missile warheads (which also are an area of Soviet advantage) as the heart of the issue to be resolved—and have addressed restrictions on slow-flying systems largely as means to meet Soviet concerns.

In the INF negotiations, we have taken a similar position. We have kept the discussion on missiles, and avoided discussion of dual-capable, tactical aircraft. We proposed the zero-zero solution for the LRINF missile problem. We have called for the similar reduction and elimination of shorter-range ballistic missiles, missiles that pose as direct a threat to our Allies and our forces deployed in support of those allies, as Soviet ICBMs do to the United States.

With respect to the Strategic Defense Initiative, my specific, stated goal has always been to make ballistic missiles obsolete. Here, again, our focus has been on promptly eliminating the threat posed by these fast-flying missiles.

In Iceland, at the critical point of attempting to find a response to Soviet concerns which would not compromise our principles, our security, or our future, I drew upon previously completed work with respect to the objective of eliminating the threat posed by offensive ballistic missiles, and I incorporated this objective into my response to the Soviet call for a ten-year period of non-withdrawal from the ABM Treaty. By doing so, we undercut any Soviet objection to our having the right to deploy defenses as insurance, since we would have committed to delay until all offensive missiles of the two superpowers should have been eliminated. By calling for the elimination of offensive ballistic missiles of all ranges, we also in one step, addressed the problem of eliminating both the last 100 Soviet SS-20 warheads in Asia (a concern of our Asian allies) and the remaining shorter-range INF missiles that still would threaten our European allies (a particular concern of our German allies).

<u>An Alternative Future</u>. Should the Soviets accept this proposal I offered in Reykjavik, we would face a substantially different future than that we anticipate today. At the end of the ten-year period specified in the offer, neither the United States nor the Soviet Union would possess any offensive ballistic missiles. When adequate advanced defenses are deployed, they should provide insurance against the return or covert retention of such missiles and guard against third country ballistic missiles. Strategic nuclear retaliatory forces, although smaller than today and of a different composition, would remain and would retain their essential role in ensuring US and allied security.

With respect to <u>strategic forces</u>, by the end of 1996 the United States and Soviet Union could retain no more than 50 percent of today's strategic nuclear offensive forces. These forces would consist exclusively of bombers and cruise missiles. Since the major portions of forces of the United States and Soviet Union would be covered by agreements that would reduce these forces to equal levels unlike the situation today), these forces should provide a sufficient strategic retaliatory capability to deter attack on the United States or its allies while eliminating the crisis stability problems inherent in the short time of flight ballistic missiles. At the same time, elimination of ballistic missiles on both sides would drastically reduce the Soviet first strike potential and, to the extent Soviet fears of a US first strike are genuinely felt, would alleviate such concerns.

With respect to our commitment to NATO, the remaining strategic nuclear systems would also provide the US nuclear umbrella over NATO which has been one of the pillars of NATO's strategy for decades. Not only would the US commitment to NATO's agreed strategy, as embodied in MC 14/3, remain, but the elimination of the ballistic missile threat to the United States and to NATO should increase the credibility of both NATO's ability to execute its strategy and the US commitment to use nuclear weapons, I necessary, in accordance with that strategy in support of the alliance.

The United States presently contributes to all legs of the "NATO triad": conventional forces, non-strategic nuclear forces, and strategic forces. That contribution would continue. Nuclear artillery and nuclear weapons on dual capable aircraft would continue to fill the twin deterrent roles of helping offset Soviet conventional superiority and serving as a link to strategic forces. Thus, while it will be essential to continue (or accelerate) current NATO initiatives to improve conventional capability, it will be equally essential for the foreseeable future to keep some nuclear forces (both strategic and non-strategic) to permit the United States and its allies to maintain the deterrence which is the heart of the NATO strategy set forth in MC 14/3.

With respect to the Strategic Defense Initiative (SDI) program, it is clear that in the alternative future that such an agreement would provide, the requirements that SDI would have to meet would be altered substantially. Deployments of advanced defenses against ballistic missiles could be sized to provide the insurance that we need against both any existing or potential third country threats and against the covert retention of ballistic systems by the Soviet Union. Even if ballistic missiles were covertly retained, only certain elements of such systems could be covertly tested (e.g., boosters under the guise of space launch systems). It would be extremely difficult covertly to test offensive ballistic missiles as integrated combat systems in a surface-to-surface mode in such an environment. Therefore confidence in the overall reliability of such systems would degrade over time. Also, without the ability to conduct developmental testing of new offensive ballistic missile systems, the problem of the defenses having to constantly stay ahead of a technologically evolving ballistic missile threat may also be greatly reduced. In short, the size, complexity, and technological difficulty of fielding a militarily meaningful defensive system against any residual ballistic missile threat will be substantially different. If the US proposal were accepted and implemented, these factors may be reduced to the point that, even based on the progress made in SDI to date, there would be little question that a scaled-down defense will be adequate and feasible under those future conditions.

We can consider the possibility of more limited requirements for defense if ballistic missiles are actually eliminated. On the other hand, even if the Soviets were to accept the proposal that I made in Reykjavik, we will continue to need the leverage and protection produced by the possibility of being able to develop a system capable of handling a much more extensive and evolving offensive ballistic missile threat.

<u>Deterrence in such a future</u>. The basic concept of deterrence in such an alternative future need not be altered.

Deterrence can best be achieved if our defense posture makes Soviet assessments of war outcomes so uncertain as to remove any incentive for initiating attack. This would require that we possess a mix of military forces, including those nuclear and conventional forces providing defensive and retaliatory capabilities, that the Soviets will view as giving us the ability to deny them their political and military objectives.

In short, deterrence of aggression is also achieved by maximizing an aggressor's <u>uncertainty</u> that he can achieve political objectives by force, and the <u>certainty</u> that he will face grave tools for maintaining deterrence will change. The challenge and opportunity that we face is to determine how best to channel that change.

<u>The potential impact of eliminating ballistic missiles on deterrence</u>. The elimination of offensive ballistic missiles offers the possibility of enhancing deterrence because the slower pace associated with the employment of bomber and cruise missiles forces makes their effective use by an aggressor in a first strike much more difficult. The effects of such an attempt are also much more uncertain. At the same time, it should be recognized that the certainty of the ability of the US to respond to a first strike with strategic forces which are not degraded by that attempted attack is considerably higher when both sides have only slow flying systems. These considerations should be factored into evaluations of the military sufficiency of alternative forces to deter and to respond to a first strike.

In today's world, or in a future that builds on today's trends, ballistic missiles are uniquely suited to be employed by an aggressor with relatively certain results. The time between the detection of a ballistic missile attack and its arrival is so short that it freezes the situation, reducing the options of the party attacked so that they can be largely anticipated by an aggressor. Facing no defense, there can be little doubt that, if ballistic missiles function reliably, they will arrive on target. Finally, predicting the specific levels of damage they can inflict on a target is largely a matter of physics. Their effectiveness does not depend on the skill, courage or training of men in the loop. It depends on the technological reliability of the system which can be tested and measured in peacetime.

If such systems were eliminated, the uncertainty in the mind of an aggressor must increase because of the loss of their unique characteristics. Provided that we take steps to ensure that other forms of attack are not permitted to rebuild that certainty over time, the result can be a significant net gain in terms of the quality of deterrence and, in turn, in our security and that of our allies. In considering the requirements for maintaining deterrence in such a future world, a high premium should be placed on identifying, determining the feasibility of, and taking such steps.

Measuring the impact on deterrence. In measuring our ability to deter in an alternative future, we must take into account the elimination of the contribution of our own ballistic missiles and the corresponding relative increase in the degree of our uncertainty in predicting the effectiveness of our retaliatory strike, should deterrence fail. But at the same time, we must also properly reflect in our measurements the contribution that this same inherent uncertainty makes in deterring an aggressor. We should also consider the even more fundamental contribution that is made to our security should we face an aggressor who is not rational or finds himself placed in an irrational situation by events that have gotten beyond his control, but who is armed only with systems against which we can build a reasonable defense should we choose to do so. We must also weigh the real and immediate benefits of removing an immense, existing threat to the United States that is literally only thirty minutes away. Nor can we forget that, unlike Soviet stated policy, US strategic and nuclear forces are intended to make an explicitly identified contribution to the deterrence of conventional attack on our Allies and our forces deployed in support of our Allies.

In accomplishing this measurement, to the extent practical, we should attempt to approach the problem from the point of view of a net assessment of all considerations involved. Our present analytic tools will fall short of resolving all the questions such an alternative future presents. Therefore, until new methods adapted to the challenges and opportunities of this new alternative future are fully developed, we will have to depend heavily on the experience, expertise, resourcefulness, creativity, and judgment of our professional military and defense community. I believe that this, too, plays into a significant aspect of our strength.

The Immediate Task Ahead. At this time, it is not clear whether the Soviet Union will have the wisdom to accept the US proposal which I made in Reykjavik. The main thrust of our national security planning and military programming should not be altered now in anticipation of such an uncertain possibility. In fact, if we were to prematurely adjust our current military plans and programs for either the modernization of our own ballistic missile forces or to limit the scope of our SDI program, the Soviet Union would certainly attempt to pocket these actions without a reciprocal response on their part. Unilateral action of this sort would be counterproductive and dangerous. It would not only reduce the likelihood of our convincing the Soviet Union to join us in the approach to a future elimination of offensive ballistic missiles contained in my Reykjavik proposals, but it would also reduce our security and that of our allies.

However, I want to ensure that we are prepared to exploit, fully and safely, our proposal should be the Soviet Union be willing to join us in its pursuit. In order to do so, the necessary foundation of detailed, careful planning must be laid now. Therefore, I request the Joint Chiefs of Staff, under direction of the Secretary of Defense and drawing upon other agencies as necessary, to provide a plan which would permit the US to safely transition to the alternative future I have proposed.

The nature of the plan. This plan should catalogue the necessary national security requirements to support the implementation of the negotiated elimination of offensive ballistic missiles by 1996 as proposed in the last US offer made at Reykjavik. It should fully take into account the discussion of deterrence that I have provided above. Having done so, it should propose programmatic and non-programmatic approaches — including changes in military strategy and tactics, force structure and posture, and additional supportive arms control/reduction initiatives — which could be used to meet and fulfill those requirements. The identification of multiple and competing approaches to meeting requirements is encouraged. If alternative paths or methods exist, they should be presented. Finally, the resource implications of all alternatives should be estimated and provided with the alternatives.

Assumptions. In developing this plan, the following assumptions should be used:

--With respect to the 50 percent reductions in strategic forces to be taken in the first five years:

1. there will be no sublimit on heavy bombers within the 1,600 ceiling on the number of SNDVs; and

2. within the 6,000 ceiling associated with ballistic missile warheads, air-launched cruise missiles, and (indirectly) other bomber weapons;

(a) there will be no sublimits on ALCMs;

(b) each ALCM on a heavy bomber counts as one warhead;

(c) all the gravity bombs and SRAM on a single heavy bomber counts as one warhead; and

(d) SLCMs will not be included in this number.

--The US and Soviet Union will eliminate all offensive ballistic missiles by 1996. As a departure point for planning, the term offensive ballistic missile should be applied to ballistic missiles of all ranges and carrying any type of weapon designed for use in a surface-to-surface mode. Air-to-surface missiles that employ a ballistic trajectory should not be included. Artillery rocket assisted artillery rounds, and rocket assisted ASW systems should also not be included. Recommendations with respect to alternative or additional limitations on the term "offensive ballistic missile" are encouraged.

--While eliminating offensive ballistic missiles, the United States will not abandon the concept of strategic nuclear deterrence.

--The strategic policy and targeting priorities of NSDD-13 should be considered as an initial baseline. They should be critically reviewed in the context of the purposes of the development of this plan. Recommendations concerning alternative formulations which may be more appropriate for a ballistic missile free world are encouraged. These alternatives should be provided as soon as possible so that they can be reviewed and, if considered appropriate, approved for use for this planning activity. [censored]

--It will continue to be a objective of US policy to [censored]

--The Strategic Defense Initiative will be given adequate [censored]

--The NATO strategy embodied in MC 14/3 will remain in effect and be fully supported by the United States. The current NATO efforts to raise the nuclear threshold through conventional improvements will continue.

--For the purpose of this plan, the total resources available to the Department of Defense will not exceed current planning levels, with a rate of growth thereafter not to exceed three percent in real terms. However, the reorientation of priorities may be considered within those totals. Should the JCS consider additional resources essential, they should so indicate as an excursion to their baseline plan.

--The military capabilities associated with this plan will be acquired under peacetime, non-mobilization conditions. Where this guideline, constraints on our industrial capacity, or constraints on non-fiscal resources (ranging from availability of trained manpower to the availability of special nuclear materials) impact upon achieving desired force levels, this fact should be explicitly indicated, with a clear identification of the governing constraint.

--In Soviet acceptance of the proposals made in Reykjavik which would open the possibility of the projected alternative future in question, the Soviet Union would also agree to monitoring as necessary to permit verification of their compliance.

Initial progress report. In developing this plan, an initial progress report should be submitted not later than December 1, 1986, which addresses the following:

--initial recommendations, if any, with respect to national policy guidance and strategy for the employment of nuclear and non-nuclear forces that should be considered in the development of such a plan;

--an explanation of the analytic methodology planned for evaluating risk and force effectiveness in support of the development of the plan, recognizing, as mentioned earlier, that military expertise and judgment will play a critically important role accomplishing the overall task;

--a description of the initial basic planning assumptions that will be made concerning friendly forces, critical missions to be accomplished; and, the general number and characteristics of the targets associated with these missions;

--a method for appropriately folding into this planning process the contribution of highly compartmented programs while maintaining their security; and

--an estimate, submitted for my approval, of the date upon which this plan will be available for my final review.

Issues to be addressed in the full plan. The final completed plan should address at a minimum:

--recommendations on the appropriate phasing of the elimination of US ballistic missiles by 1996 in the context of the US proposal, and those steps which we could take to ensure that the phasing of the elimination of Soviet ballistic missiles is accomplished in an appropriate manner (and preferably in a manner advantageous to US and Allied security);

--recommendations on specific changes in strategic nuclear force employment strategy and related force structure made necessary by the elimination of both US and Soviet offensive ballistic missiles;

[censored]

--recommendations on similar changes in the associated strategy for the employment, deployment and structural development [censored]

--recommendations on additional general purpose capabilities that may be needed (e.g., increased ASW capability);

--recommendations on additional improvements in any area needed to ensure that the effectiveness of our strategic deterrent relative to NATO and our overall military capability of this plan;

--recommendations on how we can best use technological advantage to implement competitive strategies in support of this plan;

--recommendations concerning how we can best address the US commitment to pursue in START limitations on SLCMs with the Soviet Union in the context of this plan; and

[censored]

Treatment of risk. In formulating the alternatives and making the assessments associated with this plan, the objective of the baseline plan should be to hold overall levels of risk generally constant. It is unlikely that the risk could be kept generally constant in the projected environment which will be continually changing over the ten-year period. On the other hand, every effort should be made to avoid even short periods of greatly increased risk and to remain within a band of acceptable risk using today's levels as the departure point.

An appropriate methodology for measuring risk over the period being considered will be required to ensure this objective is met. Sources of greatest risk and uncertainty should be documented as they are identified and addressed in the development of the plan.

Alternatives that reduce risk at no significant cost can and should be included within the baseline plan. Alternatives that reduce overall levels of military risk from current or anticipated levels (as measured assuming currently planned or programmed forces), and that significantly increase the cost or difficulty of achieving an executable baseline plan can also be considered and presented. However, these should be presented as excursions to the baseline plan.

Associated Taskings. It goes without saying that the assurance of effective verification is essential to our entering into the arms control agreements that are assumed as the backdrop for the above tasking. Therefore, the Director of the Arms Control and Disarmament Agency and the Director of Central Intelligence, with the participation and drawing upon the assistance of other appropriate agencies, should prepare a supporting plan which recommends a preferred path, and alternative paths where appropriate, for achieving the effective verification of the assumed arms control agreements.

Additionally, the Director of Central Intelligence should provide:

--an assessment of the Soviet Union's intentions and capability, both military and economic, to satisfy its own national strategy and strategic force objectives;

--an assessment of the intentions and potential capabilities of other countries which currently have, or could obtain, ballistic missiles; and

--an assessment of the intelligence resources needed both to monitor Soviet compliance in such an alternative future and to support the evolving projected US military requirements associated with that future.

Implementation. The objective is the optimal executable plan, with alternative paths where appropriate, which would permit me to move quickly to exploit any Soviet willingness to join us in the proposal involving the elimination of offensive ballistic missiles within ten years which I made in Reykjavik. This should be completed on a priority basis.

Access to this NSDD and to the resulting products should be limited only to those with a clear need to know about and assist in the development of each individual product.

www.ingramcontent.com/pod-product-compliance
Lightning Source LLC
Chambersburg PA
CBHW071304110426
42743CB00042B/1165